The Politics of Landscapes in

Singapore

Space, Place, and Society
John Rennie Short, *Series Editor*

The Politics of Landscapes in

Singapore

CONSTRUCTIONS OF "NATION"

Lily Kong & Brenda S. A. Yeoh

Syracuse University Press

Copyright © 2003 by Syracuse University Press
Syracuse, New York 13244–5160

First Edition 2003
03 04 05 06 07 08   6 5 4 3 2 1

All illustrations courtesy of the authors.

The paper used in this publication meets the minimum requirements
of American National Standard for Information Sciences—Permanence
of Paper for Printed Library Materials, ANSI Z39.48–1984.∞™

Library of Congress Cataloging-in-Publication Data
Kong, Lily.
The politics of landscapes in Singapore : constructions of "nation" /
Lily Kong and Brenda S.A. Yeoh.—1st ed.
p. cm.—(Space, place, and society)
Includes bibliographical references and index.
ISBN 0–8156–2961–3 (alk. paper)—ISBN 0–8156-2980-X (alk. paper)
1. Singapore—Politics and government. 2. Nationalism—Singapore. 3.
Multiculturalism—Singapore. I. Yeoh, Brenda S. A. II. Title. III.
Series.
JQ1063.A58 .K66 2002
320.95957—dc21
2002015781

Manufactured in the United States of America

For our families, for being there for us

Lily Kong is a social-cultural geographer and professor in the Department of Geography, National University of Singapore. Her research focuses on religion, music, constructions of "nation" and "identity," and constructions of "nature" and "environment." Her publications on these topics have appeared in among other publications, *Transactions, Institute of British Geographers; Environment and Planning D: Society and Space, Progress in Human Geography;* and *Urban Studies.* Among her recent publications are a coauthored book (with Martin Perry and Brenda Yeoh), *Singapore: A Developmental City-State* (1997), and a coedited volume (with Kris Olds, Peter Dicken, Philip Kelly, and Henry Yeung), *Globalisation and the Asia Pacific: Contested Territories* (1999).

Brenda S. A. Yeoh is associate professor in the Department of Geography, National University of Singapore. She specializes in social and historical geography. Her research foci include the politics of space in colonial and postcolonial cities; and gender, migration, and transnational communities. She is author or editor of *Portraits of Places: History, Community, and Identity in Singapore* (with Lily Kong, 1995); *Contesting Space: Power Relations and the Urban Built Environment in Colonial Singapore* (1996); *Singapore: A Developmental City State* (with Martin Perry and Lily Kong, 1997); *Community and Change: The Tanjong Pagar Community Club Story* (1997); and *Gender and Migration* (with Katie Willis, 2000).

Contents

Illustrations

Tables

Acknowledgments

The National University of Singapore funded the research from which this book was written (RP960044).

Some of the material in the book have appeared in several places: *Journal of Historical Geography, Journal of Southeast Asian Studies, Urban Studies, Transactions, Institute of British Geographers, Environment and Planning D: Society and Space, Asian Studies Review, Area, Cities, Habitat International, Geoforum,* and in *Contesting Space: Power Relations in the Urban Built Environment in Colonial Singapore* (Brenda S. A. Yeoh) and *Singapore: A Developmental City State* (Martin Perry, Lily Kong, and Brenda S. A. Yeoh).

The Politics of Landscapes in
Singapore

1

Introduction

Landscape Politics and the Construction of "Nations"

In an age of globalization, scholars increasingly have paid attention to questions about the continued existence of the state and nation. While some have focused on the *state's* continued existence in terms of its enduring role as an effective economic entity (Ohmae 1995; Gereffi 1996), others have focused more specifically on the continued existence of the "nation-state" as a consequence of globalization, shifting the emphasis from the economic to the cultural and political. In this literature, it has been suggested that the nation-state as the primary institution of social life has declined. Guehenno (1995), for example, argues that the "end of the nation-state" is apparent and serves as a potential threat to personal liberties, while Shapiro (1994) views such decline more positively as heralding a more emancipatory "post-sovereign ethics." Yet current wisdom also acknowledges that there is no simple one-directional process—namely, the decline of nationhood—with globalization. Indeed, it is acknowledged that population movements as a consequence of globalization can "engender absentee patriotism and long-distance nationalism" (Pieterse 1994, 165). Some even argue that this era is a "time of continuing and even heightening nation-state building processes" (Glick Schiller, Basch, and Szanton-Blanc 1995, 59), amounting to a "reassertion" and "celebration of the nation" (Pieterse 1994, 52).

   In this book, we acknowledge that at any one time there are competing centripetal and centrifugal forces shaping the formation of "nation." While we recognize that many of these forces must be contextualized and understood within larger global discourses and flows, we also assert that many attempts to construct "nation," both discursive and material, are effected within the boundaries of the state. Our concern here is to examine specifically the internal strategies that a particular state (Singapore) uses to construct a "nation," focusing on both ideological and material projects. In particular, we scrutinize the part played by landscapes in the making of the Singapore "nation."

Conceptually, we adopt the perspective that "nation" and "identity" are social constructs that are rooted in historical material circumstances. As we elaborate in chapter 2, the "nation" is an "imagined community" (Anderson 1983) and thus conjectural, but it is also rooted in the materiality of sociopolitical and socioeconomic lives. Likewise, identity comprises unstable formations and sites of differences, and it is relational rather than existing as an essence. Identity is thus subject to multiple (re)constructions. Yet, like "nation," the concept of identity is not only discursively constructed but also grounded in historically situated material conditions. Our interrogation of these conceptual ideas within the specific context of Singapore illustrates how analysis of the notion of a socially constructed "nation" must be understood within the specificities of time and place.

The social constructedness of both "nation" and "identity" suggests that their constitution can be negotiated and contested. We proceed with the notion that the idea of "nation" and "national identity" are contested by different social, economic, and political groups who sometimes actively resist powerful state-centrist perspectives in overt ways, while at other times they negotiate meanings through reinterpreting state perspectives in more ordinary ways in their everyday lives. Our emphasis in subsequent chapters will thus be as much on the state's construction of "nation" and "national identity" as on the lived experiences of other actors within Singapore.

Landscapes play an integral role in the (re)construction of "nation" and, relatedly, "national identity." Landscapes naturalize ideologies by making the cultural appear natural (Duncan and Duncan 1988). Thus, particular ideological constructions of "nation" are made to appear natural when concretized in the landscape. The (re)creation of landscapes is therefore unlikely to be an innocent event but must instead be read as being deeply ideological. At the same time, landscapes may be reinterpreted by people in their everyday lives in ways divergent from the imposed meanings of the dominant. The power relations that define and contest the "nation" are therefore often played out in and through landscapes.

Singapore: Archetypal yet Singular

We have chosen to examine the conceptual arguments outlined above within particular time-space specificities. In this regard, Singapore is an excellent case study for exploring the construction of "nation" and "identity." As a country that gained statehood as recently as 1965, contending with a colonial past (1819–1963) and then a turbulent time in union with (then) Malaya (1963–65), the imperatives of "nation-building" are compelling. As a multiracial and multicultural entity with a people of largely immigrant stock, there is more divergence than there is common ground and shared experience to draw on in the exercise of nation-building. At the same time, upon independence, the social, economic, and political problems that confronted the country were staggering, and both ideological and material battles had to be fought in the process of constructing a "nation." In these various ways, Singapore's experience is not unique but parallels that of many other newly or recently independent countries, often from Third World contexts. Therefore, an understanding of Singapore's case may in some ways throw light on processes of nation-building elsewhere. Yet Singapore's case is also unique. Within the brief time of ten to fifteen years from independence, Singapore had propelled itself out of the material difficulties of the 1960s and early 1970s. Indeed, it has moved from a developing country to a newly industrializing economy to its present status of "advanced industrializing nation." For more than a quarter of a century beginning in the 1960s, Singapore, together with the other "tiger economies" of Hong Kong, South Korea, and Taiwan, maintained the highest rate of gross national product (GNP) growth in the world, in the process winning substantial shares of the world market economy. These countries' economic and social conditions were substantially transformed. "Nation-building" has therefore taken place in contexts that have radically changed over a short period of time. Singapore's case is also unique in its small area and the consequent significance of geographical constraints on its material and physical development. This situation has led to the justification for widespread and substantial landscape change. The reconstruction and management of landscapes has become a critical factor in the material and ideological shaping of Singapore.

In the exercise of constructing a "nation," the state in Singapore has emphasized various ideological positions that, as we will illustrate in this book, often draw on the materiality of landscapes for their legitimization. Specifically, in chapter 3 we elaborate on the ideologies of survival, discipline, and pragmatism; multiracialism (and multilingualism, multiculturalism, and multireligiosity); meritocracy; and "Asian" communitarianism. The state has consolidated many of these ideologies in the form of five "Shared Values." Together, these ideological constructs are aimed at maintaining economic development, building a modern(ist) city-state, and developing a "gracious" society, all of which goals undergird the state's attempt to achieve ideological hegemony and maintain political legitimacy. In subsequent chapters, we illustrate how these ideological constructs shape and are shaped by various landscapes.

The Chapters Ahead

While postcolonial nationalism often takes on economic forms such as import-substitution and protectionist policies, social and cultural projects are equally crucial to the nation-building enterprise, even though often "the object of all this hard work [in the social/cultural sphere is to support or effect] a neo-liberal restructuring of the economy so that the ["nation"] can compete for a place in the new globalising world" (Weekly 1999, 338). Without downplaying the importance of economic projects in constructing nations or denying the interconnections between the economic and cultural spheres, we wish to give attention to a variety of landscapes that are usually considered essentially noneconomic in nature. These we call "landscapes of sentiment" (places of worship and places of final repose), "quotidian landscapes" (housing and streets), "landscapes of aesthetics" (performance places), and "landscapes of heritage" (historic areas and symbolic icons). We argue that each of these landscapes feature as a major strand running through both the imaginary and material body of the "nation." They represent landscapes borne of different social-cultural projects and illustrate varied relationships between people and landscapes—from the taken-for-granted to those of intimate significance, from the private to the public, from the functional to the iconic.[1]

Landscapes of sentiment—at both the personal and communal level—are intimately related to the core of meaning in a person's life, implicating meanings that are often central to a person's deeply held beliefs and deepest sentiments. We have chosen two dimensions of life of intimate significance to individuals: first, those landscapes associated with the end of life (deathscapes), and second, those associated with intensely held beliefs (landscapes of religion). In chapters 4 and 5, we explore how these landscapes function as centers of meaning for communal groups and how the state's anxiety to build a "nation" prompts it to rewrite these landscapes in its own terms, drawing on its range of ideological apparatuses. They include, for example, the principles of modernist and pragmatic planning, wrenching religious and racial groups away from their original orientation towards communal ties and beliefs and reorientating them toward the "nation-state." We illustrate how the rewriting of deathscapes and landscapes of religion is critical to this project, but we also examine how individuals and communal groups find ways of negotiating and resisting the state's dominant landscape meanings.

While the landscapes of sentiment we focus on often hold meaning for people in a conscious, self-reflective way, quotidian landscapes are distinguished by their taken-for-granted character. In this regard, they are critically important landscapes to examine, because their very taken-for-grantedness makes them particularly well suited to ideological appropriation. In chapters 5 and 6, we examine Singapore's public housing

1. The arguments we craft in relation to each of these landscapes are built on a range of information sources: archival material (such as parliamentary debates, ministerial speeches, and annual reports of government departments); newspaper reports; interviews and correspondence with representatives of the state in various capacities, including officers in the Ministry of Environment, the Housing and Development Board (HDB), Urban Redevelopment Authority (URA), and National Arts Council (NAC); interviews with non-state agents and civic groups, such as Chinese clan association representatives, religious leaders, and members of the artistic community; and interviews with individuals in various capacities, including religious adherents, residents of heritage districts, and HDB residents affected by upgrading programs.

landscapes and street names respectively, exploring both the state's inscription of ideological meaning in the process of constructing a "nation" and grassroots responses to such inscriptions.

Finally, we focus on landscapes of heritage and aesthetics, which might ostensibly be interpreted as being particularly distinct from our selected quotidian landscapes in terms of functionality. Whereas housing landscapes and street names are patently practical, heritage and aesthetics (here represented by artistic pursuits—in particular, landscapes for the performing arts) may be construed as "luxury" rather than "necessity." This was certainly the case in the early years of Singapore's independence, when the country faced pressing social, economic, and political problems. However, by the late 1980s the discourse was shifting. The ideological and material roles that heritage and the performing arts and their associated landscapes have played since then are examined in chapters 7 and 8.

2

Landscape Politics and the Construction of "Nations"

The Social Constructedness of the "Nation"?

As a reaction against the evolutionary determinism that regards the rise of nations as an inevitable process in the history and development of human society, scholars have argued that the term "nation" is a social construct, a concept borne of modern imagination and which emerged in specific historical circumstances (Jackson and Penrose 1993; Smith 1993). The idea of the "nation" draws on notions of common interest between heterogeneous groups; by grounding this idea in physical space and delimiting a recognizable territory, the belief in the existence, legitimacy, and inviolability of the entity is reinforced. The "nation" comprises an "imagined community" (Anderson 1983)—imagined because "the members of even the smallest nation will never know most of their fellow-members, meet them, or even hear of them, yet in the minds of each lives the image of their communion" (Anderson 1983, 15). At the same time, nations are communities "because, regardless of the actual inequality and exploitation that may prevail in each, the nation is always conceived as a deep, horizontal comradeship" (Anderson 1983, 16). In this vein, the ideology that holds the "nation" together—nationalism—is treated primarily as a political tool, that is, "a vital political discourse . . . able to mobilize different strata, uniting divergent social interests and legitimizing their political aspirations" in order to create or sustain the national imaginary (Smith 1993, 11).

"National identity" suggests that, among members of a particular entity, there is a sense of identification with and belonging to that entity (be it a state defined by political boundaries or a people defined by cultural boundaries). If the "nation" is no more than a socially constituted site and language of political interests, national identities too would be largely conjunctural and socially constructed rather than of the essence and natural (Clifford 1988, 12; Jackson and Penrose 1993; Cohen 1993). It follows that, at particular times and under particular conditions, the sense of national identity becomes especially fragile. In other words, the need to foster and assert the sense of identity may be stronger at particular times than at other times. In circumstances where heterogeneous groups are involved, where a shared history is lacking, or where any nascent sense of nation and national identity is threatened by global—sometimes interpreted as Western—forces, the bonds between members of the community and between people and place are, at best, tenuous, and require nurturing. The rise of the modern nation-state is certainly one condition under which there is a need to develop and assert the sense of identity to construct a "nation-state." In the context of Europe and America, for example, a period of rapid political mobilization and social change threatened the stability of the old orders, particularly between 1870 and 1914. Nations were created as the main mode of social control to foster group belonging and cohesion (Hobsbawm and Ranger 1983). This was achieved through the "invention of traditions," including fairly recent symbols such as the national anthem and the national flag and suitably tailored discourses such as national history, designed to "inculcate certain values and norms of behaviour" (Hobsbawm and Ranger 1983, 1).

It has also been argued that in recent times, with improved telecommunications and the growth in travel and tourism, time-space compression has led to the loss of a "sense of local place and its particularity." This broader "annihilation of space by time" has led some to reactionary responses: "certain forms of nationalism, [and] sentimentalized recovering of sanitized 'heritages' " (Massey 1993, 232). Featherstone (1993, 177) suggests that with greater globalization there is the "generation of such nationalistic, ethnic and fundamentalist reactions to globalization . . . [that there is] a strong assertion of local cultures. These might take the form of reviving or simulating local traditions and ceremonies, or inventing new ones." Attempts may be made to produce "homogeneous, integrated common cultures and standardized citizens loyal to the national ideal" (Featherstone 1993, 178) through the "establishment of national symbols and ceremonies and the reinvention of traditions" (Featherstone 1993, 178). The rites and ceremonies need not be invented *ex nihilo* because they can draw on traditions and ethnic cultures that possessed plausibility (Featherstone 1993, 178).

While "invention," "imagination," and "reconstruction" are processes integrally woven into the formation of nations, Smith (1993) cautions that it would be an error to conceive of the new world of nations as a purely constructed order borne of conscious manipulation alone and to ignore the central, historically embedded, role of ethnic, political, and religious ties as well as common institutions and rights that reinforce a feeling of belonging to a bounded territory. Similarly, it has been vigorously debated in the literature whether national identity is an "inevitable, natural outcome of community existence constructed through tradition and history" or whether it is "artificially constructed by powers that be, an insidious notion created to hegemonically control individual thought and dissent" (Das and Harindranath 1995, 499). For our purposes, we take the position that the national imaginary is necessarily rooted in and continually changing according to the materiality of sociopolitical and socioeconomic lives. For example, it was in the aftermath of the traumatic rupture of occupation by invading forces during the Second World War that a backlash of anticolonial sentiments was set off in hitherto colonized countries, where "the jelly of nationhood" (Gopal Baratham 1999) began to congeal among the polyglot populations in plural societies and "national identity" emerged. And as Hooson (1994, 368) argues, even if the most apparently "self-evident" of national identities (such as French or English identities) are made up primarily of myths and memories, this fact does not diminish the material groundings if "people are prepared to sacrifice their lives for the assertion of their national identities, and the restoration of the 'historic' lands to which they 'belong.'" Nations are hence embedded in both the "material and imaginative spatialities of collective and individual subjects" (Radcliffe and Westwood 1996, 23). The space of the nation is hence both "imagined" and "lived" at the same time, a complex interweaving of shadow and substance. To borrow the words of Jacobs (1996, 158, written in the context of the social construction of imperialist space but equally applicable in our present context), "imaginary and material geographies are not incommensurate, nor is one simply the product, a disempowered surplus, of the other. They are complexly intertwined and mutually constitutive." Lowenthal (1994, 15) puts the idea across more succinctly: "National identity is a leitmotiv of modern politics, geography and history the bulwarks of national identity."

It must also be noted that, not only do imaginaries about the national self take different forms in different places, the "imagined community" and its inclusions and exclusions are continually subjected to a multiplicity of ambivalent or even contradictory interpretations in any one place. As Radcliffe and Westwood (1996, 12) note, we cannot assume that people are automatically mobilized by ideologies about the "nation" propagated by the state; instead, there are "simultaneous yet different versions of national identity" that assume crucial significance, particularly in multiethnic, multidiasporic communities in which the task of national self-definition is fraught with contradictory tensions and diverse claims. They argue that, in the context of Latin America, while socioeconomic elites have been identified as "potential nation-builders," it was equally crucial to "refuse to take on board either a state- or elite-centred notion of the nation-building project" and instead to recognize that "the very nature of the national imagined community" is being constituted by "struggles over defining nation and identity through which different groups and institutions (whether cross-class, elite or popular) express their collective subjectivity and political projects." Even as individual subjects are (re)constituted in and through relations of state power and the discourses of nationalism produced by the state, cross-cutting, overlapping, and alternative forms of identification persist and continue to be articulated and re-articulated. In order to interrogate the multidimensionality of national identities, scholars need to give more attention not only to state discourses but also to social and cultural practices that are generative of what Radcliffe and Westwood (1993, 19) call "quotidian definitions of nationhood and affiliations to place." While research on identity formation has burgeoned in recent years, it has not moved to examine explicitly "the ways in which national cultural identity at the popular level is actually constructed, maintained or challenged" (Johnson 1995, 52). To do this work requires first an understanding of power relations that goes beyond examining the state as a regime of modern power and an instrument of control.

Power Relations Within the "Nation"

While analyses of national self-definition have often focused on the state and its disciplinary powers in the forging of the nation—from delimiting and policing national boundaries to engendering national consciousness—we argue for a reading of power relations that goes beyond a description of domination and dependence, allowing for the insertion of collusion, conflict, and collision as individual or collective subjects engage in negotiation, dialogue, and counter-strategies, often in the sphere of everyday life. It has been argued, by Foucault (1980a) in particular, that power should neither be arrogated to the state or political system nor identified with particular individuals. Instead, Foucault has argued that power emerges from "local arenas of action" and should be viewed as "a 'microprocess' of social life or pervasive feature of concrete, local transaction" (quoted in Agnew 1987, 23). The effects of power cannot simply be defined as repressive but are instead productive and enabling, "run[ning] through the whole social body" rather than remaining confined to the state or political system (Foucault 1984, 60–61). Power is not conceived as a property but is expressed in specific strategies: its effects of domination are attributed to dispositions, maneuvers, tactics, techniques, functionings. In short, this power is exercised rather than possessed (Foucault 1979).

As conceptual tools that aid in understanding the exercise of power in the making of the "nation," we explore the notions of "ideology," "hegemony," "ideological hegemony," and "resistance." "Ideology" is a complex term that, following J. B. Thompson (1981, 147), refers to "a system of signification which facilitates the pursuit of particular interests" and sustains specific "relations of domination" within society.[1] We also adopt the Gramscian notion of "hegemony" as the means by which domination and rule is achieved (Gramsci 1973). Hegemony does not involve controls that are clearly recognizable as constraints in the traditional coercive sense. Instead, hegemonic controls involve a set of ideas and values that the major-

---

1. Thompson (1981) rejects two other definitions of "ideology," criticizing the first ("the lattice of ideas which permeate the social order, constituting the collective consciousness of each epoch") for being overgeneralized and the second ("false" consciousness that "fails to grasp the real conditions of human existence") for being too narrow and pejorative.

ity are persuaded to adopt as their own. In order to persuade the majority, these ideas and values are portrayed as "natural" and "common-sense." This is "ideological hegemony." Once accepted, the ruling group has the power to shape the political and social system. In specific terms, to stay in power a ruling group must persuade people that the group is working for the general good of the country. Further, members of the ruling group must persuade people to accept their definitions of the "general, public good" and people must be convinced that the ruling group's methods of attaining this "public good" are the most natural, commonsensical ones. If policies and actions are supported, the power of the ruling group is uncontested. The more successful ruling group is the one that attains power through ideological hegemony rather than through coercion. When hegemonic control is successful, the social order endorsed by the political elite is, at the same time, the social order that the masses desire.

While gaining and maintaining political power through hegemony is desirable, Gramsci (1973) also has made clear that such hegemony is never fully achieved. In other words, those seeking to gain power or maintain power will always be challenged in some way by other groups in society. To attribute an absolute omnipotence to the "apparatus" of disciplinary power analyzed by Foucault would, as Colin Gordon (1980) has argued, confuse the domain of *discourse* with those of *practices* and *effects*. This is because that which is intended and articulated by the "powerful" within the domain of discourse (such as those of nationalist ideology or urban planning) may fail to materialize in its entirety when transposed to the domain of actual practices and techniques or may produce unintended consequences and effects. Such a situation would also amount to denying that those that disciplinary power seeks to control are capable of counter-strategies that can challenge disciplinary power and modify its effects. As Giddens (1987, 11) has contended, "no matter how great the scope and intensity of control superordinates possess, since their power presumes the active compliance of others, those others can bring to bear strategies of their own, and apply specific types of sanctions." Foucault (1980b, 142) himself admits that there are possibilities for "revolts to the gaze" and contends that instances of resistance to power "are all the more real and effective because they are formed right at the point where relations of power are exercised [and that] like power, such resistance is multiple and can be integrated in global strate- gies." Specific forms of resistance may be overt and material but they could as well be latent and symbolic. In other words, while resistance represents political action, it can be conveyed in cultural terms, for example, through the appropriation and transformation of the material culture of the domi- nating group (see for example Hall and Jefferson 1976; CCCS 1978; and Hall et al. 1978). This kind of use of cultural terms is often the means of resistance adopted by the "weak" (Scott 1985) and represents "tactics" (de Certeau 1984) and "rituals" (Hall and Jefferson 1976) rather than "strategies."

As already implicit in the above, we argue that the specificities of hege- monic control and resistance are constituted at both the discursive and practical levels of social reality within the body of the nation. Conflict and negotiation may occur as a result of the collision of discourses but, more often than not, they exist at the level of habitual practice as part of every- day life. It is in daily encounters that power can be studied "in its external visage, at the point where it is in direct and immediate relationship with . . . its object, its target, its field of application, . . .where it installs itself and produces its real effects" (Foucault 1980c, 97). It is at this level too that sub- jugation is achieved, challenged, or inflected. The "concrete space of everyday life," to borrow Henri Lefebvre's (1991) term, not only is en- framed, constrained, and colonized by the disciplinary technologies of the state, but also the site of resistance and active struggle as individual subjects challenge the hegemony of the state. The commonsensical, pragmatic cir- cumstances of everyday life not only provide the context for the "experi- ence of culture" (Cohen 1982) but also—in as much as everyday encounters are embedded within and shaped by the larger discursive/polit- ical context—ordinary people in turn affect political discourse. It must of course be added that the degree to which they are able to make a real dif- ference depends in part on the effectiveness with which they are able to (whether discursively or tacitly) draw upon coherent ideologies, institu- tional structures and resources, and schemes of legitimation that are inde- pendent of, or impenetrable to, state authorities.

The Politics of Landscapes

Central to the construction of a "nation" is the articulation of a "mystical bond between people and place," an immutable relationship between citizens and their country (Penrose 1993, 29). While there indeed may be a disjuncture between the "national place" and "national identity," identifications with a "nation" usually evoke a sense of belonging to a specific territorial space.[2] Not only are social identities such as a sense of the national self mapped onto claims over particular configurations of concrete space, we argue that such nationalized space is defined not only in terms of its physical reaches and limits but also in terms of the way it is crafted into a landscape and infused with meaning to support, represent, and reproduce a particular lifestyle. Interestingly, Olwig (1993, 331–32) observes that the word "landscape" bears similarities to the word "nation" and in fact carries the suggestion of being an area of cultural identity based, however loosely, on tribal ties or blood ties and thus bears, with the word "nation," "a counterpositional relation to the concept of the state as a more formal governmental organisation."

By "landscape" we follow Steve Daniels (1989, 206) in arguing that this complex notion may be seen as "a dialectical image, an ambiguous synthesis whose redemptive and manipulative aspects cannot be finally disentangled, which can neither be completely reified as an authentic object in the world nor thoroughly dissolved as an ideological mirage." In this sense, landscape embodies both the material and the imagined and reflects the negotiation of power between the dominant and subordinated in society, each with their own versions of reality and practice (Anderson 1983, 28). On one hand, this notion articulates the social construction of landscape imposed by the powerful—planners, architects, administrators, politicians, property owners, developers—intent on advancing state ideology or consumer capitalism. By becoming part of the everyday, landscape acts as a powerful ideological tool that masks the artifice and ideological nature of

2. For example, Radcliffe and Westwood (1996, 20) observe that the "space of a nation" can be imagined by populations that have no "place" in which to express or consolidate that identity; alternatively, a nation-in-diaspora may hark back to a "homeland" located either in the past or the future but absent under present conditions.

its form and content, making what is patently cultural appear to be as natural as possible (Duncan and Duncan 1988; Kobayashi 1989; Duncan 1990). On the other hand, landscape is also a "multicoded space" that, in its everyday usage, is constantly reinterpreted by "everyday people who may be 'reading' and 'writing' different languages in the built environment" (Goss 1988, 398). For the everyday users of a particular landscape, it is an environment of both opportunity and constraint. As Appadurai (1990, 297) notes, the suffix "scape" indicates that these spaces are not objectively constituted but are "deeply perspectival constructs" that vary with the angle of vision.

Power relations that define and contest the specificities of the "nation" are negotiated through, among other things, elements of the cultural landscape, including the landscapes and practices of everyday life. In this idea, we echo the view that social relations are constituted through as well as constrained and mediated by space (Wolch and Dear 1988). In more concrete terms, we grapple with this insight by examining how the landscape is differentially perceived and drawn upon by the state authorities and other social groups with their own versions of reality and practice, the conflicts over the production, definition and use of space, and their resolution. This point of view focuses explanation on the practical nature of everyday life and the plural and diverse readings of spatiality rather than on the abstracted nature of political organization or superorganic culture in understanding the creation and sustenance of the "nation" and "national identity," as well as their inflections.

In our conception of power relations, therefore, landscapes become an integral part of the exercise of power in the (re)making of nations and—in being drawn into relations of domination, negotiation, and resistance—reflect cultural politics at work. Part of the state's attempt to secure political legitimacy, build ideological consensus, and forge a sense of national identity depends on the imposition of what Rabinow (1989) calls "norms and forms" to shape the landscape. These "norms and forms" in turn reflect state aspirations and are used "both consciously and unconsciously, as social technologies, as strategies of power to incorporate, categorize, discipline, control, and reform" the inhabitants of the city (King 1990, 9). Toward these ends, an institutional framework that put into effect social technologies for planning, orchestrating, and controlling the organization and shaping the urban landscape had to be created. These technologies often emphasize rationality and functionalism and what might be described as a "demolish and rebuild" mentality; they parallel Relph's (1976) "objective outsideness," in which places are analyzed in terms of logic, models, reason, and efficiency. The application of rationality in planning is in effect a strategy of power and occurs at two levels: a procedural level, concerned with rationality in the process of planning; and a substantive level, concerned with the subject matter of planning such as social welfare, economic activity, and so forth (Thomas 1982, 13). The combined result is usually that rationality and pragmatism puts a premium on the "economic" use of land, often giving rise to the annihilation of place.

However, while landscapes reflect the exercise of state power to fashion a "nation," they are also sites of conflict and negotiation where individual and collective subjects of the "nation" resist or inflect the imposition of an all-encompassing structure on the landscapes in question. Such conflicts often arise as a consequence of the different ways in which people, at an everyday level, develop relationships with places and invest personal, social, and other symbolic meanings and values in these places.

This analysis of the nexus between the cultural and political, as reflected and reproduced in the materiality of the landscape as well as in its imaginative representations, reiterates the point that power relations do not simply involve political and economic coercion/resistance but also ideological and cultural impositions/oppositions that are often inseparable from the material. In the same way that cultures have political dimensions (Blaut 1980), cultural landscapes are produced at the nexus between the cultural and the political. As Fox (quoted in Cartier 1997, 577) points out, we need to avoid "a false rigidity to our conception of culture [in which we] artificially fortify our belief that cultural productions can be classified as either racial, or ethnic, or nationalist."

In the main chapters (chapters 4–9) of this book, we examine the cultural politics implicated in the construction of the Singapore "nation" through an interrogation of several material "strands" interwoven into the tapestry of landscape. In the following sections, we provide a brief review of each of these landscapes and the complex ways in which they have been harnessed to the task of constructing the "nation."

"Death" Landscapes

It has been argued that, far from being wasted space of purely esoteric interest, "the habitations of the departed invite inquiry into all manner of social and geographical questions" because the jolting, crisis-laden nature of death allows us to "peel back . . . the central layers of our community's value system—traditions and axioms rarely examined during the routine stretches of our days and years" (Zelinsky 1994, 29). On the assumption that landscapes of death are collective representations of deeply shared attitudes, values, and cosmologies among the living, the bulk of the work on these resting places for the dead have focused on the social organization and production of death landscapes and related ritual practices and artifacts, as well as the ways that groups based on ethnicity, class, or religion articulate and shape their cultural values, norms, and experiences (see reviews in Yeoh and Tan 1995; Teather 1998; Kong 1999). Taking this view to a different plane, others have argued that cemeteries represent the collective identity of the soul of a nation because they are the sacred spaces of the "nation" where those who had once toiled in the past are now laid to rest (Jackson and Vergara 1989). They are "the last great necessity" of the city and, ultimately, the "nation" (Sloane 1991).

Indeed, it has been argued that cemeteries and columbaria are repositories of not only personal but also collective memories and as such provide an ideal terrain from which to resurrect deeply rooted, fundamental values that characterize the people of a "nation" (Teather 1998). From this starting point, a number of geosophical studies (a geographical tradition that seeks to reconstruct images of "other" imagined worlds; see Lowenthal and Bowden 1975) such as Zelinsky (1975) and Knight (1985) use cemetery placenames and information culled from epitaphs to piece together conceptions of the American afterworld as a mirror image of the American "nation."

Drawing on the analytical tools of cultural politics rather than geosophy, Cartier (1993; 1997; 1998) demonstrates the way in which Bukit

China in Melaka, Malaysia, the world's largest traditional Chinese cemetery, became a landscape of contention between different versions of national culture. Her work is a showcase of how various groups—political and
nonpolitical parties, community and temple associations—negotiated with
the state to prevent the removal of some 12,500 graves from the cemetery
to make way for what might have been the largest historical and cultural
theme park in the world. Cartier argues that, against the selfconsciously
Malay-centric national culture championed by the Malaysian state government, preservationist groups drew on landscape representations of Bukit
China to press for an alternative, place-based version of national culture
that acknowledged the contributions of the Chinese community and the
active cooperation among ethnic groups. The monumental landscape of
death was transformed from "a tired Chinese burial ground" into a "nationscape," a "singular site in Malaysia to embody the history of the nation"
(Cartier 1997, 576).

Religious Landscapes

Significant attention has been paid to the nexus between religion, nation,
state, and politics, particularly within sociology and political science. Writers have examined, for example, the relationship between religion and voting patterns (Scheefers et al. 1994; Gee 1995), and the role of religion in
influencing the success of political participation (Wood 1994; Gifford
1998). More pertinent in the present context, studies have focused on the
ways in which religion reinforces or challenges attempts at constructing
the "nation" (Ludden 1996; Lee and Ackerman 1997; Ayabe 1998; van der
Veer and Lehmann 1999). These works focus on the social and political
roles played by religious groups and organizations, but they do not interrogate the roles of religious landscapes in the (de)construction of the "nation." Simultaneously, a separate body of literature acknowledges the
existence of a politics of sacred space. Chidester and Linenthal (1995, 15),
for example, argue that "a sacred space is not merely discovered, or
founded, or constructed," but "is claimed, owned, and operated by people
advancing specific interests." However, this literature on the politics of sacred space (see for example Naylor and Ryan 1998; Philp and Mercer 1999)

has remained essentially separate from the literature on the social constructedness of "nation." The conflicts over use of space by different religious groups have often been examined, for instance, apart from the
question of how such conflicts reflect divergences in particular notions of
"belonging" and "nation."

This connection is addressed more recently in a small number of works
that more frequently acknowledge implicitly rather than address explicitly
the part played by religious landscapes (including the politics of such landscapes) in the process of "nation" construction. Dwyer and Meyer's (1996)
comparison of the institutionalization of Islam in the Netherlands and the
United Kingdom through a consideration of the establishment of state-
funded Islamic schools is a case in point. In examining the conflicts over the
establishment of such schools, the authors argue that ideological constructions of "Muslim" and "integration" are at play. Specifically, some argue that
Islamic schools detract from integration because they will be populated
largely, if not exclusively, by immigrant children. Without the mixing of
children of different cultural and religious backgrounds in schools, integration is thought to be impossible. The multicultural school, in this view, is
the "site of the creation of a multicultural society." On the other hand, others argue that Islamic schools provide the grounds for the development of a
strong sense of identity, only after which integration might occur. The authors illustrate how these negotiated notions of "integration" inform decision-making (Dwyer and Meyer 1996, 235–36; see also Dwyer and Meyer
1995, in which the argument is extended to Belgium as well). Fundamentally, the issue is one of how notions of "nation" intersect with notions of
"being Muslim," an issue played out in this case in one particular site of religious practice, the Islamic school. Like Dwyer and Meyer, Jacobs's (1993)
examination of conflicts over aboriginal sacred sites in Australia reveals the
ways in which white constructions of a multicultural "nation" impose particular ways in which aboriginal practices surrounding the sacred are to be
incorporated. Whereas indigenous peoples may not want to or be able to
map the precise boundaries of their land claims because of the nature of
their beliefs, non-Aboriginal Australia insists on such precision (Jacobs
1993, 111). This has become one of the mechanisms by which legitimacy
of claims in "multicultural" Australia is established (see also Jacobs 1996).

What the above examples illustrate are the ways in which the politics of religious place form an integral part of the negotiations over what constitutes the "nation." Such religious place may take the form of religious schools or natural sites, as exemplified in the studies above, but also deserve to be extended to other types of religious places, from the "officially sacred" (for example, churches, temples, mosques, synagogues) (Leiris 1938) to pilgrimage sites, communal halls, and roadside shrines, for instance (see Kong 2001).

Housing Landscapes

There are no more quotidian and immediate landscapes in people's lives than housing landscapes—a necessary, and in some ways, often taken-for-granted dimension of everyday lives (except for the homeless). Yet, the very habitual nature of this landscape often masks its intense ideological role, certainly in the construction of the "nation." Alongside other urban policies, such as zoning codes and regulations and conservation and preservation legislation, housing policy has been a crucial instrument in the formation and maintenance of the "nation" in various contexts. Existing literature in this area illustrate how this operation might proceed along three fronts. First, housing policy may be a means by which the privileges of citizenship are exercised, thus effecting and reinforcing notions of "insideness" and "outsideness." Daly (1996, 11), for example, examines how increasing migration across western Europe has created a "marginal class of aliens working within a shadow economy," reflected in part in their relegation to the worst housing in the least desirable districts of large cities. Some of this takes the form of temporary hostels, containers, and barges for homeless migrants, but with increasing fiscal constraints and right-wing political pressures, housing inadequacies are a powerful means by which to argue for and put in place immigration restrictions, as well as to mask xenophobic tendencies that call for the deportation of foreigners (see also Faist and Haussermann 1996). Second, local and neighborhood-level conflicts over housing, both in the property market and at the level of architecture and design, are not merely conflicts over different factions of capital and different systems of aesthetics but are anchored in questions of friction between "capital and community, immigrants and long-term residents, [and often] Asians and non-Asians" (Smith 1995, 59). In several North American cities, including Vancouver and New York, for example, the disputes over housing issues are material manifestations of less tangible unhappiness over the "Asianization" of neighborhoods and cities (see also Mitchell 1997). Writ large, these are encounters in public discourses about and disputes over "multiculturalism" and "nation." A third set of housing literature examines how housing policies are actively used as instruments in the state's construction and maintenance of particular visions of the "nation." Chua (1991a, 1991b), Van Grunsven (1992), and Laquian (1996), for example, have argued that housing policy is used by the Singapore government as part of its race-relations/management strategy, a strategy in its maintenance of a multiracial "nation."

Toponymic Inscriptions of Landscapes

Within the expanding field of textual readings of the landscape, toponyms[3] have been critically "read" for a variety of purposes as "signifiers" of wider societal trends. Toponymic inquiry traditionally has been used for inferring landscape and settlement histories; the elaboration and mutation of place-names are used to reconstruct the "sequent occupance" of colonizing and sojourning groups. This fact can be seen in the inscription of imperial personalities and imagery on the landscape of colonial societies. Thus, "the sudden rash" of Tlaxcalan place-names in northern Mexico cannot be explained without understanding Aztec colonial policies of the fifteenth century; similarly, making sense of Germanic place-names of southern Chile, Brazil, and Paraguay cannot be divorced from knowledge of the nineteenth-century streams of immigrants into the region (Robinson 1989, 160). Todorov (quoted in Robinson 1989, 160) also reminds us that Columbus was "careful to name the sequence of the first five newly discovered places [in the Caribbean] in a rank order which tells us a great deal of the context of his historic enterprise: the Savior (San Salvador); the Virgin Mary (Santa Maria de la Concepción); the King (Fernandina); the Queen

---

3. "Toponyms" literally mean "place-names" (*topos* = "place"; *onomia* = "name").

(Isabela); and finally the Royal Prince (Juana)." In a similar fashion but a different context, streets christened "Victoria," "Albert," "Queen's," "King's," "Coronation," and "Princess Elizabeth" (after British royalty) ubiquitously found in major ex-colonial South and Southeast Asian cities were inscribed onto the landscape as part and parcel of the lexicon of British nineteenth-century colonialism.

Such an approach has more recently spawned fresh studies on the name-changing process with the emergence of new "nations" in the post-colonial world. For example, Robinson (1989, 160) argues that, in Latin America, "when regimes fall, empires collapse, or one local elite replaces another, very often a name-changing process is initiated in particular places" to signify the installation of a new configuration of power. Indeed, if the power of "nomination . . . is often the first step in taking possession" (Todorov, quoted in Robinson 1989, 160), place-names would constitute one of the most obvious cultural products through which we may investigate the transition from colonial to independent rule.

With the dismantling of colonial empires and the rise of nationalism in the postcolonial world, some newly independent countries have found it necessary for purposes of ideological and political legitimation to divest the landscape of colonial associations. In this process, colonial street names in some Indian and Malaysian cities have been changed to reflect local essences (Lewandowski 1984; Khoo 1993). For example, Anglicized place-names in Malaysia are accompanied by a parallel vernacular system: generic terms such as "Street," "Road," and "Lane" have indigenous equivalents (e.g., in Georgetown, Penang, "Light Street" becomes "Lebuh Light," "Transfer Road" becomes "Jalan Transfer," and "Western Road" becomes "Jalan Utama") while a few street names have taken on completely different connotations (e.g., "Northam Road" is now also "Jalan Sultan Ahmad Shah" while "Green Lane" has been renamed "Jalan Mesjid Negeri"). Clearly, place-names are "among the first to undergo a refurbishing to commemorate new regimes" (Richman 1983, 16).

In a different context, Cohen and Kliot (1992) have illustrated the way the Israeli nation-state selects Biblical and Talmudic place-names for the administered territories of the Golan, Gaza, and West Bank in order to reinforce national Zionist ideologies and project Israel as the rightful heir to the holy land. In North America, individual place-names honoring public figures have been interpreted as indicators of nationalistic fervor (Zelinsky 1983; Stump 1988; Rogers 1995), while whole new patterns of street names have been generated and inscribed in the landscape as part of the ideological process of "nation-building" in South Africa (Pirie 1984).

While the christening of places and streets reflects the power of dominant others to assign place-meanings to serve hegemonic purposes (whether colonial or nationalistic), various commentators have observed that the process is not uncontested. Pirie (1984, 51) shows how the naming process is contingent on the "social relations of deference and defiance" in the case of the naming of Soweto, South Africa's best-known black urban township. Berg and Kearns (1996, 99) argue that "the process of naming places involves a contested identity politics of people and place" and go on to show how the debate over the reinstatement of Maori names in Aotearoa, New Zealand, traded explicitly in the rhetorics of "race," "culture," and "nation." While Emmerson's (1984, 4) observation that names in "Humpty Dumpty" fashion express "the power of the namer over the thing named" is a salient one, it must be remembered that schemes of power often encounter strategies of resistance on the part of those who bear the brunt of such power. The naming process hence not only is of toponymic significance but also embodies some of the social struggle for control over the means of symbolic production of the "nation."

Heritage Landscapes

The creation of heritage landscapes forms part of the "process of cultural and geographical imagining" (Gruffudd 1994, 61) integral to the work of "nation-building." Heritage refers to the making of "an apparently immutable history present in the *now* of society—as a logic of the concrete" (Crang 1994, 341). Such a mapping of "history" onto "territory" is indispensable to the construction of a nation because "the idea of the nation as 'imagined community' presupposes a demarcated space which incorporates particular symbolic landscapes and sites . . . [which are] the repository of common memories, myths and traditions" (Edensor 1997, 175). The selective fixing of history into the firm bedrock of place to mark a "circuit of memory" (Johnson 1995, 63) gives form and shape to the nation's life-story and does so in ways that masks the artifice and ideological nature of its content. Indeed, if "the most successful ideological effects are those which have no words, and ask no more than complicitous silence" (Bourdieu, quoted in Harvey 1989, 78–79), then public icons and historic monuments, heritage sites and cultural theme parks are illustrations of these effects par excellence. As Johnson (1995, 52) argues, if the "imagination and territoriality" that go into defining a "nation" are not to appear as though they are fashioned "out of thin air" (quoting Watts 1992), we need to examine "the ways in which material bases for nationalist imaginings emerge and are structured symbolically." Heritage landscapes provide us with everyday material forms to examine the "relationships between the memorialisation of the past and the spatialisation of public memory" in the context of the ongoing task of "nation-building" (Johnson 1995, 63).

Much has been written about the (re)valorization of various landscapes as "heritage areas" or "historic monuments" in a bid to buttress a national sense of history and belonging. In the postcolonial developing world, for example, while the preoccupation with modernization and industrialization continues to dominate the way urban landscapes are shaped, historic elements—from solitary buildings to whole areas—have been revalorized. They have been appreciated anew as resources invested with symbolic values of relevance to the construction of national, ethnic, or cultural identities, as well as local assets that feed the growing heritage tourism industry, of significance in an era of globalization when places are compelled to compete internationally by selling local cultures and difference in a cosmopolitan marketplace (Dix 1990; Bromley and Jones 1995; Parenteau et al. 1995; Robins 1991). Monumental forms, whether created from artifacts of the past or made anew, are also often key landscape nodes embedded within the symbolic matrix of modern nationhood (Azaryahu and Kellerman 1999, 109). As "signatures of power" (Lasswell 1979), they are landscape forms intended to "put the viewer in awe, evoke emotions, then humble the individual before the abstract notions [of particular ideologies]" (Boddy 1983, 38) and hence have a special place in mobilizing the emotive and symbolic aspects of nationhood. Often permeated with notions of history and heroic mythology, monumental iconic forms are "sites of memory

[that] weld historical events and contemporary sights, evoking historical memories and mythical associations" (Azaryahu and Kellerman 1999, 111).

For many postcolonial societies in search of nationhood, the question of what constitutes national heritage is particularly difficult. Societies emerging from colonialism have to decide how far to divest the landscape of colonial associations by removing its stock of colonial structures and to what extent to accept the colonial legacy as part and parcel of the sociocultural baggage of the newly independent states. Western (1985, 344) notes that, in practice, postcolonial nations often "do not have the capability to rewrite forthwith a new image in their cities" as "other priorities clamor" and colonial structures are often appropriated for new purposes and reinvested with new meanings more congruent with national consciousness. Tunbridge (1984, 174–78), for example, argues that, ironically, the present city government of Harare, the capital of Zimbabwe, is more sensitive to heritage conservation in comparison to the pro-development white governments that preceded it, partly because of a need to claim a history to bolster the new nation and partly because heritage provides a profitable means to compete for the tourist dollar. Fitch (1982, 402) contends that, in the Third World in general, the balance between conservation and redevelopment is particularly difficult to maintain in the case of postcolonial "nations," not only because of "economic and political problems of staggering complexity" but also because the nations are "prisoners of a cultural ambiguity."

The fixing of "history" into "heritage" is by no means an uncontested process. What constitutes "history" in pluralistic postcolonial "nations," where the perspective of hindsight is still highly unstable? What becomes valorized and mapped as "heritage" in official imaginative geographies? Who controls the whole process of transforming "history" into tangible presences (and hence also absences) on the landscape and for what purposes? These remain fraught terrain. Hardy (1988, 333) reminds us that the term "heritage" does not simply describe an assemblage of cultural traditions and artifacts belonging to a particular community but is a value-laden concept, "embracing (and often obscuring) differences of interpretation that are dependent on . . . class, gender and locality; and with the concept itself locked into wider frameworks of dominant and subversive ideologies." For example, Jacobs (1996, 130) traces the ways in which a heritage-redevelopment project involving an old brewery in Perth, Australia, called forth complex relationships among the "indigenous," the "colonial," and the "postcolonial" imaginaries, setting in train "an anxious politics of reter-ritorialisation" that "unleash[ed] disturbing powers on the constitution of the nation."

"Arts" Landscapes

In considering landscapes of the arts, various sets of literatures have a bearing on the issues we are concerned with here. First, researchers have focused on the ways in which cultural resources may be harnessed to anchor national identities and act as a bulwark to globalizing forces. The debates on the indigenization of cultural content reflect desires to assert local/national identities in the midst of influences assumed to be homogenizing and culturally imperialistic. In the growing literature on globalization, for example, it has been argued that a homogenization of cultural forms has resulted because of improved technologies, commodification, and commercialization (Cohen 1991, 342). Adorno (1992), for example, has argued that music has been subject to such global processes, what with the proliferation of technologies such as radio, the cassette, and compact disc. With these technologies, it has become possible to involve music in mass production as part of capitalistic ventures. The result is a significant degree of standardization and homogenization as huge quantities are produced and widely distributed. Indeed, it has been argued that such border crossing has given rise to conditions of placelessness and timelessness (Wallis and Malm 1984; Meyrowitz 1985). Such arguments about the negative homogenizing effects of global forces are often equated with Americanization. Thus, a process of cultural imperialism is said to be at work in which the cultural spaces of (Third World) nations are being broken down by the "economic and political domination of the United States . . . thrust[ing] its hegemonic culture into all parts of the world" (Featherstone 1993, 170). It is argued that this process is damaging to local cultures because they give way under the relentless modernizing force of American cultural imperialism. In such a scenario, the sense of collective memory and tradition of localities will be obliterated to the point that there is "no sense of place" (Meyrowitz 1985).

Such views of the negative effects of globalization and the loss of local-cultural identity are, however, countered by other arguments about the role of local resources in anchoring the production of cultural forms. For example, in the context of musical production, it has been suggested that there are "local sounds," that is, particular sounds that are produced in particular localities with specific characteristics (Halfacree and Kitchin 1996). Such unique local sounds are the result of, among other things, the distinctive interplay of language, lyrics, melody, and instrumentation. They are also singular because of the general "feel" or sensory impact of the music. In other words, in recognizing that particular musical forms "originate within, interact with, and are inevitably affected by, the physical, social, political and economic factors which surround them" (Cohen 1991, 342), it is possible to identify unique local sounds produced from unique local milieux—in spite of broader global capitalistic forces that tend to encourage homogenization (see Kong 1996; 1997). In this way, cultural resources are a significant means by which national identity is engendered.

A second set of literature focuses on an examination of particular cultural activities and the politics surrounding them. These studies examine social conflicts in the production and consumption of these activities, offering insights into the ways in which these events form part of the maintenance of social distance between groups (Clarke 1982; Waterman 1998), or conversely, contribute to the social glue that brings different social and political groups together (for example, through the creation of spectacle; see Ley and Olds 1988).

A third set of works examines the ways by which cultural activities serve to bring together neighborhoods and communities, particularly through community arts activities. Such activities are analyzed for their role in the formation and maintenance of a sense of community identity and belonging. Writers have argued, for example, that cultural policies that are truly effective do not simply succeed in terms of income or employment generation but contribute toward improving the quality of life, particularly social cohesion and community development. The really important mission, according to Bianchini (1993, 212), is to develop a cultural-planning perspective that is "rooted in an understanding of local cultural resources and of cities as cultural entities—as places where people meet, talk, share ideas and desires, and where identities and lifestyles are formed." To do so requires that there is "an explicit commitment to revitalise the cultural, social and political life of local residents" and this should "precede and sustain the formulation of physical and economic regeneration strategies" (Bianchini 1993, 212). Others make similar arguments. Wynne (1992, x), for example, calls for the arts to be made a daily part of people's lives, socially and economically, and argues that only then will the arts "reside within the wider community associated with that everyday life, rather than existing as an appendage to it . . . in some exclusive arena outside of everyday experience" (see Kong 2000a; 2000b). Such cultural policies not only serve to develop or rejuvenate community identity but may also be viewed as constituting part of a larger agenda in the invention of a "nation."

In these three sets of literature, the role of landscapes is sometimes implicitly handled while at other times it is explicitly and integrally part of the analysis. Conflicts surrounding cultural activities may be manifested in conflicts over the use of space for such activities, while the revitalization of local/community life through artistic ventures is critically tied to the landscape resources available. Indeed, analysis of the availability of such resources, their adequacy or lack thereof, their architectural form, and a host of related issues becomes crucial in the understanding of the roles that landscapes for the arts play in the construction of the "nation."

3

Singapore

The Making of a New "Nation"

Historical Trajectory: A New State, A New Social Order

In 1965, Singapore became an independent state, a political reality that was foisted on a people under conditions beyond their control. With this rude thrust into statehood, it became necessary to construct a "nation" and a Singaporean national identity. This idea was alien to a people for whom identity had hitherto been oriented elsewhere. At the various historical moments of its "modern" past, Singapore's culture, economy, and polity had invariably been rooted elsewhere—in imperial Britain, in immigrant "homeland" China and India, or, briefly, in the Federation of Malaysia. From the time the island became a British trading post in 1819, with the signing of a treaty between Stamford Raffles of the British East India Company and the local chieftain, the Temenggong of Johor, to the time it became part of the East India Company's Straits Settlements in 1826 (together with Penang and Malacca) and then a Crown Colony under the London Colonial Office in 1867 (Turnbull 1989), Singapore was peopled primarily by immigrants whose cultural orientations were to their different "homelands." These immigrants had no intention of staying permanently, and were shown, in the case of the Chinese at least, to have had shifting loyalties at different times, although they never cast their roots locally (Wang 1988).

With the Japanese invasion of Singapore in December 1941, the beginning of the end of the myth of British superiority had been set in place. Even after the end of the Second World War and the return of the British, the trust in British protection was no longer there, and the ultimate justification for colonial rule (from the perspective of the colonized)—that is, for protection against other powers—had not been fulfilled. It was only a matter of time before a new generation of local leaders began to seek independence. In 1959, Singapore acquired internal self-governing status. By 1963, independence was granted but only as part of the new Federation of Malaysia. After two troubled years, Singapore was expelled and became a fully independent state in 1965.

Expulsion from Malaysia left Singapore with a host of potential and real problems. As Clutterbuck (1984, 158–60) has outlined, there was the loss of the potential common market, which threatened the economic survival of the city-state. This fact was exacerbated by the disruptions to trade with Indonesia as a result of that neighbor's stance of confrontation against the formation of Malaysia. Such economic challenges simply compounded existing domestic economic woes of high unemployment and social problems, such as poor housing conditions and public health, and high population-growth rates (Chan 1971). Further employment loss loomed on the horizons soon after independence when, in 1967, Britain announced early military withdrawal in 1971. These conjunctural social and economic elements were matched by potential domestic political woes. As Chan (1971; see also Chua 1995a, 18, and Hill and Lian 1995, 63) points out, the radical left was suppressed but had not lost complete influence. At the same time, "although the period of membership in Malaysia was brief, it had nevertheless given Singapore's minority Malay population a sense of its own interests and political significance as a community in the larger regional picture. This gave rise to potentially disruptive demands on communal grounds with racial riots of 1964" (Chua 1995a, 18). Together with the problem of a continuing lack of political identification with the newly independent state among the varied population, the government embarked on the tasks of building the economy and constructing a "nation." Efforts at building the economy have been documented elsewhere (see Perry, Kong, and Yeoh 1997). Our intention in the rest of this chapter is to trace the key ideological stances that the government adopted in its nation-building quest and that it sought to persuade the population to accept.

Whereas Hill and Lian (1995, 62) have identified the central tenets of the People's Action Party (PAP)[1] philosophy to be multiracialism, pragmatism, and meritocracy, we will identify several other dominant tropes in the state's ideological apparatus, making linkages between key ideas where appropriate. In what follows, we will elaborate specifically on the ideologies of survival, social and spatial discipline, and pragmatism; multiracialism (along with multilingualism, multiculturalism, and multireligiosity); meritocracy; and "Asian" communitarianism. We will then use the state's articulation of five "Shared Values" as a way of consolidating these various ideas just as the state has done. Finally, we will discuss how these ideological constructs are aimed at maintaining economic development, building a modern(ist) city-state, and developing a "gracious" society—all of which goals undergird the state's attempt to achieve ideological hegemony and maintain political legitimacy.

Survival, Discipline, and Pragmatism

One of the key hegemonic tools of the state has been its "national survival" discourse. Given the multifarious challenges confronting the city-state upon independence, as outlined above, the state was quick to use this discourse to its best advantage. Singaporeans were exhorted to behave in particular ways and to achieve specific goals if the country was to survive. They were to become a "rugged, resolute, highly-trained" (Bedlington 1978, 211), "tightly organised and highly disciplined" workforce, "efficient," "innovative and technological in outlook" (Hill and Lian 1995, 189), and were to "pull together in the same direction with a sense of public spiritedness and self-sacrifice in the national interest" (Chua 1995a, 18). This meant participating fully in the economic development programs, contributing to the industrialization of the country, subscribing to the "compelling logic of a capitalist economy" (Chua 1997a, 28), and displaying strong achievement motivation (Chua 1995a, 105). Discipline was a key trait and was deemed crucial for Singapore's capitalist success (Offe

---

1. The PAP is, in many ways, synonymous with the state, given that it has been in power by overwhelming majorities since 1959.

1984, 94). Discipline was therefore to be maintained not only in the workplace, but also in the family and society. In other words, a generalized social discipline was required (Quah 1983), a goal which sometimes translated into a quest for spatial discipline as well. As illustrated elsewhere (Yeoh and Kong 1994; Phua and Kong 1996), the state engaged almost vehemently in a "cleaning up" of people and places to remove social/moral and physical pollution. All these actions, designed to contribute to the country's overall economic development, were deemed "practical," indeed "necessary" for the survival of the nation. Such a marked orientation is what has come to be characterized as an ideology of pragmatism. As Chan and Evers (1973, 317) put it, "pragmatic" state policies, based on "rational and scientific principles," meant that any criticism of these policies would be branded as "irrational." This fact, in turn, legitimized "tight political control and eventually an authoritarian political system" (Chan and Evers 1973, 317).

5Ms

Another central tenet of the state's hegemonic ideologies is that of multiracialism and, relatedly, multilingualism, multiculturalism, and multireligiosity, dubbed in much of the literature as the 4Ms (Siddique 1989). In order to understand the abiding commitment to the 4Ms ideology, it will be instructive to explain its beginnings. The roots of the 4Ms go back to the mid-1950s. After the Chinese high school riots of the mid-1950s, a commission of inquiry was set up to investigate the causes of alienation in 1955. The report argued that Chinese nationalism was a form of "outpost nationalism," that "there was an absence of allegiance to Singapore as mother country," and that "building a nation out of a plural society was to be a top priority for long-term political stability" (Chiew 1990, 12). Many of the recommendations of the commission were adopted by the PAP after Singapore gained self-government in 1959, and they form the basis of the multiracial, multilingual, multireligious, and multicultural ideological stance of the state even today.

Some of the recommendations were:

• recognition of Malay as the national language;

- recognition of Malay, English, Chinese, and Tamil as the official languages of public administration and educational instruction;
- equal treatment of all language schools in terms of government financing and recognition of their certificates after their curricula have become nationalized;
- compulsory bilingualism at the primary school levels and trilingualism at the secondary levels;
- rewriting of all the textbooks so that regardless of language streams they should have a common content emphasizing identification with Singapore and the culture and history of the Chinese, Malays, Indians, and Europeans; and
- the reorganization of schools into districts so that multiethnic sports teams could compete against each other rather than a Chinese school football team against a Malay or Indian team.

The central concerns were the elimination of division by race or language, the forging of mutual understanding and increased interracial interaction among the young, and the elimination of discrimination against minorities (Chiew 1990, 13).

These concerns, in turn, may be traced to both domestic and foreign factors. Brown (1994, 78–79), for example, has argued that the 4Ms ideology was adopted for geopolitical reasons, to avoid having Singapore seen as a "Third China." As Chua (1998, 205) elaborates, it was the "least troublesome solution" because of both internal dynamics and external factors:

> The Chinese, though numerically dominant, morally had no proprietary right to the new island nation. Also, the geopolitical condition of archipelagic Southeast Asia placed them in a region populated by an overwhelming number of Malay-speaking Malaysians and Indonesians, who were unlikely to accept a Chinese nation in its midst with equanimity. On the other hand, the island's Malays, though regionally indigenous, were unable to dominate Singapore politics because of their numerical minority.

Given these conditions, the result has been the institutionalization and bureaucratization of the 4Ms ideology in Singapore.

Multiracialism in Singapore is the ideology of "cultural equality" between groups wherein "equal status is accorded to the cultures and ethnic identities of the various 'races' " (Benjamin 1997, 67) and each is assured the group right to cultural maintenance and continuity. This is translated to mean that the "responsibility for promoting racial/cultural activities is entirely dependent on volunteered individual and/or collective efforts of each officially constituted racial group. The cultural vibrancy of each group is dependent entirely on its members, with the state providing an equal administrative support role; no preferential claims can be made on any state agencies on the basis of race" (Chua 1997a, 26). In other words, "racial cultural practices are relegated to the realm of private and voluntaristic, individual or collective, practices" (Chua 1995a, 106). At the same time, the state polices the boundaries of cultural expression and defines what is to constitute acceptable "racial cultural practices."

The state often conflates—or at least treats as closely related—race, language, culture, and religion. As Chua (1998, 190) points out, "a person's racial descent defines his or her 'culture' (multiculturalism); the racialized culture is assumed to be embedded in the language of the race which is assured continued existence through compulsory school instruction as the 'mother tongue' language of the student (multilingualism)." Similarly, Chan and Evers (1973, 308–09) argue that the state defines multiracialism not simply in terms of equality before the law and equal opportunity for advancement for each racial community but also as acceptance of differences in religious practices, customs, and traditions of the different communities. Hill and Lian (1995, 94) also point out how the terms multiracialism and multiculturalism are used interchangeably in state discourse. Such conflation between race/language/culture/religion has the effect of reducing differences among the population. Chua (1998, 190) illustrates this fact:

> In the case of language, for example, dialect differences which created sharp divisions among the Chinese, have been suppressed by the exclusive promotion of Mandarin as the "language of the Chinese" in the mass media. Language differences among Malays, Javanese, Bawaenease, and Arabic are officially ignored and the speakers of these languages are to "re-emerge" under a common formal "Malay" language. Differences be-

tween Indians were initially eliminated by privileging Tamil, a south Indian language, as the "race" language. Subsequently, in response to protests from other Indian language speakers, Hindi, Punjabi, and Bengali have been made available as official "mother tongues."

Overlapping religious affiliations and differences are also subjected to a process of simplification and symbolic representation. Malay as a "race" is further defined by Islam; all Malays are by constitutional definition Muslims; Hinduism is identified with "Indians," although less than 60 per cent of the people grouped under the "racialized" group are Hindus, the rest are either Muslims, Buddhists or Christians; while religion is completely excluded as a marker of Chinese, whose religious affiliations are as varied as the Indians.

This situation has the effect of making manageable a widely diverse population with potentially divisive claims. The state positions itself as a neutral actor vis-à-vis three "clear" categories ("Chinese," "Malays," and "Indians") and a residual category ("Others") of citizens.

One of the effects of adopting a multiracial policy is that race actually has been foregrounded. The first thing that a Singaporean typically wishes to know about another is whether he or she is a Chinese, an Indian, or a Malay. Other possible criteria (for example, class, age, or degree of educational attainment) become less important in placing someone in the scheme of things. This fact is reinforced in the identity card that every permanent resident must by law possess, which identifies the "race" to which the holder "claims (or is asserted) to belong" (Benjamin 1997, 72). Benjamin goes on to argue that, to be a Singaporean under the state's ideological framework of multiracialism, one will have to be able to "claim membership" of one of the four "races," and to that end, "we should expect that actual behaviour would show a tendency to conform to the expectations that derive from those 'racial' stereotypes. In other words, Singapore's multiracialism puts Chinese people under pressure to become more Chinese, Indians more Indian and Malays more Malay, in their behaviour" (Benjamin 1997, 75).

While anthropologically ironic, from a political perspective the state has carved out a space of autonomy for itself in which it is to be untouched by "racial" claims, that is, "race cannot be constituted as a legitimate basis of

special claims on the state without violating the norm of multiracialism"
(Chua 1995a, 106). At the same time, the state can consult any racial group
without having to act in the interests of any particular group. Those who do
seek to make claims on the grounds of race are said to be subjecting the nation to wreckage from within and are liable to face severe legal action and
even detention without trial under the Internal Security Act.

We began this section by reference to the 5Ms as opposed to the common designation of 4Ms, which we have hitherto sought to explicate. It
will be incomplete to discuss the 4Ms without relating it to meritocracy—
the fifth "M." Meritocracy and the 4Ms are firm bedfellows because meritocracy facilitates social mobility purely on the basis of hard work and
achievement. It gives no special advantage to any single community.
Race—and relatedly, language, religion, and culture—are suspended as the
basis for resource distribution, whether it be housing, education, or health
services, for example. As with the 4Ms, meritocracy has come to dominate
Singapore's ideological landscape, although Betts (1975) argues that, as a
guiding ideology, it was only fully articulated in 1969, just after explicit
adoption of the 4Ms ideology.

"Asian" Values and Communitarianism

Throughout the 1960s and 1970s, the government held the view that cultural products, particularly popular cultural products from the West, constituted "unhealthy" "yellow" culture that "destroy[ed] [young people's] sense
of value, and corrode[d] their willingness to pay attention to serious
thought" (Lee 1967). As a parliamentarian, Inche Sha'ari Tadin argued,

> It is important to have a rich, established cultural tradition particularly at
> this time of Singapore's development. This is because there is the danger
> of our Republic being inundated by undesirable influences from the out-
> side world. Already many young people are mindlessly aping foreign
> mannerism. They think that the process of modernisation simply means
> drug-taking, a-go-go dancing and pornography. Once our youths have
> adequate cultural anchorage, they will be less prone to these modern ex-
> cesses. (*Singapore Government Press Release* 26 Apr. 1973)

Concomitant with the concern that Singaporeans would adopt "un-healthy" "Western values" associated with "yellow culture" and decadent lifestyles, the state also began in the late 1970s and early 1980s to caution against what it saw to be an "excessive material consumption" that belied "excessive individualism" on the part of younger Singaporeans in particular. It read, as the first signs of such individualism, job-hopping, believed to be the result of a constant search for more money and a deficit of loyalty to the employer. The trend among single young professionals applying for gov-ernment-constructed middle-income flats in increasing numbers was also taken to be indicative, apparently, of a desire to leave the parental home and shed familial responsibilities (Chua 1995a, 117). In part, this situation may ironically be attributed to the success of the state's ideological cam-paigns: meritocracy, together with the strong achievement motivation and social discipline that had been so strongly encouraged, had led to the de-velopment of a materialistic orientation among the population. Education, for example, was not an end in itself but was understood in instrumental terms, as a ticket to a better job and a more comfortable material life. In part, this fact also stemmed from the orientation of a largely uneducated immigrant population (Chua 1995a, 110).

Whatever the precise complaint against "Western values" and their ef-fects on Singaporeans, it was a matter of time before the state took an ex-plicit stand to promote "Asian values." This first took the form of moral and religious education beginning in 1984, designed to inscribe a set of "desir-able" values. The program was, however, curtailed when it was thought to have contributed to heightened religious commitment and thus potentially dangerous religious divisions (Kuo, Quah, and Tong 1988). The state also prompted the introduction in 1984 of a Speak Mandarin Campaign in the belief that Mandarin (as a "mother tongue") would root young (Chinese) Singaporeans in their traditional cultural values. The annual campaign con-tinues even today. To further keep "Western liberal values" at bay, the state moved toward a public discourse on re-inculcating "Asian values" in the population. This move paralleled the interest among Western social scien-tists in the successful economic transformations of East Asian societies (Japan, Hong Kong, South Korea, Singapore, and Taiwan) and the con-struction of "Asian values" as an explanatory factor. The key "Asian values" that the Singapore state subscribed to in the middle to late 1980s were essentially Confucianist in character—or at least, the "positive" elements in Confucianism, primarily, "collective orientation" (or communitarianism) and social discipline (Hill and Lian 1995, 8–9). This project, too, was aborted in favor of a new one with "an 'integration' of selected elements of supposedly traditional values of the Chinese, Indian and Islamic cultures," "proposed and consecrated as the cultural essence of 'Asia' " (Chua 1997a, 32). This change took shape in the Shared Values in which Singapore became re-inscribed as an "Asian" society.

In October 1988, First Deputy Prime Minister and Minister for Defense Goh Chok Tong first raised the notion of an explicit national ideology to guide the governance of the "nation" and the behavior of its population. Relying on the two major concepts of "individualism" and "communitarianism" used in George C. Lodge and Ezra F. Vogel's (1987) book, *Ideology and National Competitiveness: An Analysis of Nine Countries*, Goh argued that during the last decade "there ha[d] been a clear shift in our values" from communitarianism to individualism, especially among younger Singaporeans. The transformation of values of Singaporeans was viewed with concern by the government because it was believed to "determine our national competitiveness, and hence our prosperity and survival as a nation" (quoted in Quah 1990a, 1).

In January 1989, President Wee Kim Wee in his address at the opening of the seventh sitting of Parliament outlined the raison d'être for a national ideology and identified its four core values:

> If we are not to lose our bearings, we should preserve the cultural heritage of each of our communities, and uphold certain common values which capture the essence of being a Singaporean. These core values include placing society above self, upholding the family as the basic block of society, resolving major issues through consensus instead of contention, and stressing racial and religious tolerance and harmony. We need to enshrine these fundamental ideas in a National Ideology. Such a formal statement will bond us together as Singaporeans, with our own distinct identity and destiny. We need to inculcate this National Ideology in all Singaporeans, especially the young. (*The Straits Times* 10 Jan. 1989)

On the basis of feedback, the four initial values identified were re-crafted and a fifth value was added to arrive at five core values encapsulated in a white paper on Shared Values adopted by Parliament in 1992. They are to serve as the guiding principle for the ongoing governance of the country, and are:

- nation before community and society before self;
- family as the basic unit of society;
- regard and community support for the individual;
- consensus instead of contention; and
- racial and religious harmony.

Because these values were believed to be "compatible with Chinese, Malay, and Indian cultures, and with the values taught by the major religions," they were deemed legitimate, serving as handmaiden to the long-standing 4Ms ideology (Lee Hsien Loong, second deputy prime minister, cited in Quah 1990b, 92).

Chua (1995a, 22) argued that the emphasis on these core values (the word "ideology" was eschewed because the state did not want any association with its purported Marxist connotations) appeared to move the ideological discourse somewhat away from the earlier emphasis on pragmatism and economic survival. Similarly, Hill and Lian (1995, 11) argue that "the 'crisis' and 'survival' motifs of the early and traumatic years of independence have not been entirely abandoned . . . but their resonance has weakened within a generation of citizens which has not experienced the bitter struggles of the 1950s and 1960s." This loss in the ideological purchase of economic success has been used by the ruling party and some scholars to explain the significant loss in the percentage of votes in the 1984 general elections (Chua 1995a; Perry, Kong, and Yeoh 1997). However, from another perspective, we would argue that the focus on the core values made room precisely for a return to the ideology of "survival," this time in social and cultural rather than economic terms, precisely because it allowed the state to call on the notion of "vulnerability"—cultural vulnerability—a condition that is said to confront Singapore as it faces increasing "Westernization" and risks undermining its Asian heritage and values. Besides, in revisiting the first deputy prime minister's words in 1988 (quoted above), Singaporeans' perceived value transformation from communitarianism to individualism was being viewed with concern because it affects "national competitiveness and hence our prosperity and survival as a nation" (Quah 1990a, 1). These words hark back to the pragmatism expressed in the 1960s by Prime Minister Lee Kuan Yew, whose primary concern with values was in relation to their contribution to economic development. His words bear repeating here: "By right values I mean the values that will ensure you a reasonably secure, a relatively high standard of living which demands a disciplined community prepared to give of its best and ready to pay for what it wants" (quoted in Tamney 1988, 111).

Of the five core values, the call to racial and religious harmony is not new and echoes the stance of multiracialism and multireligiosity. A common refrain is that

> While the communal threat is not serious in Singapore today given the absence of communal riots over the last two decades, it should not be forgotten that the road to nation-building is a long and arduous one, and along the way many things can happen which can hinder progress. No plural society like Singapore can be immunized from the threat of racial riots; but such a threat can be minimized if not eliminated when there is also a strong sense of national identity to reinforce the racial harmony that already exists in Singapore. (Quah 1990b, 97)

The appearance of "racial and religious harmony" in the Shared Values is explicit endorsement of the multiracial and multireligious ideology that has persisted for decades.

The call for consensus instead of contention is interpreted to mean that the leadership should rely on consensus to solve the problems that face the country. Quah (1990c, 95) argues that this situation has been made more possible because of the shift in leadership style of the political leaders from a more paternalistic one to a more consultative one from the mid-1980s onwards. Whether this does in fact translate to more room for civil society is, however, left to be seen.

Regard and community support for the individual was not one of the original four values outlined in the president's presentation but was added after consultation and public input. Because Singapore is a meritocratic society and has an efficient free-market economy, the system rewards individuals according to their contributions. While this situation generally works well, it is acknowledged that there will always be those "who are less able and do less well" (*Shared Values* 1991, 6). As such, it is believed that there is also a need to strive to become a caring society in which each member of the community will care for others so that the lesser off may benefit as well. The needy should be assisted through "helping to meet some of their pressing needs, training and equipping them with skills to uplift themselves, and giving their children a better start in life, especially in terms of their education" (*Shared Values* 1991, 7). In this sense, Singaporeans are exhorted to put society above self by participating directly to help the needy. Individuals volunteering to do community work and contributing to welfare programs are encouraged as enabling practical solutions to help the needy. Such community efforts also are believed to help "strengthen the sense of togetherness, cohesion, and self-reliance of the society" (*Shared Values* 1991, 7). Here, the state calls upon previous forms of community support as being exemplary, namely, Chinese clan associations and the Malay concept of *"gotong royong."* In elevating this value of regard and community support for the individual as it is expressed in particular forms of help, the state subscribes to the belief that the problems of the welfare state as experienced by many developed countries will be eliminated.

Arising most directly out of the concern that Singaporeans have become too individualistic is the value identified as "nation above community and community above self." It is believed by some in government that Asian and Western societies differ primarily in terms of the relative importance of the individual and the group; whereas the former places more emphasis on the group, the latter tend to emphasize the individual. This dichotomy is captured in Lodge's (1987) "ideal types": individualism and communitarianism. Individualism suggests

> an atomistic conception of society, one in which the individual is the ultimate source of value and meaning. The interests of the community are defined and achieved by self-interested competition among many, preferably small, proprietors. Communitarianism, however, takes a more organic view, regarding the community as more than the sum of its indi-

viduals and requiring explicit definition of its needs and priorities. (Quah 1990b, 92–93)

Given the evaluation that Singaporeans have become too individualistic, the desire to stress communitarianism or community above self as one of the core values is understandable.

The fifth shared value that the state has chosen to emphasize is the family as the basic unit of society, a value that appears to have struck resonance with various communities. When feedback initially was sought on the core values suggested, there was unequivocal support from various groups such as the Tamil Representative Council, Eurasian Association, and the Joint (ad hoc) Committee of Muslim Organizations (Quah 1990b, 94). The cornerstone of this value is that an orderly and stable family unit is a prerequisite for a sound and stable society because the family is believed to be the bearer of traditional cultural values and carries the primary responsibility for socializing children with the desired values. In this sense, the family is an important mediating structure between the individual and the state and is a source of moral values in society (Hill and Lian 1995, 141). Indeed, as Kuo and Wong (1979, 11) argue, in such a situation, the family is "not just a passive recipient of the impact of economic and social development but may become an active agent of socioeconomic change." This idea has been reinforced as one of five key ideas that form the Singapore 21 Vision (see later discussion).

The state's conviction that the family plays a significant role not only in nation-building but also in economic development (through inculcating the desired values and ethics) is evident in concerted efforts to articulate and propagate "family values." In early 1994, a draft document on family values was released for public discussion, prepared by the National Advisory Council on Family and the Aged, which was initiated by the Ministry of Community Development the preceding year. The draft document identified five family values, which were subsequently modified after public discussions. The final document listed five core family values: love, care, and concern; mutual respect; commitment; filial responsibility; and communication (Hill and Lian 1995, 155). It also asserted, among other things, that children should continue the family line, and should reciprocate the care and concern shown by their parents and elders by showing respect and deference towards them (*Singapore's Family Values* 1994, 6–8). Further, it was claimed that strong ties between relatives would contribute to the strength of the family. These stances reflect some of the core values of the Confucian family (Kuo 1987, 1), including filial piety, ancestral worship, family continuity, and extended kinship network. At the same time, the document also prescribed that "the relationship between husband and wife should be egalitarian and that siblings should regard each other as companions" (Hill and Lian 1995, 155). This approximates more closely a liberal Western view. Hill and Lian (1995, 155) therefore conclude that the family values espoused represent a "mix of 'Asian' traditional and 'Western' middle-class elements," and where they drew from Confucianist precepts, the ethnic content was carefully left unmentioned to render them acceptable to a multiracial population.

In contradistinction to the explicit espousal of family values, a related ideological position pertaining to the role of women in family and society has been left relatively unstated. However, the ideological stance adopted in this regard is clear and unequivocal, has found expression and maintenance through various landscapes, and deserves some elaboration here.

The statement below illustrates clearly the overt and unapologetic patriarchal stance of the state:

> Most societies are organised in such a way that there is a clear male or female line of authority, descent and inheritance. In a few, it is the women who are dominant, but in most it is the men. In matriarchal societies, the men accept that the women are more equal. In a largely patriarchal society, minor areas where women are not accorded the same treatment should be expected so long as the welfare of women and of the family is protected. I would not regard them as "pockets of discrimination" or "blemishes" but as traditional areas of differential treatment. (Prime Minister Goh Chok Tong, 13 June 1993)

It is on this basis that researchers have time and again argued strongly that the state in Singapore is guided by an unabashedly patriarchal ideology. Kandiah (1987), for example, has argued that Singapore's brand of patriarchy is a nondiscriminatory one; that is, women are ostensibly given the same legal rights as men almost all the time although they may find their movement into male-dominated areas of society curtailed by less overt but nonetheless strong patriarchal values, borne of familial socialization and governmental attitudes and perceptions. Thus, while "many of the legal barriers to women entering public life have been removed. . . , underlying the facade of equality is a patriarchal ideology which keeps male domination alive" (Kandiah 1987, 8). The effects of nondiscriminatory patriarchy, Kandiah argues, can be easily observed although its mechanisms are subtle. Kong and Chan (1997) argue that Kandiah focuses too narrowly on legal rights and therefore came to the conclusion that Singapore is a nondiscriminatory patriarchy. Kong and Chan's analysis illustrates how, when moving beyond the confines of legal rights into the realms of housing, education, and medical policies, Singapore is seen to be, in fact, a discriminatory patriarchy.

Chua (1995a, 121) argues that the Shared Values remain "a floating signifier without any institutional site because they are constitutionally of unclear status, being neither enshrined as a preamble to the national Constitution nor as an actionable piece of legislation." It would appear, therefore, that the worth and purchase of these Shared Values are doubtful. Yet we will argue that, while there is no one institutional site, there are in fact multiple sites that promote and enshrine these values in the psyche of Singaporeans. As Chua (1995a, 119) himself points out, the state's ideological efforts are invariably backed by legislative measures of various manner to "police their propagation and entrenchment where necessary." This situation is borne out in various existing analyses of Singapore's nation-building efforts, in which various ideologies are shown to be translated into policies, which are in turn matched by fiscal and legal measures to ensure "propagation and entrenchment" (see, for example, Chua 1995a; 1997b; Hill and Lian 1995). Indeed, some have examined, as we seek to do in this book, how landscapes have been used to achieve these same hegemonic goals in post-independence Singapore (Kong 1993a; 1993b; Yeoh and Kong 1994; Kong and Yeoh 1997). As we will illustrate in the remainder of this work, the Shared Values have multiple institutional sites in the sense that they have been translated into policy and action and no doubt will continue to exist, not least through their effects on landscapes.

Defining "Nation"

In embracing the various ideologically hegemonic positions outlined above, the state seeks to achieve particular versions of the "nation." Drawing from the public rhetoric and discourse in which the state has engaged, we draw together in what follows this vision of a modern "nation," characterized by economic wealth and translated into development for the "nation" and affluence for the individual; a modern(ist) city that is technologically advanced, with all the comforts and trappings of a "city of the 21st century" (*Living the Next Lap* 1991); a people with a sense of history, heritage, belonging, and sense of place; and a "gracious society." Such goals have, at various historical junctures, been articulated in piecemeal terms, but some elements have also found expression in Vision 1999, an explicit, deliberate, and consolidated effort to set the goalposts for Singaporeans in the construction of a "nation." These have been repackaged, re-articulated and refined subsequently in the *Singapore 21 (S21) Vision*, a document completed in 1999 by a high-level (ministerial) Singapore 21 Committee, which contains "the vision of Singapore in the 21st century . . . a compass to guide us through the challenges of the next century" (1999).

Vision 1999 had its roots in 1984, in which the goal was set to achieve a Swiss standard of living by the year 1999. Vision 1999 was to be measured by, among other indicators, per capita income. The target was to reach S$31,550 by 1999, equal to what the Swiss had achieved in 1984. It was believed that the achievement of such growth would cap Singapore's development into a modern and impressive city. Vision 1999 represented a clear articulation of what the state had always sought to do: to continually move Singapore in economic developmental terms. Whereas in the 1960s and 1970s the challenge of such development was to achieve full employment, by the 1980s and 1990s the goal was to achieve increased per capita income.

The focus on economic development and wealth acquisition has come to be such a marked feature in the state's construction of the "nation" that it has come to be characterized as a developmentalist state. According to Castells (1992, 56), a state is developmental when "It establishes as its principle of legitimacy its ability to promote and sustain development, understanding by development the combination of steady high rates of economic growth and structural change in the productive system, both domestically and in its relationship to the international economy." While economic development is a priority in all types of countries, a developmental state is distinguished through the absolute prioritizing of economic growth and its use as a prime indicator of government performance. In the case of Singapore, evidence that economic development is given the highest priority takes various forms, including the privileging of land for economic use; the status of state economic agencies and administrators and the coordination of planning at the highest levels of government; and the continuous fine-tuning and multiplication of incentives and economic programs, based partly on the detailed monitoring of industry needs and development intentions.

Several of these principles are effected through urban planning policy in Singapore. For example, the privileging of land for economic use and the coordination of planning at high levels is patently evident in urban redevelopment and the manner in which it is carried out. Urban redevelopment primarily has meant demolition of the old and construction of the new on the basis that such a program provides better employment and investment opportunities, improves living conditions, and leads to physical, social, and economic regeneration. Such an interpretation of urban redevelopment places value on "efficient," "rational," and "pragmatic" use of limited land resources. In essence, it characterizes modernist notions in planning theories, where places are analyzed in terms of logic, models, reason, and efficiency. As Lewis Keeble described it, modernist planning principles involve "the art and science of ordering the use of land and the character and siting of buildings and communication routes so as to secure the maximum practical degree of economy, convenience and beauty" (cited in McConnell 1981, 72–73). Indeed, such an approach suggests that, in some places, urban planning becomes no more than a "technical problem of clearance and construction" (Ley 1989, 51). As Robert Moses, a student of Le Corbusier's, put

it, "more houses in the way . . . more people in the way—that's all. . . .
When you operate in an overbuilt metropolis, you have to hack your way
with a meat axe" (cited in Ley 1989, 51).

To understand how these planning principles are effected, it is critical
to situate them within the context of Singapore's larger political-cultural
ethos—in particular, the extent of state powers in urban policy and planning, the nature of decision-making, and the role of public participation.
For a long time, public participation has been minimal and a "top-down" approach has been taken to decision-making. The attitude is what Fonseca
(1976, 7) regarded as the "Master Plan attitude," in which decision-makers
treat public discussion on planning policy as "threats to a cherished vision"
rather than as "efforts at participation and a need for involvement." As Chen
(1983, 22) pointed out, "citizen participation" in Singapore implies participation at the stage of program implementation rather than decision-
formulation. This situation reflects the wider political scenario, in which
public participation in general policy-making has been limited. Chan
(1985, 55), in terming Singapore an administrative state, described it as one
that "believes that time spent by groups and counter-groups to lobby, influence and change policy outcomes are a waste of time that detract from the
swift implementation of the plan and programme." Her argument that participation is allowed only if it is directed through "approved channels"
echoes Cockburn's (1977) view that public participation in planning in
Britain during the 1960s was permissible only if the terms of participation
were dictated by the authorities. In Singapore, this scenario has been mod-
erated in recent years with a greater involvement of the public through
feedback sessions, although decisions are invariably still made by those
who are not directly affected by the proposed changes. In part, it is anchored in the continued view that policy makers and planners have the
necessary professional expertise and technical knowledge and are therefore
best placed to make decisions about urban form. It is thus hardly surprising
that they are astonished when their decisions are challenged (Eversley,
cited in Burgess 1979, 319).

In many ways, the scenario described above is symptomatic of what
Scott (1998) calls a "high-modernist ideology," which places confidence in
the progress of science, control and mastery over nature, and rational plan-

ning of the social order. Scott (1998, 89) argues that high modernists "envisioned a sweeping, rational engineering of all aspects of social life in order to improve the human condition." This, in turn, is made possible by a state that uses the power of its authority to achieve certain actions because civil society is weak and unable to resist state action. In the Singapore context, the developmentalist and modernist stances are justified on the grounds that they contribute instrumentally to better, modern living conditions, which Singaporeans must work to enjoy.

While this situation meant the provision of roofs over people's heads, a hygienic city, and an adequate transport system in the 1960s and 1970s, by the 1980s and 1990s the time had come to develop a "world class city." In 1991, the government launched *Living The Next Lap*, a document to guide the city's development and that covered all the key areas of life, from housing and education to defense. In 1992, the PAP used it as its election manifesto. A key component of this vision is the Revised Concept Plan, a planning blueprint put together mainly by the Urban Redevelopment Authority. Some aspects of the revised plan are already being implemented, while others are still futuristic. They include the creation of an improved city for business (with a new downtown, new business parks and technology corridors, and regional centers to bring jobs closer to people), living (a greater variety of high-quality housing) and leisure (more social, cultural, and community amenities, with the development of, among other things, a "world class" performing arts center, and increased sporting facilities and theme parks). The city is also one that should have a world-class transportation system and be endowed with nature so that it becomes not only a "garden city" (an approbrium of the 1970s and 1980s) but also a city in a garden (a late 1990s characterization). If achieved, all these strategies would help Singapore "make a quantum leap" in the quality of its environment (*Living the Next Lap* 1991, 3).

However, while the state strives to develop a community of people who will be rooted to Singapore, attracted by the comforts of affluence and the modernity of the city, the question arises as to whether higher incomes alone will be enough for Singaporeans. The challenge that the state acknowledged was how to "tie the emotional hearts of Singaporeans" so that, while Singapore may lose people for short periods for economic reasons (especially given Singapore's regionalization drive), "ultimately, their hearts will still belong to Singapore" (Jumabhoy 1994, 6). The challenge, the state believes, is to develop in Singaporeans a sense of emotional bond and an appreciation of living in Singapore because it is a harmonious, socially gracious, and culturally vibrant society. Singaporeans would thus return even if they have studied or worked overseas and defend the country when circumstances require it. It is in this light that the vision of a "nation" as a community of people with "character, culture, community, courtesy and commitment" (George Yeo, quoted in *The Straits Times* 15 July 1996) has emerged, rather than one that places emphasis on the more materialistic five C's that have been said to consume Singaporeans' aspirations—condominium, cash, credit card, car, and club membership. This vision of a united people has been articulated in terms of the "Singapore heartbeat" in the S21 Vision, wherein "all citizens unite in a common passion for the country" (1999). In emphasizing the idea of rootedness and emotional bonds, the S21 Vision also has as a chief tenet the notion that Singaporeans must be "active citizens" who have a passion for, and commitment to, building a better Singapore, and who are participants, not just observers, in the process. In this regard, "every Singaporean matters," the S21 Vision declares, and the important factor is that every Singaporean does his or her best in whatever chosen field. In turn, the state undertakes to create conditions where opportunities are available to all who are willing to participate and give of their best (Singapore 21 Committee 1999).

While there is no serious suggestion that the "nation" that has come to identify and be identified with economic growth faces extinction, the idea that the "non-tangible aspects of life" need greater priority is gaining wider currency, as expressed in the prime minister's view that there is more to being a successful country than having lots of money. Rather, a successful country is one in which its people are able to appreciate the finer things in life and are concerned for one another and public property. As he articulated explicitly in his dialogue with youths, "I myself do not regard material wealth as a measure of success. It is more than that, it is the value system of society. . . . If Singaporeans are rich but crude, rich but selfish, rich but uncaring, the society cannot hold together for many years because we are going to have internal conflict, tension, and very quickly, the whole place will fall apart" (*The Straits Times* 22 Apr. 1996).Reminding the people that Singapore had achieved "advanced developing nation" status, the prime minister urged, "Let us now complement our economic achievements with social, cultural and spiritual development" to achieve a "gracious society" (*The Straits Times* 22 Apr. 1996). It is, he argued, these less tangible qualities that will help provide the social "glue" to hold Singaporeans together and anchor them in their "homeland."

The state also believes firmly that part of the rootedness in the "nation" must derive from a sense of history and heritage, which provides people with a sense of place. Reflecting the ideological position that Singapore must not be overwhelmed by "Western values" but should be rooted in "Asian" ones, First Deputy Prime Minister Goh Chok Tong declared the state's vision of the "nation" Singapore: "We are part of a long Asian civilization and we should be proud of it. We should not be assimilated by the West and become a pseudo-Western society. We should be a nation that is uniquely multiracial and Asian, with each community proud of its traditional culture and heritage" (Goh 1988, 15). It is argued that, when such heritage and traditions are internalized, a "nation" will have successfully evolved. Multiple efforts, therefore, have been made on the part of the state to draw upon history for "social and psychological defense" in the construction of a "nation."The state's vision for the "next lap" is therefore a multifaceted one. It is a vision of a "nation" with a strong economy, a "world-class" city that is efficient and beautiful, a people who are gracious and cultivated. It is, to use the prime minister's words, "a near ideal home . . . not just the best house, but the best home for Singaporeans" (*The Straits Times* 5 June 1996). It is a place where citizens will feel a bond to their "nation" and will not dream of migrating elsewhere. Above all, it will be led by a government that is both clean and capable, but more importantly, one that would rule by the political legitimacy it has gained through hegemonic use of various ideological positions, illustrated in this chapter. Such hegemony is often achieved through the naturalization of these ideologies through the concretization in landscape features. It is to these landscapes that we turn in subsequent chapters.

4

Making Space for the Dead in the Body of the Living "Nation"

Landscapes of Death

It has been argued that, not only is the phenomenon of death a radical breach in the social fabric of human societies, "the issue of death throws into relief the most important cultural values by which people live their lives and evaluate their experiences. Life becomes transparent against the background of death and fundamental social and cultural values are revealed" (Huntington and Metcalf 1979, 2). In this chapter, we argue that expressions of such deeply rooted values and norms—undergirding what has been said to be "the most private, and at the same time most public, of human experiences" (Tong and Schiller 1993, 2)—are not hermetically sealed in by purely cultural parameters but often respond to and are challenged by the broader context of the construction of the "nation." Precisely because landscapes of death—burial grounds, cemeteries, columbaria, and crematoria—are landscapes invested with the most fundamental and possibly the most sacred of human sentiments and values, they become singularly important sites from which to take the pulse of the "nation" and examine the constitution of national identity.

In this chapter, we argue that, particularly in the immediate postindependence period in Singapore, landscapes of death were implicated as important focal points of debates in the developing discourse on "nationhood" and "nation-building."[1] After a brief discussion of "traditional" Chinese

---

1. This follows on previous work (Yeoh 1991; Yeoh and Tan 1995) that attempted to situate burial landscapes in the context of colonial Singapore as contested spaces within

concepts that frame an understanding of the salience of Chinese burial grounds, we discuss the powers of the state in shaping the world of death for the Chinese community through interventions in the landscape.[2] The form and architecture of material landscapes of death are not only shaped by traditional rites and rituals (such as funerary rites and disposal practices) often associated with the realm of culture and sentiment, they are also sites of negotiation staked out by multiple claims as to what constitutes the place of the dead in the living body of the "nation." From the perspective of the modern state, these habitations of the dead are often treated as remnant landscapes of sentiment with no real place in the forward-looking task of constructing a "nation." In contrast, among citizens of the "nation," other views may predominate. Indeed, the social organization and production of landscapes of death may be particularly salient in affirming a sense of identity, whether this is understood in social, religious, ethnic, or national terms. In a penultimate section in this chapter, we examine collective and individual subjectivities as articulated in people's responses to state strategies of control over Chinese landscapes of death.

---

broader sociopolitical developments. It was argued that the site, location, and morphology of burial landscapes were invested with different meanings by different individuals and social groups. For example, over and alongside the priorities that immigrant and indigenous groups of different faiths accord to places for the dead are the perspectives of the colonial state, which shape and control urban form and structure through successive measures of urban regulation. The clash of priorities is often resolved through a complicated process of conflict and negotiation among individuals, groups, and the state: on one hand, "dominant" groups construct the burial landscape as a site of control; on the other hand, other "subordinate" groups may also use the burial landscape as a site of resistance to combat exclusionary tactics and to advance their own claims.

2. In a multiethnic, multireligious society such as Singapore, there is great diversity in the death rituals and burial customs associated with different ethnic and religious communities. We focus primarily on state interactions with the Chinese community not only because the Chinese constitute the majority ethnic group in Singapore but also because the debates over how landscapes of death should be incorporated into the materiality of the nation with its space constraints were most intense with this particular community given the extensive nature of their burial grounds on the eve of independence.

The "Traditional" Discourse on Chinese Burial Grounds: Chinese Geomancy and Ancestor Worship

Among Chinese communities, death is an important rite of passage—for both the dead and the living. Watson (1988, 4), for example, argues that "proper performance of the [funeral] rites . . . was of paramount importance to determining who was and who was not deemed to be fully "Chinese." Beyond ushering the deceased into a different world, these rites also reinforce values associated with Chinese social structure such as filial piety and the maintenance of lineage, affirm that participants (both the dead and the living) belong to their ethnic community, and help restore them to their everyday worlds.

In traditional Taoist belief, the liberty to select propitious burial sites according to the principles of "feng shui" and sepulchral veneration is an important part of ancestor worship. "Feng shui," or Chinese geomancy, was considered central to the Chinese faith because it was believed that it was possible to locate the grave in relation to the configuration of the landscape and the vicinity of watercourses in such a way that benign influences were drawn from the earth and transmitted to the descendants of the deceased. In general, a favored burial site was one situated at the conjunction between the "azure dragon" on the left and the "white tiger" on the right, the former signifying boldly rising "male" ground and the latter emblematic of softly undulating "female" ground. The site should ideally contain three-fifths "male" and two-fifths "female" ground and should be open in front to breezes, shut in on the right and left, and with a tortuous, winding stream running before it. Such ground contained an abundant supply of beneficial "vital breath," which augured well for descendants. On the other hand, flat, monotonous surfaces or landscapes characterized by bold, straight lines such as the presence of a straight line of ridges, watershed, railway embankment, road, or water running off a straight course tended to concentrate malign influences and were avoided as burial sites (Lip 1979; Eitel 1985). Once sited according to geomantic principles, both the tomb and its sepulchral boundaries were considered inviolable because any interference with them would spoil the efficacy of the feng shui and imperil the welfare

4.1. Chinese cemetery with omega-shaped tombs.

and prosperity of living descendants. As a material expression of ancestor worship, the burial site serves to link in inextricable ways the world of the living and that of the dead. Its centrality in Chinese belief is further strengthened by the fact that the various strands of Chinese religion converge in the institution of ancestor worship: while the rituals pertaining to the burial of the dead and the art of divining in grave site selection have Taoist roots, ancestor veneration is also given support from Confucianist perspectives (Tham 1984, 7). As "sacred" sites, burial sites are also traditionally considered immune from government intervention or other external interference.

Centered on the ancestral altar and the grave, the Chinese institution of ancestor worship provides a means by which the living are made aware of their "membership in the groups within which they worship" (Freedman 1967, 87). For the Chinese, the idea of continuity of kinship beyond death and the notion of exchange between the living and the dead were central to their death rituals (Tong 1988, 340–42). The dead were reciprocally linked to the living: on the one hand, the dead received veneration at the ancestral tomb; on the other hand, the grave provides the living a chance "to force their ancestors to convey good fortune" (Freedman 1967, 88). The Chinese burial landscape might thus be seen as a site through which the Chinese could cement kinship ties and group loyalties and exercise power over their own fortunes independently from the state. Once geomantically sited, Chinese burial grounds were considered sacrosanct, not only out of reverence for the dead but also in order to ensure the well-being of the living. As such, these geomantically powerful landscapes could not be arbitrarily disturbed, or worse still, destroyed through exhumation. The seeming lack of order in the way Chinese burial grounds are laid out thus disguised complex layers of meaning grounded in the practice of feng shui and ancestor worship among the Chinese.

State Discourses on Chinese Burial Grounds

Beginning in colonial times, Chinese burial grounds that occupied large stretches of land both within and close to the city had been a major source of contention between the municipal authorities and the Chinese community (Yeoh 1991). In particular, with the emerging pressure for Western-style sanitary reform at the turn of the twentieth century, Chinese burial grounds were perceived as being hazardous to public health, particularly given the persistence of the miasmatic theory of disease (coupled with the prevailing image of the unhealthy tropics), which attributed epidemics to pestilential emanations arising from common graves. With the advent of modern urban planning in the twentieth century, burial grounds were further represented as a threat to the economic principles of space management and were viewed as "major space wasters" (Yeoh and Tan 1995). For a variety of reasons including the lack of alternative means of disposal, the weakness of the legislative machinery to enforce grave removal, and the concerted effort on the part of the Chinese to protect their burial sites, the campaign to stop the proliferation of Chinese burial grounds and to free land for urban planning was largely ineffectual during the colonial era. But in the postwar colonial era, the debate over the "burials question" took on a different dimension. In 1952, a Burials Committee was set up to consider, among other things, the idea of encouraging cremation as an alternative means of disposal, and in line with this, the construction of a municipal crematorium (*Report of the Committee Regarding Burial and Burial Grounds* 1952). This action, however, failed to gain the cooperation of the Chinese community and prior to Singapore's independence in 1965 the vast majority of the Chinese dead (89.8 percent) were buried with only 10.2 percent opting for cremation (Tong 1988, 34).

After the attainment of independence, Singapore state discourse on burial grounds showed clear lines of continuity with previous concerns and constructions. Questions of hygiene and rational land-use development continued to feature prominently on the state's agenda in discussions on Chinese burial grounds. However, while there was little change as far as the substantive issues were concerned, the rhetoric surrounding state policies relating to burial grounds had shifted. Not only were burial grounds construed as "obstructive" in a physical sense (as previously advanced), they were also at odds with and should be cleared in the name of "national interest" (*Parliamentary Debates* 7 Apr. 1978). Burial grounds became a national problem to be tackled and eradicated along with the eradication of disease and slum problems in central areas, as covered in chapter 6.

The official attitude toward cemeteries as hazardous sources of disease-causing vectors such as mosquitoes must thus be seen in the context of intensified state efforts to upgrade the health of the general populace through large-scale national health-planning measures. For example, the health threat that the Choa Chu Kang cemetery posed in spite of nationwide sanitary measures was frequently raised in Parliament. P. Gowindaswamy, Member for Anson, described the cemetery as "an excellent breeding ground for mosquitoes" in spite of a "very active anti-mosquito campaign" and related to Parliament how "a great number of mourners had to fight through *lallang* as tall as a man, and thick undergrowth . . . there were many muddy potholes and pools of water all over the place—ideal for mosquitoes to breed" (*Parliamentary Debates* 20 Mar. 1975).

Similarly, the state's view that the expansive abodes of the dead were an extravagant form of land waste was given more weight in view of the urgent national concern to build "homes for the people" (*Homes for the People* n.d.; chapter 6). For example, in 1962, four Chinese cemeteries near the existing Queenstown housing estate, part of the nation-state's first satellite town, were deemed by the Housing and Development Board (HDB) as "a logical extension of the Queenstown development" and acquired for the construction of high-rise housing.[3] The need for rational land-use planning was further underscored by the rhetoric of national development: in the words of E. W. Barker, minister for law, environment, science, and technology, "The needs of Singapore's young population must require the use of sterilised land, for the economic and social good of all citizens of Singapore" (*Parliamentary Debates* 7 Apr. 1978).

In a similar vein, earlier on, in the 1965 Master Plan designed to guide land-use development in Singapore, cemeteries (together with military land, agriculture, quarry and mining, and vacant land such as swamps) were identified as land "considered available for development" (*Singapore Planning Department* 1967, 11). Given "the needs and pace of national development," privately owned burial grounds must be cleared and the "scarce and valuable" land freed for "maximum use" (*Parliamentary Debates* 7 Apr. 1978).

By the 1970s, national development, the common good, and the future of the "nation" became the main rallying points and the most explicit reasons advanced by the state for clearing private burial grounds in the central area. In 1972, the state made it clear that it would close all cemeteries in and around the city area "to conserve land" (Appendium to Presidential Address, *Parliamentary Debates* 20 July 1972). State power over cemeteries was considerably strengthened by an alteration in the law imbuing the commissioner of public health to "close cemeteries without having to assign reasons for doing so" (*Parliamentary Debates* 3 Nov. 1972). As alternative means of managing the disposal of the dead, the state offered burial space in a state-owned public cemetery complex at Choa Chu Kang in the western part of the island, although it also made clear that it considered cremation as the only viable long-term solution. In the same way that the state provided for the welfare of the living in the form of public health and housing programs (chapter 6), it also tended to the abode of the dead. This was an important maneuver in constructing the "nation" out of multiethnic fragments. To encourage the new citizenry to become "public spirited," to acquire "a sense of national identity," and to adopt the view that "the success

---

3. *Housing and Development Board Files* (hereafter *HB*), 1018/57/50, 11 Oct. 1962, acting lands manager to CEO.

and failure of the nation [was] the responsibility of all," the leaders of the new nation-state felt that the functions of Chinese voluntary associations "includ[ing] building funeral parlours, cemeteries and schools" should be turned over to the "popularly elected government," which "naturally had the responsibility of looking after the basic necessity of the people" (Lee 1991, 6).

The clearance of private burial grounds not only undermined the control and functions of the community-based associations that controlled these grounds, it also transferred responsibility for the dead to state organizations, serving to reshape the Chinese community's orientation away from parochial and toward national concerns.[4] As Cheng (1985, 62) rightly pointed out, many of the functions of clan associations have since been taken over by the state because "in the process of nation-building, the government has been concerned with the creation of more common denominators . . . which [pose] direct challenges to the associations." Private Chinese burial grounds stood against "nation-building" in more than one sense: not only did they alienate land from the purposes of national development, their persistence also signified the existence and strength of ethnic-, dialect-, or clan-based as opposed to national loyalties.

Changing Landscapes of Death: State Strategies

While only about 10 percent of the Chinese dead were cremated in the closing years of colonial rule, the number of cremations began to climb

---

4. Historically, Chinese voluntary associations were a strong force in fostering ties among the Chinese in Singapore (Cheng 1985; Yen 1986). The varied roles of these associations include the provision of recreational and athletic facilities, the establishment of mutual-help programs, and the promotion of education and charity. Such associations, which can be constructed along the lines of locality/dialect, clan/surname, trade/occupation, mutual help, recreational/cultural/athletic/alumni, or religious lines, played an important role in drawing the community together along ethnic, if not dialect or clan-based, lines. In constructing the new "nation," these ties must be broken down and replaced with social relationships that derive their meaning from "the nation-state framework" (Benjamin 1988, 36). The process of "nation-building" requires that the state interfere with the consciousness of its new citizens, turning people's attention away from more parochial concerns and toward the "nation-state."

steeply from the early 1970s. By 1988, the majority of the Chinese dead, 68.1 percent to be exact, were cremated, while the remaining 31.9 percent were buried (Tong 1988, 34). In 1993, the equivalent figures were 9,669 (67.6 percent) cremations and 4,625 (32.4 percent) burials. In the 1990s, for the total Singapore population, cremation was preferred by four in five of those for whom burial is not required by their religion (i.e., all communities apart from the Muslim, Ahmaddiya Jama'at, Jewish, Parsi, and Bahai populations) (*The Straits Times* 9 Aug. 1994).

The reasons behind such a major change of funeral rites of passage within such a short span of time are complex. Jupp's (1993) study of the rapid passage from burial to cremation as the principal practice in the disposal of the dead in postwar England concluded that a range of factors were significant in affecting social attitudes toward death and funeral practices. In religious terms, the major Christian denominations hold the position that the mode of disposal has no consequences for the afterlife. Changing residential patterns, increased social mobility, and a decline in forms of communal solidarity have reduced the role of neighbors in funerals and increased the latitude of freedom that families have in the mode of disposal. With the institutionalization of death and disposal, "deathwork" (nursing the terminally ill and mourning the dead), which used to be the responsibility of the family (and particularly the women) has increasingly devolved to hospitals, nursing homes, funeral directors, and local authorities. This change has also promoted "simpler" forms of disposal. Most critically, the transfer of control over the spaces for the dead from the church to local secular authorities has encouraged cremation as the more practical and financially attractive option.

In part, the change from burial to cremation as the main mode of disposal among Chinese Singaporeans is a reflection of the weakening hold of "traditional" ideas and beliefs concerning death and the afterlife. According to Tham (1984, 60–61), three sets of beliefs are particularly salient in the performance of traditional funeral rites: the expression of filial piety and family and clan solidarity (e.g., the ostentatious, collective expression of grief at funerals and the elaboration of customs concerning mourning); the idea of pollution (e.g., the need to shield family members and others against contagion and to perform cleansing rites); and the belief in the continuing potent influence of the dead on the welfare and fortunes of the living (e.g., the burning of paper money and other paraphernalia are intended for the deceased but also done in expectation of reciprocity). Tham's (1984) survey inquiring into the religious beliefs of Chinese Singaporeans shows that in general, while about two-thirds of the sample continue to observe ancestor worship, adherence to ritual is highly variable. He writes that, while the central beliefs remain potent and continue to shape ritual behavior, there is an "overriding indeterminacy" because "the practice of rites is dependent on who happens to know something about them and whether their observance complies with 'customary' expectations" (Tham 1984, 64). Specifically, the fear of retribution from the dead (an important reason for "proper" burial and geomantically favorable sites) seems to hold much less sway than in the past.

An important factor in explaining the decline of ritual practice—thus paving the way for a greater acceptance of cremation as an alternative to burial—is the diminished role that regional, dialect, and clan associations play in Chinese social life after independence. Once "the warp and woof" of Chinese society overseas (T'ien, quoted in Tham 1984, 4), these associations played an important role in the social organization of death, collecting funeral subscriptions to ensure Chinese immigrants of proper burial, supervising funeral rites and ritual observances pertaining to the grave, and maintaining clan graves and burial grounds as focal points for clan identity. With independence, however, in order to reorient the new citizenry away from the more parochial, ethnically bounded concerns toward acceptance of the nation-state framework, many of the functions of these Chinese voluntary associations including control over funeral and burial matters were transferred to the government, which assumed responsibility for the welfare of the people (Yeoh and Tan 1995, 187). By the 1970s, the rhetoric of "national development" and the release of "sterilized" land for socioeconomic development became the most explicit reasons for closing and clearing privately owned Chinese burial grounds. Such rhetoric was backed by considerable powers, most crucially in the form of the Land Acquisition Act, which gave the government the right to compulsorily acquire land for "any public purpose" as well as absolute discretion to decide what that "public purpose" entailed (Khublall and Yuen 1991, 193). The most pressing de-

4.2. Mount Vernon columbarium-*cum*-crematorium complex.

mand for land in the urban area was for public housing; in the decades following independence, numerous large Chinese burial grounds were cleared
for the purposes of New Town development, including at Queenstown,
Tiong Bahru, Redhill, Kampong Silat, and Telok Blangah. It was hence no
surprise that the HDB, the state agency in charge of housing, became a
major player in state attempts to clear Chinese burial grounds.

As alternative means of managing the disposal of the dead, the state
makes it clear that it considered cremation as the only viable, long-term solution (Yeoh and Tan 1995, 191). The earliest government crematorium,
situated on Mount Vernon, began operations in 1962 with only one funeral
service hall and about four cases of cremation a week. By 1995, it had three
service halls and ten cremators and was averaging twenty-one cremations a
day, with operations beginning each day at nine o'clock in the morning
with cremations scheduled at intervals of forty-five minutes until about six,
seven, and occasionally eight o'clock in the evening (Tailford 1995). The
site also includes a columbarium built in several phases, comprising niches
either arranged in numbered blocks, some of which also feature Chinese-
style green roofs, or housed within a nine-story "pagoda-style" building or

a two-story "church-style" building. Toward the end of the 1970s, the Mount Vernon complex, which was primarily meant for the storage of ashes from recent deaths, could no longer cope with the scale of exhumation projects fueling the demand for columbarium niches. The HDB, for example, was then undertaking the exhumation of some 17,000 graves from the Kwang Teck Suah cemetery at Chye Kay Road. A new columbarium with 16,720 niches was built and opened for the storage of cremated remains in 1978. Another crematorium-*cum*-columbarium complex was also built at Mandai. This commenced operations in 1982, equipped with eight small and four medium-size cremators and a total of 64,370 niches for the storage of cremated remains.[5] In addition, Chinese voluntary associations such as the Pek San Theng association were allowed to build columbaria to house cremated remains of the dead exhumed from clan-owned cemeteries acquired by the government (*Pek San Theng Special Publication* 1988, 118–19), while Taoist and Buddhist temples and Christian churches were also allowed to offer amenities for accommodating cremated remains. Financial incentives were also provided to promote cremation vis-à-vis burial. The announcement of adjustments in burial (currently standing at S$700–$840 for those for which burial is not required by religion) and cremation rates (S$80–$100, the fee for a single columbarium niche being S$500) are usually accompanied by statements such as the following: "The Government's policy is to encourage cremation rather than burial in order to conserve land, so cremation and columbarium niche fees are deliberately kept lower than those for burial" (*The Straits Times* 14 Aug. 1997).

Opposition to cremation among the Chinese did not assume public form but remained an undercurrent throughout the years. In the immediate years after independence, there was considerable difficulty persuading the people to accept cremation and the storage of cremated and exhumed remains in a columbarium. Private burial grounds were still available for the reburial of exhumed remains even after the government had ceased providing land for reburial, so families could choose to purchase private plots for reburying their ancestral remains. However, as available plots in private

5. Information given by the Land Clearance Unit, Housing and Development Board, 20 Sept. 1997.

cemeteries were gradually taken up and these cemeteries were closed against further burial, those who objected to cremation had few courses of action open to them. Most were forced to accept cremation, although some sought reburial plots away from Singapore, in neighboring Malaysia and beyond that, in China. Even in a recent exhumation exercise affecting a large Chinese cemetery at Bulim, there were "numerous requests" for the exhumed remains to be transported out of Singapore for reburial; these requests were generally acceded to on condition that applications for import permits from recipient countries and health regulations (e.g., transportation of the remains in airtight containers) were complied with.[6]

While the move toward cremation was largely enforced by the government's stringent control of land use and circumscription of permissible burial space, strategies of persuasion and negotiation were also in place, mainly to show that cremation was in accord with Chinese religious beliefs or ritual practices. To do this, the state depended on the role played by funerary middlemen, the expert managers of the rites of death and disposal.

Within the Chinese community, the power relations between the funeral specialists—be they exhumation contractors, caretakers of funeral parlors, priests, or geomancers—vis-à-vis the ordinary Chinese were such that ritual practices were directed by the specialists while the people paid for their expert knowledge on the varied rites of each Chinese dialect group. An informant, a caretaker and funeral parlor owner, pointed out that "the government cannot very well say that everyone in Singapore has to be cremated since there is supposed to be religious freedom in Singapore . . . so they ask us [funeral specialists] to promote cremation."[7]

Because they were directly in contact with the Chinese masses and held positions of respect and authority given their "expert" knowledge, these middlemen were more successful in eroding the distrust of cremation without any semblance of coercion. The same informant, who also ran a coffin-making shop near Kampong San Theng in the early 1970s, related some of the difficulties with cremation in the initial years, difficulties of a

---

6. Information given by the Land Clearance Unit, Housing and Development Board, 20 Sept. 1997.

7. Personal interview, 20 July 1992.

practical nature but also of deeper significance. For example, the typical Chinese coffin of that time was not suitable for cremation because they were too thick and the only ones available for the furnace were the "Catholic religious coffins." The Chinese objected to the use of the latter because these were designed with the Christian cross prominently positioned on the coffins. The informant had to alter the coffin design into a form acceptable to the religious sensibilities of the Chinese. As he explained, designs that were considered neutral or auspicious had to be found: "When we first tried to alter them, it was difficult—the suppliers said they did not have those with the 'flowers and grasses' design so we then had to find bronze 'lion head' design plates, color them white and then put them together ourselves."

These funeral specialists were thus crucial as mediators, being both recognized experts in the realm of Chinese cultural and religious beliefs and in a position to modify these beliefs in acceptable ways. These middlemen were instrumental in converting the Chinese to the idea of cremation because, as traditional managers of death, they were able to draw on their specialized knowledge of Chinese death practices. At the same time, they were in a better position to persuade the Chinese people to turn to cremation because, unlike state officials, they were considered insiders holding positions of authority in the community rather than "others" who distanced themselves from the intricacies of Chinese funerary beliefs. As mediators of funerary practice, they were able to frame Chinese religious beliefs in a way to accommodate the shifts in practice in the move from burial to cremation.

Changing Landscapes of Death: Collective and Individual Negotiations

As state control over Chinese landscapes of death strengthened with time in the era of independence, they also continued to be contested sites at both the collective and individual levels. In terms of collective agency, clan-based associations, the traditional providers and organizers of Chinese burial grounds, attempted to protect their burial lands from state acquisition and, where they failed, negotiated hard for concessions. This is clearly illustrated in the case of extensive cemetery land acquired for the development of Queenstown, Singapore's first satellite town.

In 1962, four cemeteries near an existing housing estate in Queenstown were evaluated by the HDB for their development potential. They were deemed to constitute "a logical extension of the Queenstown development" to complement existing neighborhoods that were already being built.[8] Compensation for acquired land was assessed at current (that is, as a cemetery) rather than potential value, so the HDB sought the Planning Department's cooperation to refuse to grant any planning permission and thereby prevent the lands from being developed until they could be acquired by the HDB.[9] Because "cemetery land [had] no market [value]" and any proposed commercial development would require "an alteration of the Master Plan Zone" for which there appeared to be no justification,[10] the Board could arrange matters such that "no high claims [could] be admitted for loss of development value" when they were ready to acquire the land.[11]

Many of the cemeteries acquired at this time were run by the various Chinese clan associations. For example, three of the burial grounds at Queenstown were managed by the Hakka association *Ying Foh Fui Kun* (YFFK) (*Ying Fo Fui Kun* 1989, 26), while the cemeteries at Kampong Tiong Bahru and Redhill belonged to the *Singapore Hokkien Huay Kuan* (SHHK).[12] In attempting to clear these burial grounds, the HDB often met with resistance from the associations.

The YFFK, for example, "objected strongly to the compulsory acquisition of their only cemetery in Singapore."[13] The association members, however, added that they would not "stand in the way of progress by the government."[14] Instead, they requested several concessions from the government. First, they asked that a licence for another burial ground elsewhere be granted. Secondly, that a portion of about four and one-half acres of their burial ground be returned to them for the purposes of constructing a memo-

8. *HB1018/57/50* 11 Oct. 1962, acting lands manager to CEO.
9. *HB1018/57/50* 11 Oct. 1962, acting lands manager to CEO.
10. *HB1018/57/50* 11 Oct. 1962, report by Johnny Loh, lands officer.
11. *HB1018/57/50* 11 Oct. 1962, acting lands manager to CEO.
12. *HB25/59/II: Kampong Tiong Bahru Redevelopment of i) Fire Site, ii) Cemetery Site, iii) Exhumation of Graves* 3 Oct. 1964, CEO, HDB to permanent secretary, National Development.
13. *HB1018/57/50* 10 Aug. 1966, collector of land revenue to E.M., CEO, chairman.
14. *HB1018/57/50* 10 Aug. 1966, collector of land revenue to E.M., CEO, chairman.

rial and reburial of existing graves. They also wished to keep their existing temple on the burial ground. Finally, the association requested that exhumation be delayed for another five years.[15] According to the association, the four and one-half acres was to be used for reburial because their members would object to using the government cemetery at Choa Chu Kang for reburial and would not like to see the only cemetery "extinguished."[16]

The state authorities did not accede to the requests to grant a reburial ground elsewhere and to delay exhumation.[17] The other request for four and one-half acres as a reburial site was granted in view of the fact that the Hakka people had "no other cemetery." The proposed site on the southern fringe of the lot was deemed not to affect the board's "comprehensive development of the land,"[18] but in order "not to create a precedent," the land was to be designated as a public burial ground with no fresh burials permitted.[19] In other words, the ownership of the land was to be effectively vested in the state, which would in return alienate on a state lease for a term of ninety-nine years, the four and one-half acres to the association at a nominal annual premium of S$1.00.[20]

Thus while the state effectively managed to acquire the cemetery for housing development, it also had to take into account some of the wishes of the Chinese clan associations. In fact, it was admitted that the concession was granted in view of "public sentiment as regards [the] government's many acquisition[s] of private burial grounds."[21] On another level, the government also had to alter the zoning of the Master Plan to accommodate the reburial site and the fact that this was a "concession to the [a]ssociation" was noted by the HDB.[22]

When reinterment had almost been completed, the association re-

15. *HB*1018/57/50 29 Nov. 1965, *Penolong Setiausaha (Undang²)* to *Ketua Pegawai Pentadbir.*

16. *HB*1018/57/50 10 Aug. 1966, collector of land revenue to E.M., CEO, chairman.

17. *HB*1018/57/50 29 Nov. 1965, *Penolong Setiausaha (Undang²)* to *Ketua Pegawai Pentadbir.*

18. *HB*1018/57/50 10 Aug. 1966, collector of land revenue to E.M., CEO, chairman.

19. *HB*1018/57/50 2 Dec. 1965, *Penolong Setiausaha (Undang²)* to *Pegawi Tanah Melalui Pengurus Tanah.*

20. *HB*1018/57/50 25 Feb. 1969, Teh Cheang Wan to permanent secretary, National Development.

21. *HB*1018/57/50 29 Nov. 1965, *Penolong Setiausaha (Undang²)* to *Ketua Pegawai Pentadbir.*

22. *HB*1018/57/50 10 Aug. 1966, collector of land revenue to E.M., CEO, chairman.

quested that the stone tablets from the original burial ground be reset to conform more closely to geomantic requirements because the original layout was thought to be geomantically unfavorable. The state agreed to this request and absorbed the additional cost of the alterations (*Ying Fo Fui Kun Singapore* 1989, 30). At the same time, the authorities made arrangements to enable affected families to conduct private exhumations for reburial elsewhere and also, if they wished, to be informed of the date of exhumation so that they could witness the exhumation together with a representative from the association.[23] The clan associations were hence involved at various points in the clearance process and, while unable to prevent the alienation of their main burial lands, they managed to wrestle several concessions from the state.

In the main, however, clan-based control of the burial landscape was generally weak after independence because the state had to a large extent usurped the role as guardians of habitations for the dead. Extensive burial grounds had given way to several large state-run crematoria as the main resting places for the dead. While the Chinese burial ground reflected the social organizational structure of the Chinese clan association, the crematorium/columbarium complex, with its space-saving features and efficient processing of bodily remains, is clearly shaped by the rationality of the modern state (and in fact bears several salient resemblances to the high-rise, high-density, state-developed housing estates for the living, discussed in chapter 6).

Negotiations over landscapes of death, however, continued at other levels, including at the interface between state policies and the individual citizens and families. Death is often an event of crisis proportions, which draws the extended family together in expressing at least some semblance of collective loss and grief. At the same time, the decision to cremate or bury the dead may also become a literal "bone of contention" (to use the phrase of one of the interviewees), subject to negotiation in the context of family circumstances. For Koon Teck (a Chinese Taoist in his fifties), the cremation of one of his uncles some ten years ago has gone down in family history as a highly regrettable event that has caused rifts in the family clan:

23. *HB*1018/57/50 11 Apr. 1959, Johnny Loh, lands officer to acting manager, SIT.

When my fourth uncle died ten years ago, he never mentioned that he wanted to be cremated but he was the first one to be cremated in our family. His children wanted a simple job and cremation was faster and easier. Then, my father made helluva noise. He said [to his brother's children]: "Why didn't you ask? They said, "Ask who? Someone has to make a decision." As a result, nobody [no other member of the extended family] came to the funeral. I went to help with the funeral but the rest boycotted the family.

Five years later, when Koon Teck's father passed away, there was no question of cremation. He recalls, "My mother didn't believe in cremation so we chose burial. She said, 'Why should we burn? We Chinese don't dispose of the body in that manner.' "

For Chinese such as Koon Teck's parents, a proper burial is non-negotiable because it signifies one's ethnicity and culture. When pressed further as to why it is not "Chinese" to burn, few were able to articulate their feelings apart from constant recourse to the idea that besides being "unChinese," "burning" is "too painful a way to go." Jenny (a Chinese woman in her mid-twenties who finds herself "in between" religions), however, seems to be able to elaborate much more fully on these commonly held notions:

I have a definite preference for burial. It's more whole, I think. I don't think the person really goes away if you don't really burn the person. You feel their lingering presence. And then you put it in an urn and stick it in a wall. It's a bit too practical. Maybe I have very romantic ideas about death in a morbid way, but at the end of the day, you look at death and think about life. Perhaps you would want to be a bit philosophical. You won't be totally practical about these things. I think it is also steeped in our culture. We've always had this impression that, in China, people are buried more than not. They don't really get burnt. The only anomaly I've ever heard of are the sky rites of the Tibetan monks. They feed them to the vultures and stuff! But so far, we Chinese traditionally don't burn people, we bury people. In Singapore, we burn them for lack of space.

Despite a definite preference to be "buried" rather than "burned," however, Jenny (unlike Koon Teck's parents) echoes another commonly held view in accepting the inevitability of cremation in the context of Singapore: "There is not much land in Singapore," Jenny says. "I can understand why the government is worried. So I think practically, burial is out of the question when my time comes."

While Jenny explains the aversion to, but inevitable need to accept, cremation and columbaria, Li Cheng (a Chinese agnostic in her late twenties) focuses on the significance of the grave and suggests the possibility of other scenarios. For Li Cheng, a visit to the grave of her ancestors—her paternal great grandfather and his two wives—in the Hock Eng Seng cemetery (a Hokkien burial ground located in Lorong Panchar and surrounded by prime landed properties in what is today one of the most expensive residential areas in Singapore) was a taken-for-granted event every Qing Ming (the annual Chinese festival of grave-sweeping) ever since she could remember. The annual occasion was a daylong affair involving the entire family clan and made memorable by the difficulty in locating the grave:

> The cemetery was very overgrown and not well-kept. . . . [It was essential] that everyone went together at the same time because it was like all over the place, [the grave was] very hard to find. This uncle who died nearly five years ago was the only guy who knew how to navigate through the whole labyrinth of graves . . . It was like, north of the tallest tree if you go straight on the road, and then travel thirty steps till you come to a big trunk and then turn left. But, of course, it never works out because there was like, oh no! There are fifty trees in this place! [The graves] were not numbered and it was impossible to find unless you really remembered that place. So there were years when we lost it completely. So we went there and couldn't find it, and go back quite dejected.

Each member of the family clan was involved in the Qing Ming rituals, from finding the grave, to the actual work of cleaning and cutting the grass, and preparing and making offerings of ritual food:

> My father and my uncles would wear army kind of gear with long sleeves, hats, proper shoes, really hardy clothing, and I would have to do the same, and then we would load up the car with sickles and everything. The full works. And then when we reach there, we put down the food and start

cutting the grass. Not just on the omega grave itself but all around it as well. And then we start making the offerings. I never knew what the offerings were supposed to be. I think it was more of a gesture than anything. And my aunt would have gone shopping a few days before to buy the right food. Not that she knew what it was. She would just go to the shop and say "For offering for the dead." And they would give her the stuff. My aunt's Catholic, you see, but because she is the wife of the eldest son, it's her duty to coordinate the food for these outings.

In 1995, the cemetery was acquired by the Urban Redevelopment Authority (URA) and by early 1997, all graves were exhumed and the majority of the remains transferred to columbarium niches in Mandai. Li Cheng explains what the "moving house" (her own phrase) episode means for her:

> All these years, everything sort of revolved around Lorong Panchar. It was the epicenter, and somehow that sort of spatial center has been taken away. It's sacred ground that should not be violated because it's a space from which we orientate ourselves all the time . . . Then you suddenly realize, after all those years, you can't go back any more.
>
> I don't want to go to the columbarium any more because the meaning would have been lost. I think it's really stupid to think that these things can be transferred. For me, space is space. I don't think you can transfer something from one space to another space and think that everything will be the same. . . . That trip to that very first epicenter, it is important at the subconscious level. The fact that it [the columbarium niche] is not the original burial spot makes all the difference although you can pretend it doesn't make a difference. The actual physical structure [of the grave], the actual trip of getting lost in the woods and then finding it, navigating by trees and all that. That is what gives the place significance. In the columbarium, it's quite easy [to find the niche]. There are block numbers and all that. It's not a problem, and no longer an adventure. And then it all becomes purely ceremonial.

The whole exhumation and "moving house" experience has ironically confirmed Li Cheng's own personal choice in favor of cremation, partly because this is a "safer" option in the Singapore context, in which burial may lead to exhumation. But she does not accept the state's rhetoric that exhumation is justifiable and cremation preferable to release "sterilized" land or to conserve "scarce" land. As Li Cheng explains, "I suppose it [the loss of the ancestral grave] made me decide that I am not willing to pay the price for progress. In the end, what is it all for? More land so that there could be a better standard of living? In the end, if there ever was a referendum on this issue, I know how I would vote . . . To say that the cemetery is dead and has got no significance is a stupid reason."

Li Cheng attributes the general lack of resistance to the exhumation of burial grounds and the "easy" acceptance of cremation and columbaria among Singaporeans to what she sees as the people's abdication of responsibility in matters of life and death (literally) to the state:

> I asked my aunt, "So do you think they will be angry?" I didn't specify who the "they" were, but she knew immediately. And then she just sort of lapsed back into the typical Singaporean response of "But it's beyond us! The government wants it, so what can we do?" A sort of absolving of responsibility . . . While many people are afraid that if you don't pay your respects properly (i.e., providing a proper burial and maintaining the grave), "they" will not give you good luck for future generations, they also think that if you are doing as much as you can up to a point and within all the constraints, you will still be rewarded with good luck. I think that is how most people reconcile themselves to cremating or exhuming their dead.

While Li Cheng prefers cremation as the "safer" option, she is also adamant that death and disposal must be "space-locked." By this she means that she would still want to claim a space in death, a space whose "meaning" is vested both in its beauty as well as permanence (for her, cemeteries in Singapore only give an illusion of permanence because they are not immune from exhumation; columbaria are artificial and unattractive simulations that fail to match both the complexity and significance of the Chinese burial landscape). As she explains, "For myself, I am going to be cremated and maybe scattered in some beautiful landscape somewhere that doesn't change much, some parkland or something, possibly abroad. I don't like the Singapore landscape at all because space here doesn't have any value . . . but I do want to be scattered in a particular space where that space can still be a meaningful space."

It must be remembered that the general acceptance of cremation and the columbarium landscape does not signal the end of traditional Chinese funerary rites. For example, the discourse on feng shui has been resurrected in relation to the siting of cremation urns in columbaria. In 1983, the government had to change its previous practice of allocating niches at the Mount Vernon Complex sequentially using serial numbers and to allow for some degree of free selection for an additional fee, "following requests from families, some [of whom] would keep ashes until they can get a niche of their choice" (*The Straits Times* 23 Dec. 1983). The upper rows at eye-level are usually preferred to the lowest two rows, which are perceived to be "unfavorable" because these niches are in danger of being touched by sweeping brooms as well as being exposed to dust and dirt. Instances of people consulting professional geomancers to determine the most favorable niches to locate cremation urns are also fairly common (*The Straits Times* 9 Apr. 1986). Even without professional consultants, many Chinese will attempt to adapt geomantic considerations as a means of individualizing the selected niche, as seen in the care Tina's (a Chinese Christian in her early forties) father took in choosing an appropriate niche as a resting place for her mother's cremated remains:

> My father and I walked all round Mount Vernon. In those days [1985], there were only the slab-like structures, some with a little roof on the top. Neither the pagoda nor the church-like structure was there. My father chose a niche on what he considered to be [good] feng shui. He first chose a block that didn't have something else blocking it. It wasn't blocked by another block, and it faced an open area, greenery. Wide open space, a field basically. And in the horizon, you can see greenery, trees basically . . . This was important to him because at our apartment [a high-rise block], there was also a good view, a view of the sea. So he wanted the same thing for my mother.

Conclusion

While one would have expected landscapes of death to remain the last bastion of resilience against the imperatives of rationality championed by the modern state, this is clearly not the case. Precisely because they represent a central focus for the most fundamental of values and the way individuals and groups organize themselves, landscapes of death become staked out as major battle sites as the constituents of the nation compete for ideological hegemony. The control of Chinese burial grounds was thus implicated in the state's bid to modify traditional ritual practices so as to fundamentally revamp the consciousness of its people to ensure congruency with the overarching needs of nation-building.

Over the years, the statistics charting the relative importance of cremation vis-à-vis burial, the increasing familiarity of crematorium/columbarium landscapes, and the lack of organized protest against cremation clearly point to the success of state policies promoting cremation as the "space-saving" means of disposal as an alternative to the traditional but "space-wasting" burial. Hidden from view, if one were to simply take into account the figures, the material expressions on the landscape, and the absence of a collective voice on issues of death and disposal, however, are the constant negotiations that take place—on occasion championed by clan-based associations but more often than not privatized within the family. These negotiations often represent individual strategies to come to terms with a particular "choice" of mode of disposal within "constraints" that are clearly written into both government regulation and rhetoric. A minority of Chinese (some 20 percent according to statistics) still hold on to traditional beliefs in burial and resist even considering cremation as an option, justifying their choice on grounds of "culture." Others clearly view the shift from burial to cremation, from cemeteries to columbaria, with a sense of loss. This may be expressed in terms of a deterioration in rites that signified the strength of the family clan; the disappearance of an "original" landscape sedimented with the notion of "going back to one's roots" (either traced to an actual ancestral grave or imaginatively to China as the "home" of ancestors), or a dilution of "symbolic meaning," where such meaning can only reside fully in traditional ways of doing things, which have evolved over time and across space and which cannot be transplanted to quick-fix, human-designed landscapes.

In general, however, these sentiments do not override the acceptance of either the practicality or the inevitability of cremation as the "norm" for the future. Indeed, cremation is often described by interviewees as the "faster," "easier," "cleaner," or "simpler" mode of disposal, which accords with the dictates of "modern times." More crucially, however, many interviewees not only accept but support the government's "land scarcity" argument. Alternatively, some fear that no burial space will survive the inexorable logic of scarcity and burial today will only lead to exhumation and possibly cremation (to reduce undecomposed human remains) in the future. In the words of one of the interviewees, "Why get buried today to be burned tomorrow? It is like dying twice!"

While some interviewees lament the loss of "meaning" with the shift to cremation, it is also clear that individuals continue to devise strategies to conserve some of this "meaning." The columbarium still serves as a material landscape that, with various adjustments, supports the practice of ancestor worship.[24] Traditional beliefs such as feng shui can also be retailored to suit the columbarium landscape. Alongside considerable change in ritual practices, there is both an inflection and a resilience of meaning as individuals adapt and adjust deeply held beliefs vis-à-vis newly constituted landscapes of death in the context of the "nation."

24. Essentially, unlike the grave, there is no individual space in front of each niche for the performance of rites of worship. Instead, these rites (e.g., the burning of joss paper) take place in adjacent communal spaces (e.g., drums for joss paper are placed next to each block of niches).

5

For "Nation," for Religion?
Harnessing Sacred Landscapes

State and Religion

In spite of increasing modernization in many societies, secularization has not invariably followed suit. Indeed, modernity has not simply led to the demise of religion but has revitalized it in some contexts and among some peoples for whom religion remains or has become an anchor of meaning in a shifting, changing world. To that extent, the investment of meanings and values in religious landscapes renders them landscapes of sentiment for religious adherents. However, this personal and sometimes collective engagement with a belief system must be understood within a broader context of social, economic, and political systems that structure and sometimes constrain the full expression of religious sentiment. In this chapter, we begin by outlining Singapore's state policies pertaining to religion, which form the framework within which religions are practiced; we then focus our discussion on policies that deal specifically with the demolition, relocation, and preservation of churches, temples, and mosques. We will illustrate how these policies endorse especially the vision of a pragmatic and developmentalist "nation," as well as a multireligious/multicultural one in which communitarian values of "nation" above community and self prevail.

Singapore is characterized by a high degree of religious heterogeneity. The 2000 census recorded that the population is composed of Buddhists (42.5 percent), Taoists/Chinese traditional believers (8.5 percent), Christians (14.6 percent), Muslims (14.9 percent), and Hindus (4.0 percent). In addition, 0.6 percent of the population adhere to other religions, and 14.8

percent have no religion (Lau 1994). With such a variation, the state has adopted a secular position. Four specific tenets form the cornerstones of its policy. Singapore is a secular state in the sense that no single religion is identified as the official state religion, unlike in Malaysia, for example, where Islam is officially declared the state religion. In Singapore, all the major world religions are represented and so the state argues that "to accommodate such totally different spiritual and moral beliefs among the people without being torn apart, Singapore must be a strictly secular state" (Ho 1990, 2). But this "secularism" in no way implies that there is official disinterest in religion (Siddique 1989, 565), nor does it imply that the state is antireligion. In fact, the state allows for freedom of worship, and Articles 15 and 16 of the Constitution of the Republic of Singapore (henceforth, the Constitution) set out the rights of individuals and groups with respect to such freedom. Specifically, every person has the right to profess and practice his or her religion and to propagate it. Every religious group has the right to manage its own religious affairs, to establish and maintain institutions for religious or charitable purposes, and to acquire, own, and hold and administer property in accordance with the law. Every religious group also has the right to establish and maintain institutions for the education of children and to provide instruction in its own religion, but there must be no discrimination on the grounds of religion only in any law relating to such institutions or in the administration of any such law.

Closely related to the principle of freedom of worship is that of multiculturalism. The state is committed to all cultural groups and, in this instance, all religious groups, without prejudice to any group in particular whether they are majority or minority groups. This principle is enshrined in the Constitution in two ways. First, a general clause protects the fundamental rights of the individual and citizen and prohibits discrimination by race, language, or religion (Article 12). Second, the Presidential Council for Minority Rights established under Article 69 of the Constitution has the general function of considering and reporting on matters, referred by parliament or the government, affecting persons of any racial or religious community in Singapore. In particular, the council's function is to draw attention to any bill or subsidiary legislation if it is, in the opinion of the council, a differentiating measure.

The last tenet of the state's secular policy is the view that religion and politics must be kept strictly separate. Religious groups should not venture into politics and political parties should not use religious sentiments to gather popular support. If members of religious groups are to participate in the democratic political process, they must do so as individuals or as members of political parties and not as leaders of religious groups. In this, former Prime Minister Lee Kuan Yew has been most emphatic; he argues that religious groups should look after the spiritual, moral, and social well-being of their followers but should leave the economic and political needs of people to nonreligious groups such as political parties. The Maintenance of Religious Harmony Bill, passed in November 1990, is designed to differentiate between behavior that is acceptable and that which is not. Specifically, the bill allows the minister in charge to issue prohibition orders should any individual engage in any of four categories of harmful conduct. These are when a person causes feelings of enmity or hatred between different religious groups; when, if under the guise of religion or propagating religious activity, a person carries out political activities for promoting a political cause or the cause of any political party; when a person carries out subversive activities under the guise of propagation of religion; and when a person instigates and provokes feelings of disloyalty or hatred against the president or the government.

However, in spite of the general secular position and the specific stance of multiculturalism, the state also recognizes the special position of the Malays, and, relatedly, of the Muslims in Singapore. Article 152 of the Constitution focuses on minorities and, in particular, on Malays. It spells out clearly that the government must care for the interests of the racial and religious minorities in Singapore; particularly, it must "recognise the special position of the Malays, who are the indigenous people of Singapore, and accordingly it shall be the responsibility of the Government to protect, safeguard, support, foster and promote their political, educational, religious, economic, social and cultural interests and the Malay language" (Constitution 1985, 73). This consideration for the Malays is a legacy of the politics of the 1950s. Specifically, in the negotiations for the coalition government of 1959, one of the agreed conditions was that the Malays, as the indigenous population, should have special rights, which would be en-

shrined in the Constitution. This consideration could also be an acknowledgment of geopolitical realities—that is, of Singapore's position in Southeast Asia, a predominantly Malay world. Recognizing that the Malays are
the indigenous population and according them a special position could
help to avert any suspicions on the part of Singapore's neighbors that it is
trying to be a "Third China" (Chua 1983, 38).

Apparent Contradictions: Religion in a Pragmatic, Developmentalist "Nation"

While religion may more commonly strike one as relating to the ethereal,
the Singapore state's secular ideological imprint on religious landscapes
links the religious unequivocally with the pragmatic and developmentalist.
This situation is clearly reflected in policies pertaining to the establishment, relocation, demolition, and preservation of religious buildings,
which reflect general characteristics of land-use policy in Singapore, and at
a broader level, values of pragmatism and economic rationality. As we highlighted in chapter 3, "efficiency" and "orderly growth" form the guiding
principles in land-use planning. As a result, urban renewal generally has
emphasized demolition and reconstruction rather than conservation and
preservation. At the same time, a centralized approach has often been taken
toward planning and decision-making. These planning principles are reflected in policies regarding the establishment of new religious buildings.

In the establishment of religious buildings, the state specifically sets
aside parcels of land for tender by religious groups. These parcels of land
are usually found in the new towns built by the Housing and Development
Board (HDB) on the basis of the neighborhood principle, adapted from
British and European town-planning practices. The basic planning philosophy is to give maximum self-sufficiency with respect to basic community
needs, and so within each neighborhood there will be shopping facilities,
community centers, recreation facilities, schools, medical care, and so on to
cater to the needs of residents. If there are more than three neighborhoods
close together, then a town or district center will be built to provide higher
order goods and services, such as banks, theaters, cinemas, and department
stores (Drakakis-Smith and Yeung 1977, 6; The 1969, 175). It is clear,

Table 5.1
Planning Standards for the Provision of Religious Sites

Religious Building	Approximate site area (square meters)	Planning standard (dwelling unit)
Church	3,000–4,500	1 per 12,000
Chinese temple	2,000–3,000	1 per 9,000
Mosque	2,500	1 per 20,000
Hindu temple	1,800–2,500	1 per 90,000

Source: Correspondence with Systems and Research Department, Housing and Development Board, 2000.

therefore, that a strongly modernist stance is adopted in town planning in which the successful formula is based on efficiency and functionalism (Ley 1989, 47–51). The description of "good" town planning, as outlined in a 1923 article "Reasons for Town Planning," would apply well in the context of Singapore: "Good city planning is not primarily a matter of aesthetics, but of economics. Its basic principle is to increase the working efficiency of the city" (quoted in Ley 1989, 50). In such a context, religious building sites are provided in the new towns as another amenity that sections of the population require. Precise planning standards guiding the minimum provision of such sites are drawn up in the same way as for other amenities (Table 5.1). For churches, mosques, and Chinese temples, these guidelines are made on a new town basis. For example, for every 12,000 dwelling units in a new town, a church site will be set aside; and for every 9,000 dwelling units in a new town, a Chinese temple site will be designated. However, Hindu temple sites are made on a regional basis because it takes two or three new towns to make up 90,000 dwelling units. Factors taken into consideration when drawing up these guidelines include "demographic characteristics," "religious habits," as well as space requirements and architectural design for the different religious groups.[1] These planning standards are reviewed periodically in the light of demographic and social changes. The

1. Correspondence with Strategic Planning Branch, URA, and with the Systems and Research Department, HDB, 1990.

precise sites are usually proposed by the HDB and submitted for consideration to the Master Plan Committee and for the approval of the Ministry of
National Development.

While the state pursues its policies on establishment of religious buildings based on "pragmatism," "rational" planning, and "efficient" use of land,
religious groups have a different set of perceived needs. As one Hindu
(cited in Kong 1993b, 347) argued, "The trouble is we don't get land where
we want it, and they offer us where there is no need for a temple, and if you
do go and build a temple, and it's not frequented, it'll just be a white ele-
phant." A second set of evidence of the pragmatic approach to religious
buildings may be found in the regulations set up to control the conversion
of existing buildings from secular to religious use. Whether such a conversion can take place is not based on the perceived needs of the religious
community. Instead, it depends on several planning considerations, such as
the location of the building, whether the area is a predominantly residential
one (and therefore likely to be disturbed), whether too much traffic is
going to be generated as a result of conversion to religious use, whether
there will be parking facilities nearby, and other such practical considerations (Kong 1993a). This has meant that only certain sorts of secular buildings "fit the bill," a situation reflected in the fact that, in the last decade or
so, churches in search of a "home" have only managed successfully to obtain approval to convert old unused cinemas into places of worship.

Perhaps the most pointed evidence of the state's emphasis on pragmatism and developmentalism is the position it has taken with regard to the
relocation and demolition of religious buildings. Commonly, relocation or
demolition takes place when buildings are affected by public schemes.
Specifically, a policy statement was made in 1973 that asserted that "as people move out from old areas to be redeveloped, temples, mosques or
churches will have to give way to urban renewal or new development, unless they are of historical and architectural value" (*Singapore Government Press
Release* 25 Nov. 1973). Indeed, the stand taken is that religious buildings will
be treated as any other building that may come in the way of development.
This fact was clearly spelled out in a statement by Tan Eng Liang (then Senior Minister of State for National Development), who declared, "The resettlement policy is clear-cut, irrespective of religions, irrespective of

owners and irrespective of organisations" (*Singapore Government Press Release* 16 Mar. 1978). In putting this policy into practice, between 1974 and 1987 the government had acquired and cleared twenty-three mosques, seventy-six *"suraus,"*[2] seven hundred Chinese temples, twenty-seven Hindu temples, and nineteen churches for public development schemes (*Singapore Government Press Release* 3 Oct. 1987).[3]

The above scenario is not unique to religious buildings: the state has always maintained that "rational" and "pragmatic" decisions must be made so that Singapore can progress, a belief which is translated here as "economic" use of scarce land. Hence, many areas in Singapore have undergone massive redevelopment, which, more often than not, involves demolition of the old and construction of the new. It is this rationality that has caused cemeteries to be exhumed, as we discussed in chapter 4, and religious buildings to come under the bulldozer, as we illustrate in this chapter. Like these places of worship, many other buildings have been knocked down to give way to Mass Rapid Transit (MRT) stations, new housing projects, and other symbols of modernization and development. This process of urban change is presented as being inevitable, as extracts from two speeches by Othman Wok in 1974 (then Minister for Social Affairs) show:

> Progress in Singapore cannot be achieved without change. The numerous development schemes such as oil refinery, public housing, etc. have necessitated the resiting of burial grounds and religious institutions. These have affected all sections of the community. It is not a deliberate policy of the Singapore Government to demolish places of worship. The process of urban renewal has necessitated the moving of population from one area to another. However, every effort has been made to ensure that the way of life of the people concerned is not adversely affected both economically and spiritually. In fact, the object of development is to upgrade the living standards of the population as a whole. In the process of development,

2. A *surau* is a small mosque.

3. Attempts to obtain updated information on this point have not been successful. Such information is considered confidential because of its sensitivity. These figures were released because the state was keen to illustrate that all religions in Singapore were affected by resettlement and that no single religion was being discriminated against.

the old must make way for the new and demolition of some *masjids*, temples and churches affected by redevelopment is inevitable.[4]

Such action has only been resorted to when absolutely necessary and unavoidable (Wok 1974a). In other words, development projects that are for the benefit of Singapore society as a whole must go on, and if any building is in the way of such development, obviously it will have to go if this is unavoidable (Wok 1974b).

In these arguments it is assumed that there is only one form of rationality. However, rationality is ultimately ideological. What the state has presented is only one construction of rationality. There is an alternative position, one which begins with the premise that religion is important for a modern, fast-changing society because it provides a spiritual anchor and moral imperative. This view has been recognized, for example, in Ho Kah Leong's (then Senior Parliamentary Secretary, Ministry of Communications and Information) statement that "in our progressive but materialistic society, religion provides the much needed spiritual and moral support" (*The Straits Times* 19 June 1989). Extending from this belief, it is also true that religious institutions and buildings are important because they help people to focus on their religious lives and act as physical reminders of people's faith in the bustle of urban living. Seen in this light, the rational option would be to keep these buildings—particularly when they have a long-shared history with the people. The fact that the state's conception has been presented as the only rational and pragmatic option indicates that the state is seeking to persuade people that its beliefs and actions are the only natural and commonsense way of doing things. In other words, the state seeks to be ideologically hegemonic in its construction of the "nation."

Exemplifying the success of hegemonic control, there are religious individuals who do come to terms with the destruction of their religious places by accepting the ideological arguments put forth by the state. They argue that state actions are "rational" and "necessary." For example, some argue that there are religious buildings that have to go because they are old and in a bad state anyway. From this point of view, rehabilitation does not

4. A *masjid* is a mosque.

seem to be an option. Others point out that old buildings are replaced with new and better buildings. Demands are still met. Some buildings are unused or underused and do not deserve to remain standing. Demolition is all part of "pragmatic" planning and contributes to a more efficient use of space. Growth and change are inevitable. All these ideas reflect the adoption of modernist arguments in planning, which recognize the observable functions of places but not the intangible meanings and values often invested. There are even those who deny the sacredness of religious places and refuse to demarcate space as sacred or profane (see Kong 1993b). These forms of rationalization reflect how people have become persuaded to accept that, for the Singapore "nation" to progress, it is necessary to act "pragmatically" and "rationally."

Not all individuals and groups buy into this version of "nation," though. Indeed, relocation and demolition prove to be the most sensitive and potentially most divisive state actions, since places that are of great value and importance to people are being destroyed. It is here that the tension between the "rationality" and "pragmatism" of the state clashes head-on with the individual's conceptions of sacredness and sacred space. The "objective" outsider mentality conflicts with the "subjective" and intense insider experiences. As Kong (1993b, 348) illustrated, insiders (individuals) are left

> feeling a sense of "anger and resentment," "a sense of loss and deprivation," "like something was suddenly taken away from you." Intense reactions are expressed by Prema who sees the Hindu temple as "almost like god's embassy." Destroying a temple is like tearing down god and "that is painful, particularly when you put something that's steel and chrome up. You're not quite sure that on sacred ground they're treating it as holy."

Such actions seem particularly unacceptable because symbols of "modernity" ("steel and chrome") are put in place of the old and treasured.

Such intense emotions may translate into attempts to counter the decisions of the state. Kong (1993a), for example, illustrated how, in 1978, the Sikh community's Central Temple site was to be acquired because the area in which it stood was largely occupied by prewar shophouses and was due for urban renewal. A Ministry of National Development statement pointed out that "comprehensive development compatible with good planning is not feasible if the site occupied by the temple is to be excluded" (*The Straits Times* 17 Jan. 1978). Hence, the land was to be compulsorily acquired to make way for three blocks of eight-story flats and one block of nineteen-story flats on a two-story shopping podium. Although there is no compulsion for the government or its agency (the HDB) to provide alternative sites for religious buildings affected by public projects, it made an exception in this case because the temple was the main Sikh temple catering for all sects. The government therefore helped the community to look for a suitable site for its relocation (*The Straits Times* 17 Jan. 1978). A first site was offered but was turned down. Another site was subsequently offered, but it was again rejected. At that point, 750 members of the community attended a meeting, at the end of which three resolutions were passed. The first resolution was that the state should preserve the temple as evidence that it was treating all religious groups even-handedly. In the second resolution, participants at the meeting urged the government to protect the religious rights and interests of the Sikh community. The third was a unanimous resolution that the temple should remain on the Queen Street site and that there was therefore no question of accepting an alternative site or selling or exchanging it (*The Straits* Times 9 Feb. 1978). The resolutions were sent to then President Henry B. Sheares and then Prime Minister Lee Kuan Yew. In May 1978, the prime minister met with nine Sikh community leaders and stressed two points. One was that all religions were and would continue to be treated equally. The other was that Singapore's "progress through redevelopment must go on," meaning that the "old must give way to new—and this covered churches, temples, mosques and so on" (quoted in *The Straits Times* 18 May 1978). He also obtained from the Sikh representatives an agreement that there had been no discrimination against the Sikh community in Singapore. After the meeting, a spokesman for the group expressed confidence that the matter would be resolved amicably soon, "as the Sikh community wants also to contribute to the progress of the nation" (*The Straits Times* 18 May 1978). Eventually, the community moved out of the premises into temporary buildings until 1986, when it moved into a new temple in Towner Road.

Even while the pragmatism and rationality of state logic do not comfortably reside with all communities or members of the "nation," the state continues to pursue quite unflinchingly its rationality and pragmatism in yet other policies pertaining to religious buildings. The resettlement of religious groups is one such example. Religious groups to be resettled are offered alternative sites by the policy implementing agencies (usually the HDB, Urban Redevelopment Authority, and the Jurong Town Corporation). However, such alternative sites are not always offered on a one-to-one basis because "it is not possible to have a temple for temple, a mosque for mosque, a church for church substitution. This is uneconomic, impractical and, in the limited land space of Singapore, impossible" (*Singapore Government Press Release* 25 Nov. 1973). Hence, religious buildings affected by clearance are primarily allocated land on a joint basis. In other words, one site is made available to two or more existing buildings of the same religion.

The closure of religious buildings may also illustrate how pragmatism and developmentalism cause market forces to prevail even in the realm of the spiritual. For example, the lease may run out for a religious site just as redevelopment is about to take place. In such instances, the lease will not be extended, and those affected may not be allocated land. They will then have to tender and pay market value for sites set aside by the HDB for religious use or for sites put up for sale by the Urban Redevelopment Authority (URA) to religious groups and associations. This situation has caused some smaller religious buildings to close down completely because they could not find suitable alternative sites or because the cost of new sites was not affordable (*The Straits Times* 15 June 1979).

On the other hand, it may be argued that the state's construction of a pragmatic and developmentalist "nation" takes a backseat when attention is turned to the preservation of religious buildings. This circumstance occurs when religious buildings are deemed to be of historical and architectural value and are gazetted as national monuments.[5] However, from another perspective, preservation articulates and supports in practice those very

---

5. To date, twenty religious buildings have been designated national monuments and have been preserved. They are Sultan Mosque, Abdul Gaffoor Mosque, Al-Abrar Mosque, Hajjah Fatimah Mosque, Jamae Mosque, Nagore Durgha, Sri Mariamman Temple, Sri Perumal Temple, Siong Lim Temple, Hong San See, Tan Si Chong Su Temple, Thian Hock

values that the state seeks to perpetuate, such as entrepreneurship, economic prosperity, and progress. This is because these preserved buildings are incorporated into the tourist industry as exhibits and showcases of Singapore's multireligious setting. It is evident in the ways in which the Singapore Tourism Board (STB) and its predecessor (Singapore Tourist Promotion Board—STPB) appropriate and "sell" these preserved monuments in their promotional literature on Singapore (STPB 1989, 32–39; 1990, 26–29, 49–50, 58–63; 1999, 54–60). A systematic analysis of the official guidebooks and other promotional material produced by the STPB over the years reveals the importance attached to Singapore's multireligious heritage in the exercise of "selling Singapore." Of the seven categories of attractions promoted in this literature, one category is explicitly focused on places of worship, and churches, synagogues, temples, and mosques are promoted as places to visit. In another three categories focusing on "interesting streets," "cultural heritage," and "islands," the religious factor also features as a strong drawing point. Hence, "streets that talk" draw their character abundantly from places of worship: the "majestic" Sultan Mosque lends character to North Bridge Road and the "humble little Burmese Buddhist Temple" characterizes Kinta Road, for example. Similarly, in the brochure enticing visitors to Kusu, an island to the south of mainland Singapore, the "poignant moments" when "devotees to the shrines and temples throw coins into the wishing well or pond" are promoted alongside the "blue lagoons and pristine white beaches." This is further reflected in the training program for tour guides in Singapore. In order to qualify as licenced guides, individuals are required by the STB to undergo a training program conducted by the Centre for Tourism-Related Studies. In both the classroom and field sessions of these courses, Singapore's religious heritage features significantly. For example, many aspiring guides are taken on field trips to Singapore's ethnic districts, namely Chinatown, Little India, and Kampong Glam, and in all these visits religious places (such as Sri Mariamman, Thian Hock Keng, Sultan Mosque, and Masjid Hajjah Fatimah)

Keng, Yueh Hai Ching Temple, Cathedral of the Good Shepherd, St. Andrew's Cathedral, St George's Church, Telok Ayer Chinese Methodist Church, Armenian Church, Maghain Aboth Synagogue, and Chesed-El Synagogue.

are a compulsory part of the itinerary. The importance of religion to the tourist industry is further reinforced in the ways in which festivals are highlighted in the STB's promotional literature. Of an average of fifteen different festivals promoted every year, only two to three are nonreligious in character. Whether it is the Festival of the Hungry Ghosts for the Chinese or the fire walking festival (Thimithi) of the Hindus, colorful brochures have been produced, encouraging tourists to partake in the "spectacle" and welcoming tourists to "any of the temple ceremonies."

In the preservation of religious places, it would appear that little tension can be generated between the state and religious individuals and groups. Ostensibly, the preservation of such buildings also means that places cherished by individuals and communities have not been destroyed. However, preservation does not ensure that the meanings invested in these places remain the same. In fact, religious buildings that become recognized as "national monuments" take on new meanings, as historical and cultural artifacts and as tourist attractions. In other words, these places are appropriated and their meanings are redefined by the Preservation of Monuments Board (PMB) and the tourist authorities. Certainly, the meanings invested in these buildings by tourists are often different from the meanings invested by religious adherents who worship at these places. Such appropriation and redefinition are not totally rejected by the individuals and communities affected, for some accept that tourists may like to visit their places of worship. For example, Chia (1997–98, 38–39) discovered how, for some worshipers, the cultural value of their places of worship is enhanced precisely because of the presence of tourists; that is, the very fact that tourists are interested in them lends value to these sites. Indeed, as Chia (1997–87, 39) quotes, concern is expressed by the secretary of the temple Po Chiak Keng when visitor numbers drop: "[after the renovations are completed] we expect not only more worshipers, but also more tourists to visit our historic temple, which at the moment, has touched bottom with only a few people visiting a day." However, there are reservations that indicate potential underlying tensions. For example, some believe the private, personal relationship between an individual and his or her deity becomes open to the public eye and made an object of curiosity through tourism. As one interviewee put it, tourism should not be encouraged by external groups for it is not their religious places and religious activities that are invaded. There is also another concern that shrines, statues, and the like become treated as pieces of art. For some interviewees, such shrines and statues are imbued with a sacredness, indicating a god's presence. It is the height of insult and affront to worshipers when tourists begin to put their arms around the statue of a god for a photograph. Such tensions revolving around preservation efforts reflect broader arguments within the literature on heritage (such as Binney and Hanna 1978; and Lowenthal 1985), which address questions such as who decides whose heritage is conserved and for whose benefit (chapter 8).

Religious Buildings: Beacons of Multiculturalism and Multireligiosity

In as much as policies pertaining to religious buildings uphold the construction of a developmentalist and pragmatic "nation," the construction of a multicultural "nation" is also in part sustained by rhetoric, policy, and action that surround religious buildings in Singapore. Specifically, religious buildings serve to endorse constructions of a "nation" committed to multiculturalism and, relatedly, equality of treatment, as well as to religious tolerance and harmony. The state's construction of a multicultural "nation" draws in many ways on its policies toward religious buildings. First, some space is provided for all religious groups in planning guidelines and no group is denied at least some space (evident in Table 5.1). This fact is upheld as evidence of a genuine commitment to multireligiosity, seen to be one dimension of multiculturalism, as discussed in chapter 3.

At the same time, resettlement and demolition policies also apply to all religious groups—churches, mosques, Hindu and Chinese temples have all been affected—and so the state can hedge itself against potential accusations that it has not been fair in its treatment of different groups. In a statement from the prime minister's office (*Singapore Government Press Release* 3 Oct. 1987), it was spelled out that the state is evenhanded in all its dealings with religious groups. In the case of land clearance for the Mass Rapid Transit (MRT) stations in the Orchard Road corridor, for example, a variety of religious buildings were similarly affected, including Angullia Mosque, Ngee Ann Kongsi land, Bethesda Chapel, Chek Sian Teng Chinese Temple, Sri

Sivan Temple, and a Sikh temple at Kirk Terrace. In short, the state puts into practice its principle of equality of treatment in the relocation and demolition of religious buildings. Such specific policies and actions help to bear out the state's claim of commitment to multiculturalism and give substance to broader constitutional provisions that protect the citizen against discrimination on the grounds of religion, race, descent, or place of birth. The state's keen desire to portray its commitment to multiculturalism and multireligiosity is captured in Lee Hsien Loong's (then minister for trade and industry and second minister for defense) acknowledgment in 1989 that any treatment on the part of the state that is less than even-handed will have dire consequences: "Should any group feel threatened . . . because they receive less than evenhanded treatment from the Government, then that group too must respond by mobilising themselves to protect their interests, if necessary militantly. Tensions will build up, and there will be trouble for all."

In spite of such claims, the construction of a multicultural "nation" is not without contradictions. As part of the claim to indigenousness, the Malays enjoy certain privileges. This fact is translated into privileges for the Muslims. For example, Muslims do not have to tender for the first mosque site, unlike other religious groups, because it is a policy to have one mosque in every new town developed (*Singapore Government Press Release* 3 Oct. 1987). A site is therefore allocated to the Majlis Ugama Islam Singapura (Muslim Religious Council, or MUIS) at a price determined by the chief valuer. This is usually three to four times lower than the market value (*Singapore Government Press Release* 3 Oct. 1987). This contradiction is not lost on non-Muslims. As Kong (1993b, 347) illustrated, mosques appear to some non-Muslims to be "ubiquitous" and "imposing," and are constructed as evidence of discrimination in favor of the Muslim community. A Hindu interviewee whom Kong (1993b, 347) quoted expresses the underlying tension that is felt among non-Muslims: "We all get the feeling that we all see a mosque everywhere; in every town, you see a mosque, a real imposing structure, but you don't get to see a temple and all that . . . the temples that are being built nowadays are being built in real out of the way places." This resentment is potentially dangerous because it builds up unhappiness between religious groups. As another interviewee argued, the only way not to create or exacerbate such tensions is to ensure that all groups are treated equally:

> I think it's got to be either all or nothing. Either we have a separation of church and state or we don't. And I think that particularly, and again, this is very dangerous ground, but singling out one particular racial or religious group, for benefit or otherwise, can only work to that group's disadvantage, because what that means is everyone else is going to resent them. And, understandably, it's been done all along to protect them [the Malays] and to protect the preservation of their culture, and to make sure they didn't get swallowed up by the rest of us, because they were here first. But after, what, we've got a couple of hundred years of history, it's enough. And I think the real problem that we have here now is that everyone else is going to resent it so much, in the sense that, don't the rest of us have a culture that is worth preserving? (quoted in Kong 1993b, 347)

Constructing a multicultural "nation" yet privileging Malays and Muslims thus presents potentially thorny issues about equality that may threaten the hegemonic version of the "nation."

Communitarianism and Religious Values

As we discussed in chapter 3, one of the key tenets of the state's construction of a Singapore "nation" is the call on communitarianism, a sense of putting "nation" before self. This is nowhere more evident than in the call on religious groups and individuals to think of the "nation" rather than the "kingdom [of God]" when conflicting needs and wants arise. Thus, even if the destruction of a religious building means some personal loss or if it affects one community in particular, Singaporeans are encouraged to think in terms of "public" and "national" interests and the overall good of the country. This reflects wider calls to Singaporeans to subordinate personal and sectional interests for the common good in order that multiracial and multireligious Singapore can enjoy successful community living (Wok 1971). For example, Chan Chee Seng (1975), then parliamentary secretary, Ministry of Social Affairs, spoke of how "religion can and must play a part to get people to think in terms of nation, rather than sectional interests" (see also Ahmad Mattar 1977; 1988). This fact is further illustrated in the controversy surrounding the introduction in 1969 of the Abortion Bill, which liberalized abortion laws to allow for legalized abortion. This was done at a time when family planning and population control were primary goals on the state's agenda. Religious groups, particularly Christian and Muslim groups, objected to the bill on religious grounds, but the bill was passed with few amendments. At the height of the population-control policies in the 1970s, the Ministry of Education gave priority in school enrollment for children whose parents were sterilized. Catholic schools protested that sterilization went against their religious teachings, a fact which meant that Catholic children were likely to be systematically discriminated against. Minister Chai Chong Yii replied to criticism by saying, "We have no intention to meddle with religious beliefs. But national policy should take precedence over other policies" (quoted in Kho 1979–80, 75).

Although the "public interest" is often invoked speedily to counter any objections to policies, there has been little discussion of what constitutes "public interest" and who defines such interests. As Simmie (1974, 121–25) argued in the context of urban planning, there is no such thing as "the public interest." Rather, there are a number of different and competing interests, defined by different groups. In such a context, it is fallacious to pretend that "policy makers acting alone can determine and safeguard the 'public interest' " (Burgess and Gold 1982, 2). By contrast, as Vasil (1988, 123–24) points out, the ruling People's Action Party (PAP) view is that, in a developing society where there are many ethnic groups and economic classes, each group or class has its own distinctive views of what the common interests are. As a result, there will be no "accepted consensus on the interests of the nation." Given this, the PAP works on the premise that the government "alone [has] the legitimate right to represent the whole nation. Its perceptions of the national interest must prevail." It is such definitions of public interests that the state invokes to persuade people to accept its actions.

Further evidence that religion is to have particular nation-building responsibilities may be found in the roles that the state demarcates as being acceptable for religion, namely, to serve the "national" community through serving some of the social needs of particular "needy" groups. Homes for the aged and destitute, care for the poor and less fortunate, counseling for the "misguided" (such as drug addicts), and childcare services are said to be some acceptable areas of activity for religious organizations. This belief reflects the state's version of a "nation" in which religious groups serve the social needs of the larger community. On the other hand, the state is adamant that religious groups have no place to make any comments on economic issues; economic policy should be the purview of the state. As the former Prime Minister Lee Kuan Yew (*Singapore Government Press Release* 13 Dec. 1988) has pointed out, religion looks after the "moral and social well-being" of a people but it should not be concerned with the economic and political needs of the population. Indeed, the former premier spelled this out in no uncertain terms after Catholic church para-organizations were alleged to have been used as a front among Marxist conspirators set to overthrow the government:

> What we want our religious and para-religious groups to do is to give relief to the destitute, the disadvantaged, the disabled, to take part in activities which will foster communal fellowship. Emphasis on charity, alms-giving and social and community work . . . And priests [had] better stay out of espousing a form of economic system, or challenge the way we do things, social policy or theory. (*The Straits Times* 17 Aug. 1987)

Conclusion

If the state intends the Singapore "nation" to be a pragmatic, developmentalist, multicultural, and communitarian one, it certainly harnesses religious landscapes to naturalize these constructions. It does so by persuading Singaporeans that Singapore's land-scarce and multiracial condition means that the only commonsensical way for Singapore to survive and develop economically and socially is by adhering to certain operating principles. These concepts include pragmatic and economic principles in the allocation of land for religious buildings, the willingness to demolish or relocate those which stand in the way of development, and the acquiescence of religious landscapes to the tourism industry. Religious groups must then call upon their sense of "nation above community" to accept that the "general public good" transcends their sectarian interests. In this scheme of things, it is also critical that religious adherents believe that all religious groups are evenhandedly treated.

Clearly, not all Singaporeans accept these conditions as "natural" and "commonsensical." Offering their religious place to the tourist gaze is not always voluntary; relocation is sometimes resisted and then grudgingly accepted; sites allocated for religious buildings are sometimes recognized to be less than ideal or satisfactory; and the claim of evenhandedness in the treatment of all religious groups is sometimes queried. However, even while some question the policies and actions of the state and hence the state's version of the "nation," there have been no instances of conflict that have not been contained. This suggests that, while hegemony is not total, the state has been sufficiently successful in its ideological makeover that it can continue on its trajectory in "nation" construction and political legitimation. Religious landscapes thus play an integral role in this exercise, in the same way that various other landscapes are also harnessed to press home the vision of the "nation."

6

Housing the People, Building a "Nation"

The Development of Public Housing in Singapore

The dominance of public-sector provision in Singapore's housing environment is striking. In 1998, 86 percent of the population lived in public housing (Housing and Development Board 2002) provided at subsidized rates by the HDB. Indeed, by comparison with many other large cities in the world, modern public housing in Singapore has achieved impressive results. From old, badly degenerated, overcrowded slums in the 1950s, characterized by, among other things, poor sanitation and lack of hygiene, high-rise public flats of varied designs and sizes now characterize the skyline. Whereas tuberculosis was rife and buildings posed fire hazards just a few decades ago, Singaporeans today enjoy high standards of public hygiene and safety as well as numerous luxuries in high-quality housing symbolic of modernity.

These changes in the housing landscape have taken place over a short period of time. Up to the 1950s and early 1960s, Singapore was still plagued by varied problems. Kaye (1960, 5), for example, documented the living conditions of a typical street in Chinatown in 1954, describing it as "among the most primitive in the urban areas of the world." Goh (1956) similarly found in a study conducted in 1953–54 that 73 percent of surveyed households lived in badly overcrowded conditions. In another estimate, it was suggested that one-quarter of a million people lived in badly degenerated slums in the city center and another one-third of a million lived in squatter areas on the city fringe in 1960 (The 1975, 5). This fact is significant, considering that in 1960 the total population was only 1.6 million (Department of Statistics 1983).

Given the severe shortage of decent housing in that period, the Housing and Development Board (HDB) was established in 1960, replacing its predecessor, the Singapore Improvement Trust (SIT),[1] tasked with the job of housing Singaporeans. The HDB's top priority was to build as many housing units as possible within a short time. By the end of its First Five-Year Plan in 1965, the HDB had exceeded its construction target of 50,000 units by 5,000 and was able to house 23 percent of the total population in public flats. However, while the targets pertaining to quantity had been satisfied, the flats were very basic in nature, and little attention was paid to quality. Indeed, many were one-room "emergency" flats, with about 140 square feet of bed-cum-sitting room and a 80 square-foot service area consisting of a combined bathroom and toilet, cooking area, and a balcony for eating, washing, and drying purposes (*HDB Annual Report* 1961). Some of the one-room flats even had communal or semicommunal toilet and kitchen facilities. By its Second Five-Year Plan (1966–70), however, the HDB's success in meeting its quantitative targets meant that it could now pay a little more attention to quality, a direction that has persisted and has become most important today. So successful has Singapore's public-housing program been that the HDB has been recognized for the excellence of its management. In 1995, it received the Asia Management Award in Development Management from the Asian Institute of Management in recognition of "excellent achievements of Asian management," which were said to have created "substantial positive impact on target beneficiaries through innovative, sustainable and effective management" and to have improved the quality of life of people (*The Straits Times* 17 Oct. 1995). This award was also a recognition of how rapidly the HDB had turned around housing conditions.

In this chapter, we illustrate how the public-housing landscape, while serving functional needs, has also been the state's means by which to construct and reinforce particular versions of the "nation." The hegemony of the state is mediated by individuals' negotiated meanings of the same land-

1. The SIT was set up in 1927 to supervise urban improvement and development. It was only in the 1930s that it ventured into public housing in recognition of the shortage of housing for lower-income groups. While the SIT attempted to address the housing problem, its achievements were small in comparison with the magnitude of the problem.

scapes, where, in the everyday microprocesses of social life, different versions of "nation" are lived out. At times, these are conscious acts of resistance; sometimes, Singaporeans simply do not share the same vision. At
other times, Singaporeans subscribe to other ideologies, consciously or
subconsciously, and life pans out in ways that the state does not intend.

A "Nation" Built on Sense of Place

One of the key planks on which the state seeks to construct a "nation" is to
develop a sense of place and belonging among Singaporeans; the public-
housing landscape is called to play. In the 1960s, this idea found nascent
form in the introduction of a Home Ownership Scheme, which has become highly successful. By the late 1970s and right up to the 1990s, efforts
to promote a sense of place and community identity through the public-
housing landscape have taken the shape of new building designs.

In 1964, the Home Ownership Scheme was introduced to encourage
Singaporeans to buy their flats as part of the drive to create a property-
owning democracy extending to the lower middle-income groups (*HDB
Annual Report* 1964). The scheme initially met with slow response, but was
given a boost in 1968 when purchasers were permitted to use their Central
Provident Fund (CPF) savings to pay for both the downpayment and
monthly installments if they desired.[2] This fact meant that housing purchase might entail no extra outlay beyond their existing CPF contribution.
Not surprisingly, the scheme became an attractive option. In addition, existing tenants enjoyed a concessionary downpayment of 5 percent of the
purchase price of the flat rather than the regular 20 percent (*HDB Annual Report* 1968). Other incentives to encourage home ownership were introduced in later years, including periodic revision of the household income
ceiling for eligibility, first to S$1200 in 1969 and up to S$8000 in 1996.

The ideological roots of home ownership lie beyond economic considerations and extend to a hegemonic effort at building a sense of commitment to both the neighborhood and, at a larger level, the "nation." It was

2. CPF is a state-operated savings and pension scheme. CPF contributors can use their
savings in this fund for downpayments as well as installment payments for the purchase of
HDB flats.

believed, among other things, that people would look after their own properties better than after rental units, thus reducing estate-management problems in the long run (*The Straits Times* 26 Feb. 1984). It was also believed that
people would have a greater sense of commitment to Singapore if they had
a direct stake in it. They would thus be committed to maintaining a viable,
harmonious society and would defend it against aggressors. This belief is
clearly articulated by Prime Minister Goh Chok Tong: "The best stake we
can give to Singaporeans is a house or a flat, a home. It is the single biggest
asset for most people, and its value reflects the fundamentals of the economy" (*The Straits Times* 27 Aug. 1995).

While Singaporeans have by and large embraced home ownership, it
remains a moot point whether this attitude translates into a greater sense of
commitment to the neighborhood and to Singapore. The keenness with
which Singaporeans seek to upgrade by moving from smaller flats to bigger
ones, even if doing so entails moving to a quite different area of Singapore,
suggests a lack of sense of place. Writ large, the HDB property, when sold,
in fact offers the owner a significant sum with which to migrate.

In the late 1970s and 1980s, when the Home Ownership Scheme was
fully entrenched, the state began other means of attempting to root people
to place and community. Perhaps the most significant effort, reflecting a
sense of architectural determinism, was the use of new building designs to
grant new towns distinctive identities in the hope that residents would feel
a sense of identity and belonging. For example, varying building heights
were combined to break the monotony of the skyline. Greater use was
made of traditional forms such as pitched roofs, overhanging eaves, and tall
windows typical of a tropical building (Teo and Huang 1996). In addition,
the precinct concept, initiated in 1978, was further encouraged in the
1980s to enhance a sense of community spirit and neighborliness. Each
precinct consists of 600 to 1,000 dwelling units and is linked to other
precincts by pedestrian paths, meant to encourage meaningful social interaction among residents. The idea is to try to create a community-activity
focal point in the form of a landscape square with recreational facilities,
kindergarten, eating places, and local shops among a cluster of blocks.
Precincts are also made more compact with closer spacing between buildings to enhance a sense of community spirit and neighborliness.

6.1. Neighborhood precinct.

In a case study of one of the most recent new towns, Pasir Ris, Teo and Huang (1996) illustrated the HDB's qualified success in its attempt to inculcate sense of place and identity through the housing landscape. Their survey suggested that, while residents recognized the distinctiveness of their physical surroundings—imageable skylines, unique and striking paintwork, and a resort ambience—far fewer exhibited a real sense of belonging developed through a depth of relationship with people and place, perhaps in part because it is a relatively new estate of less than ten years. Certainly, precincts with their focal points for activity did not seem to attract residents as they were intended to. In contrast, community and social life built on spontaneous, interpersonal ties, as well as on the strength of organized vernacular associations in old estates, have developed among residents a sense of place and community (see also Yeoh and Kong 1994; 1995).

Developing a Gracious Society Within a Pragmatic and Developmentalist "Nation"

In various ways, public housing has helped to focus Singaporeans on the goal of economic growth and survival, thereby upholding the ideology of pragmatism and perpetuating the construction of a "nation" based on developmentalist principles. First, subsidized public housing has kept operational costs low for multinational investors since cheaper public housing lowers the costs of living. By keeping rents and prices low, the pressure on wages is relieved without lowering the quality of labor. At the same time, another attraction for multinational investors is the fact that Singapore's public housing includes a complete network of urban infrastructure, such as the provision of factory sites for light and nonpolluting industries in the new towns and the construction of transport networks (expressways and roads). Second, because most individuals rely on their CPF contributions for house purchase, it is possible to control inflation by controlling the housing supply and the supply of financing. At the same time, when wages increase, CPF contribution rates increase, so that the net increase in wages is effectively reduced and spending power curbed. Third, public housing provision creates employment in the construction sector. Because the construction industry is highly labor-intensive, and because it demands both skilled and unskilled workers, it was an extremely important employer in the 1960s when unemployment was high (Pugh 1989, 837–38). The building and construction industry employed an average of 10 percent of the total nonprofessional labor force between 1960 and 1965, and about 7 percent between 1966 and 1970 (Yeh 1972, 189), as well as generating multiple effects in transport and other related industries. In addition, the HDB provides sites for employment within new towns so that labor-intensive industries have ready access to labor living in the new towns—particularly female labor. It was reported, for example, that ten major factories in Toa Payoh, a new town of the 1970s, provided employment for about 16 percent of the working population living in the estate in 1972 (*HDB Annual Report* 1972). Finally, home ownership ties purchasers into a regular mortgage structure that requires monthly payments. This can be met only by steady monthly salary that can be earned through participation in the work force, a fact which helps to maintain a disciplined attitude to work (Salaff 1988).

In all these various ways, then, public housing has been harnessed by the state to materialize its pragmatic and developmentalist ideologies. This situation has, in turn, enabled it to fulfill its version of a progressive "nation" committed to and realizing economic development. Such adherence to pragmatism and developmentalism is apparent not only in state ideologies but also among Singaporeans—evident in the premium placed on material possessions and economic advancement. This fact is revealed in a 1996 survey of 418 young Singaporeans ages 21 to 30 years, in which they were asked what was most important to them in their lives. As it turned out, the "Singapore Dream" was predicated on expectations of good jobs and higher salaries, better housing, the ability to afford private transportation, and, generally, a better quality of life. Indeed, a large proportion (44 percent) of those surveyed cited a good career as the area of their life of most concern to them. However, alongside their higher expectations of life (vis-à-vis the older generation), their attitudes belie a "paradox of affluence," one in which there is a reduced drive to work and sacrifice that has arisen out of relative affluence (Wong and Ng 1993, 318). At the same time, while absolute deprivation may have been eliminated, there is a sense of relative deprivation among those who cannot achieve their "Singapore Dream." In this way, the public-housing landscape, rather than being a symbol of progress and modernity, may in fact become a symbol of entrapment and class and status immobility for the Singaporean aspiring to private housing, for example.

We have argued in chapter 3 that, while pragmatism and developmentalism pervade state constructions of the "nation," the state has also recently introduced the idea of a gracious society for balance. Such a gracious society, in the prime minister's book, is measured by, among other things, the level of public consideration—for example, the concern that Singaporeans have for public property. Quotidian living in public-housing estates provides one of the best microcosms in which to observe the realization—or otherwise—of this constructed vision.

Life in the HDB "heartlands," in fact, often negates the state's vision of the "nation" as a gracious community. The many shared problems of everyday living in high-rise buildings are indicative of how the social construction of "nation" as a gracious, cultivated one remains at the level of ideology and construction. For example, residents are far from free of problems in the maintenance of cleanliness of common properties such as lifts and staircases. Problems such as irresponsible people urinating in lifts, leaving rubbish at lift landings, and throwing "killer litter" (the act of throwing out of windows of higher floors fragile, large, or heavy items such as flower pots, thus endangering the lives of those passing by downstairs) are common enough trials that residents must battle. They point to a people lacking in social graces, common courtesy, and consideration for others, indicating the slippage between construction and reality. This situation is further evidenced in measures that are required to encourage more considerate behavior, from competitions organized by town councils to encourage cleanliness in neighborhoods, complete with prize monies (*The Straits Times* 25 Oct. 1996), to the establishment of task forces to fight antisocial habits in neighborhoods (*The Straits Times* 25 Oct. 1996), to exhortations at the discursive level that physical upgrading programs would be incomplete if residents did not change their social behavior (Peh Chin Hua, Member of Parliament, Jalan Besar Group Representative Constituency, quoted in *The Straits Times* 22 Nov. 1996).

A "Nation" in a Modern Cityscape

In many ways, the public-housing landscape has been one of the state's most important tools for realizing the vision of a modern, developed city. Examples abound of how, through the HDB, the state continually seeks to improve the cityscape, reflecting a relentless drive towards modernity. When the HDB first embarked on its task of housing the population, its main concern was to build as many housing units as possible within a short time. This, it achieved remarkably well and very quickly (Perry, Kong, and Yeoh 1997), and by 1965 the backbone of Singapore's housing problem had been broken. By the late 1960s, therefore, the concern was not only to put a roof over people's heads but also to pursue the provision of living conditions suited to an age of modernity.

The HDB began by building bigger units, replacing the minimalist one-room "emergency" flats of the early 1960s (see Teh 1975). Attention during this period was also paid to the living environment in toto, with greater emphasis on the provision of open spaces, landscaping, car-parking facilities, and recreational facilities such as playgrounds and sports facilities. By the end of the first decade of public housing, the HDB had constructed more than 110,000 units and provided residents with modern amenities such as direct water and electricity supplies, sanitation, and rubbish disposal systems, which made for much better public hygiene. Gross overcrowding became a thing of the past. In 1951, the average number of rooms per household was 0.8; by 1970 it was 2.2 (Gee and Chee 1981, 102). As a consequence, health conditions were significantly improved. In a survey conducted by the HDB in 1968, 26 percent of residents felt that life had become very much better; 44 percent said that it was somewhat better; 18 percent reported that conditions had remained the same as before; 11 percent indicated that things had changed somewhat for the worse; while 1 percent felt that change had made life very much worse (Yeh 1972, 107). Where dissatisfaction existed, it typically arose from the perception that the HDB had failed to protect a sense of community, neighborliness, and identity, and had contributed to the breaking up of the extended family. Other complaints had to do with the inadequacy of communal facilities, inefficient lifts and public transportation, and noise (Yeh 1972). These issues were all to be taken up in subsequent decades. In essence, though, the vision of a modern city was well on its way to being realized through continued improvements in the housing landscape by the late 1960s.

In the 1970s, further pursuit of modernity took the shape of even bigger and better-designed flats in choicer locations, as well as good infrastructure support in the form of efficient transportation, adequate retail and recreational facilities, and other amenities (Teo 1986). At the same time, architectural variations were introduced in the design of the flats, thus creating more attractive external designs. Between the late 1970s and 1980s, existing estates were also upgraded on an ad hoc basis as part of the effort to improve quality. Old flats were demolished so that land could be available for redevelopment. Old one-room flats were converted into larger three- and four-room self-contained flats by knocking down the walls between the old flats. Additional facilities for the older estates such as a commercial complex with fast-food restaurants and offices, a new bus interchange, an MRT line stopping in the town center, and a government mini-hospital were provided to ensure that they too had a share of better facilities found in the newer estates. At the level of individual buildings and units, new lifts were added, casement windows were installed in flats with open balconies, central television antennae were added, and rewiring and reroofing took place (*HDB Annual Report* 1979–80). Rules on flat alterations were liberalized so that owners could make minor alterations themselves. For example, owners of five-room flats were allowed to install windows in their open balconies; residents on ground floors were permitted to extend their courtyard shelters to keep out the rain (*The Straits Times* 3 Mar. 1988; 6 Jan. 1990); the space in recessed entrances and along common corridors could also be sold so that residents could turn them into small gardens or playgrounds and have improved security and privacy (*The Straits Times* 25 Feb. 1989).

In the 1990s, the emphasis on maintaining a modern cityscape took the form of providing even bigger flats, but most significantly, more comfortable and up-to-date physical environments through further upgrading. In July 1989, a formal, large-scale program was introduced that aimed to allow "a complete change in the perception of public housing" (S. Dhanabalan, then national development minister, quoted in *The Straits Times* 12 July 1989). The project is intended to last fifteen years (beginning in 1991) and benefit 95 percent of HDB dwellers (see Perry, Kong, and Yeoh 1997). It involves various changes in pursuit of modernity, including architectural improvements to make each block distinctive and addition of an extra toilet or the expansion of the kitchen area. In addition to this formal upgrading program, individual older blocks around Singapore's central area are also subject to selective upgrading under the Selective En Bloc Redevelopment Scheme (Sers), introduced in 1995. New blocks are erected in selected areas. Nearby residents then move in before their old flats are demolished and new ones built in place. In this way, the physical living environment can be improved and the community kept intact. Yet another example of the way in which the housing landscape, as a key component of the urbanscape, is used to exemplify modern living is the introduction in 1995 of executive condominiums, designed to approximate the standards in a private development but at cheaper rates. For example, these HDB executive condominiums come with swimming pools and tennis courts, similar to private condominiums.

While the precise notion and exemplification of modernity is historically specific and clearly differs between the 1960s and 1990s, evidently the state has employed various strategies to develop a modern cityscape in

6.2. Upgraded block of flats.

Singapore—in part through the development and continued improvements of public-housing estates. This urbanscape has become symbolically useful as evidence of the commitment of the state to a particular version of the "nation." However, the ways in which Singaporeans have responded to these constructions of city and "nation" reveal how intended meanings may become translated in diverse, and sometimes divergent, ways. It is to these different readings that we now turn.

Symbols of modernity, when translated into bigger, better, and posher living conditions, are indeed welcomed by Singaporeans. The constant reminder to Singaporeans to work hard to achieve economic growth for the country and material wealth for themselves has turned Singapore into a materialistic society in many ways. As discussed earlier in the chapter, part of the Singapore Dream entails home ownership, with all its trappings of modernity. The survey cited earlier reported that 27 percent of the respondents were already home owners while 90 percent of the rest of the respondents planned to buy a home in the short- to medium-term future. This importance placed on home ownership reflects the success of the government's policy of encouraging home ownership so that Singaporeans may have a stake in the country. However, the irony lies in that this desire to own one's home now takes on a different complexion from such desires in the past. Singaporeans now wish to own private property, whether it is private condominiums or houses, a dream cherished by many, particularly the younger generation. As indicated in the results of the survey, 25 percent of the respondents felt it very important to own private property, while 35 percent felt it quite important to do so. Only 40 percent felt it to be unimportant. These sentiments were endorsed by the view of 46 percent of the respondents that the government should exercise more control on private-property prices. There were already many who felt that their dream would be extremely difficult, if not impossible, to achieve, a source of discontent among Singaporeans. Among the reasons cited by those Singaporeans who wish to migrate elsewhere, one is the sense that, no matter how hard one worked, the prohibitively expensive private-housing market would always remain out of reach (Sullivan and Gunasekaran 1994). This fact suggests that the effort to construct a modern cityscape (and by extension, a modern "nation") has raised expectations to a level that may not be fulfilled, with somewhat divergent results from those originally intended.

Nevertheless, for those who remain in Singapore, the various strategies of upgrading housing conditions represent the government's way of delivering living standards for a population with growing aspirations. Upgrading also raises the value of the flats, which allows Singaporeans to share some of the country's economic growth (Teo and Kong 1997). At the same time, because upgrading entails residents both voting for and financially participating in the program, the individual's stake in society is raised. This, the state hopes, will translate into Singaporeans' commitment to stay and work for Singapore's success.

By far, upgrading has received the most overall unequivocally positive response from those affected. While many complain about the inconveniences during the process of physical construction, the quality of workmanship, and the failure to adhere to schedules, the effects at the end of the day are welcomed. The results of a questionnaire survey conducted in late 1994 involving 100 randomly selected households in Lorong Lew Lian, one of a batch of six housing estates identified for an early phase of upgrading in

1992, bears this out (see Low 1993–94). About 90 percent of the estate household heads interviewed said they were pleased with the block facade design as well as the fixtures and finishes to their flats, especially the additional balcony space. Almost 80 percent expressed the view that the provision of precinct facilities like the children's playground, barbecue pits, and residents' corners had brought residents closer together.

However, apart from such responses to upgrading at very local and personal levels, some residents also interpret the exercise in ideological terms, recognizing the state's appropriation of the upgrading exercise for political purposes. This was evident in 1992, for example, when Prime Minister Goh Chok Tong made public the government's intention to link the choice of housing estates to be upgraded to the strength of votes for the PAP in the general elections (*The Straits Times* 11 Apr. 1992). In 1996, Community Development Minister Abdullah Tarmugi further outlined the three criteria that the government would use in deciding which HDB blocks would be upgraded: surpluses, a good spread, and support. Specifically, upgrading could be carried out only if the government continued to enjoy budget surpluses. The HDB would also try to ensure a good geographical spread of the precincts being upgraded. Finally, by way of garnering support, he suggested that "if you want your blocks and precincts to be upgraded earlier, you know what to do at the next election. The answer is in your hands" (*The Straits Times* 29 Jan. 1996).

Some Singaporeans responded to such instrumental rationality by criticizing the blatant use of public housing for party political ends. One resident, for example, went as far as arguing that public housing in Singapore was like a "public good, a public utility," and that it was unconscionable to use it for political purposes. In the face of criticisms, and by way of assurance, Prime Minister Goh Chok Tong asserted subsequently that all HDB residents would benefit from upgrading. Objective criteria such as the age of flats, their location, and the level of resident interest (as indicated by votes in favor of upgrading) had been and would continue to be used, and only when two constituencies had HDB flats of similar ages would the level of support for the PAP government be used as a "tie-breaker" (*The Straits Times* 5 Feb. 1996). While the state appeared to respond to overt criticism of its strategy, the fact remained that political support was still to be used as one of the criteria, albeit a last criterion, for deciding which blocks would be upgraded. In one sense, then, the ultimate triumph lay with the state. This fact may also be true from another perspective: when it is argued, as some interviewees did, that upgrading could be a political issue for the PAP, but for ordinary people the politics of the matter were not important because to them "upgrading is a matter of economics." Such proclamations perhaps belie the success of the state's hegemonic effort.

Unlike the upgrading exercise, the response to Sers has been less enthusiastic. Given that residents' views are not sought in the decision as to whether to redevelop, many homeowners are left guessing whether they would be relocated at relatively short notice. This is particularly a problem when they have spent large amounts of money on home renovations, only to find that they are to be relocated. While residents feel they have no way of contributing to the decision-making process or to reverse decisions, they nevertheless seek means of ameliorating the potential negative effects of the decision by seeking information and confirmation of plans through their members of parliament and grassroots leaders, and by seeking to minimize potential losses by not spending money on house renovations, in case they have to relocate. The vision of modernity that Sers is meant to help achieve, however, does not treat all citizens equally, nor does it contribute to the sense of a "deep, horizontal comradeship" (Anderson 1983) that makes up community and "nation." This situation is because different segments of the population feel they are impacted differently. The dissatisfaction lies particularly among the older generation, who do not have the means to take up the offer of a new, more expensive flat and may have to find alternative residence elsewhere, thus breaking the stability of their residence. They have also expressed the view that a bigger flat meant little to them in their old age, and what mattered was the sense of community and neighborliness that had developed in their original settings (*The Straits Times* 1 May 1996). The vision of modernity may appeal to the younger generation, but for the older generation, it signifies dislocation.

Initial response to executive condominiums was lukewarm, mainly because the price was more than double that for an HDB executive flat, even though the latter is one-sixth to nearly one-half larger. Those expressing interest in the executive condominiums are drawn by the prestige of private property and the private recreational amenities (*The Straits Times* 31 Aug. 1995). However, subsequently, as the HDB lowered prices, public response reached "overwhelming" proportions (*The Straits Times* 10 July 1996).[3] But observers have expressed the view that the state is pandering to the demands of a small group of young Singaporeans with aspirations to own a condominium and using taxpayers' money to subsidize these educated, young, often graduate couples. This created an inequitable situation in which the middle class was being subsidized. The vision of improved, modern living in this instance benefits a small segment of the population and creates crevices in the construction of a "nation" constantly in search of improved modern living.

A "Nation" Rooted in Multiracialism

When Stamford Raffles arrived in Singapore in 1819 and founded the island as a base for the British East India Company, one of the first landscape changes he effected was to introduce town planning, which took shape in an 1822 document. The town plan was based on racial segregation, with accommodation of the principal races in separate quarters. Specifically, Raffles demarcated the town into "divisions" or "*kampungs*" for particular racial and occupational groups: the European town was allotted the expanse to the east of an area reserved for government while the Chinese, Bugis, Arabs, Chulias, and Malays were relegated to more peripheral locations in well-demarcated *kampungs*—Chinatown for the Chinese, the Kampong Glam area for the Malays, and so forth. Such racial segregation was to last through Singapore's colonial history. With independence and new attention paid to the need for "nation-building," racial desegregation and peaceful coexistence became one of the concerns of the new government. HDB new towns were intended to be one of the major means by which racial mixing could be encouraged. With public housing and different races being housed in the same block of flats, it was believed that opportunities for intercommunity mixing would become higher at a daily interpersonal level,

3. Two of the earliest developments (Eastvale and Westmere) were oversubscribed by about eighteen times (*Business Times* 10 July 1996).

thus contributing to the development of healthy race relations. By the 1980s, however, it was observed that different racial groups were congregating in particular housing estates. For example, Ang Mo Kio and Hougang had a larger share of Chinese than did the national profile, and there was a larger-than-average concentration of Malays in Tampines, Marine Parade, and Bedok. In 1989, rules were introduced to ensure that racial mix in HDB estates should reflect roughly the racial proportion in the total population. Where a particular group was over-represented, any flat that was to be sold must be sold to someone in the racial group that was under-represented (Ooi 1993). This goal is enforced by rules that require all sales of HDB property to be processed through the agency.[4]

Interpreted ideologically, the state has attempted to write a particular version of the "nation" in the public-housing landscape, one rooted in a multiracial ideology. At the same time, by introducing controls to ensure a racial mix in each new town—and even in each block of flats—it has also attempted to prevent the development of communally based politics, furthering the multiracial platform that the ruling party has consistently campaigned on since it came to power.

How successful have these attempts been to enhance interracial mixing, thus contributing to the vision of a multiracial nation? Ostensibly, Singapore has managed to maintain a peace and harmony that escapes other multiracial societies like Sri Lanka. However, in the local arenas of action, there are situations that risk racial and religious tension if not carefully handled. Lai (1995), in her ethnographic observations of one HDB housing estate (Marine Parade), highlights, for example, the clash of a Malay wedding and a Chinese funeral wake in the use of HDB void decks.[5] Any party that wishes to use this space must make a booking in advance with the town council that manages the estate. Malay families are one such group. The

4. This deliberate effort at racial mixing is paralleled in deliberate class mixing. Within estates—and indeed, within blocks—different income groups are mixed through the construction of differently sized flats. This practice reduces the "ghetto effect" (Chua 1995a, 141) while providing opportunities for the better educated to offer their leadership and services to the lower-income and less-educated groups.

5. This is the open space on the ground floor of HDB flats, which is often used for various functions by different groups.

celebration of a Malay wedding in an HDB void deck—elaborate, ceremonious, colorful, and accompanied by music—is part of the rhythm and life in an HDB estate. Such celebrations may run into conflict when these void decks are needed for Chinese funeral wakes as well, which, due to the contingency of the situation, do not allow for advance booking. Chinese custom further dictates that if a coffin is already placed in one spot, it must not be moved. Thus, it is entirely possible that a Malay couple may have applied to use a void deck on a particular day, only to find that an hour earlier a coffin had been placed there due to a neighbor's sudden demise. In handling such a situation, the authorities run the risk of being accused of discrimination if the inviolability of Chinese custom is upheld against the Malay's needs. The solution has been to privilege bureaucratic rules over cultural beliefs, so residents are expected to abide by pragmatic booking procedures. This requires of the Chinese a spirit of acceptance and a subordination of their own religious beliefs.

A further example of how the rhythm of everyday life reveals the cracks and crevices of multiracial and multireligious living and the fact that the ideological construction of a harmonious multiracial and multireligious community is not as seamless as desired can be seen during the seventh lunar month or the Hungry Ghost Festival celebrated by the Chinese. Joss papers are burned, very often on grass verges; marquees are pitched, sheltering offerings of diverse sorts; and stages for street performances are set up, with Chinese operas or singing at night for the "hungry ghosts" who visit this earth in the seventh month. Complaints of noise, incense ash, and burned grass are not uncommon during this period, and can well be the occasion for religious tension and strife if not for continued counsel of religious and racial understanding and accommodation. The persuasion afforded by an ideological vision needs therefore to be constantly reinforced.

While the microprocesses of social life throw up occasions of potential challenge to the construction of "nation" rooted in multiracial and multireligious harmony, there are also other arenas of local life in public-housing estates that support such state constructions. The state's vision of multiracialism appears to find resonance in the context of living and growing up in public housing among youths, for example. Here, the sharing and negotiation of play spaces (for example, playgrounds and multipurpose courts) as a

way of life highlights the absence of a clear-cut racial identification or mo-
nopolization of spaces. Instead, there is a sense of equity and ethics, with
certain basic principles that operate: first-come-first-served, ground-
sharing for simultaneous play, joining forces if the game is the same, or
agreement on the duration of a game or day and time of play or practice
(Lai 1995). In the mutual understanding and give-and-take attitudes evident, it may well be said that the accommodation and negotiation practiced in this microcosmic way reflects a synergy with the state's constructed
notion of a harmonious multiracial "nation."

A "Nation" Built on Firm Family Ties

In chapter 3, we outlined the state's construction of the "nation" as one built
on strong family ties in which a stable society and community can develop
only if the family is the basic unit of society. The notion of "family" is an
ideological construct. A "normal" family is difficult to comprehensively
characterize, but PuruShotam (1993) highlights some of the characteristics
of such a family as constructed by the state: its rootedness in Asianness; the
authority and power structure of such families, which is essentially age- and
gender-based; and the "normalcy" of people getting married, having children after marriage, and raising girls to be women and boys to be men. Perhaps the most extreme expression of this ideology is captured in the views
of Chan Soo Sen, parliamentary secretary in the prime minister's office and
Ministry of Health, who defined the family as "man, wife and children living in the same household" (*The Straits Times* 27 May 1999). On this basis,
contrasting versions become "abnormal," such as having children outside of
marriage and same-sex partnership, or even two unmarried siblings living
together.

Public-housing policies have been some of the most successful in reinforcing the continuance of the "normal" family, not least in favoring marriage over singlehood. Since the establishment of the HDB in 1961, it has
been more difficult (and even impossible at times) for singles to purchase or
rent public housing. For at least a whole decade of the HDB's existence, it
was impossible for singles to buy an HDB flat because it was believed that
to make public housing available to singles was to help in breaking up fam-

ilies prematurely. The first sign of a relenting of this policy in 1972 was a
cautious one: an unmarried woman could buy or rent a flat only if she joined
with two or more women and at least one was older than 40 years. Such a
woman was viewed as a "confirmed spinster" (*The Straits Times* 20 Aug. 1972).
The regulation thus did not contradict the state's pro-family policy. In fact,
in allowing such sale or rental of an HDB flat, the state was in fact introducing one of its first responses to an aging population, which was its preferred
solution of using care from friends and relatives for the aged population as
an alternative to state assistance (*HDB Annual Report* 1978–79). In this sense,
principles of pragmatism prevailed.

In 1976, another regulation was introduced, which clearly signaled the
HDB's firm stand on keeping families together and which also made it more
difficult for unmarried women to choose singlehood and to be able to live
apart from their parents or siblings. This regulation made it impossible for
unmarried applicants to pay for their HDB flats using their full CPF savings
while allowing married applicants to do so (*The Straits Times* 7 Mar. 1976). A
further signal that the HDB endorsed marriage and family living above singlehood came in 1978, when it stipulated that an unmarried flat owner could
transfer ownership of the flat to his or her parents or other blood kin and
apply for a second flat so that he or she could move out upon marriage (*The
Straits Times* 7 Oct. 1978). This had the effect of making it easier for young
people who wanted to marry and set up their own home to purchase flats.

In the late 1970s and 1980s, the HDB turned its attention to other aspects of family living, namely, encouraging the establishment of extended
families. Further reinforcing the "normal" family as the cornerstone of society, the HDB uses allocation priorities to keep such families in close contact. In 1978, two new schemes (a joint balloting scheme and the mutual
exchange of flats scheme) were introduced to help married children and
their elderly parents live in adjoining flats or blocks within the same estate.
Those who applied for a flat as a three-tier family were given incentives,
such as a three-year retrospective priority over other applicants, a longer
loan-repayment period, and a smaller deposit payment for those with insufficient CPF savings (*HDB Annual Report* 1978–79). These policies underscore the view that care for the elders and children should come from the
family (keeping families intact or in close proximity is viewed as a way of

ensuring this). What remains unspoken and taken for granted is that such care often comes from women in the family, so much so that any attempt to promote intra-family caregiving directly promotes the traditional role of women as caregivers. In this sense, in emphasizing the centrality of the "normal" family and the importance of support within the extended family the state is in effect promoting a gendered version of the "nation," a construct which has real material consequences for gender roles and relations (see Radcliffe 1996).

In 1990, the state returned to review policies pertaining to marriage and singlehood. While the minimum qualifying age for unmarried women who wanted to jointly buy or rent a new flat from the HDB was lowered to 35 years, both applicants now had to satisfy the age requirement, as opposed to the earlier requirement that one be older than 40. Thus, while purchase or rental of flats by unmarried women was made possible at an earlier age, finding two people older than 35 was also probably more difficult than finding one (*The Straits Times* 7 Aug. 1990).

In 1995, revision of an earlier Transitional Rental Housing Scheme made it easier for first-time HDB flat-buyers to rent flats while waiting for their own, thus encouraging young couples to start their families earlier. As Prime Minister Goh Chok Tong noted, many first-time buyers were young couples who delayed their marriage until they had their own flats. It was hoped that, by improving their rental opportunities, the delay in marriage and child-rearing would be reduced (*The Straits Times* 27 Aug. 1995). Among the incentives were reduced rentals; priority over those seeking to upgrade in the selection of rental flats; and better units with more fittings such as a kitchen stove, water heater, and refrigerator—in addition to those already available, namely, kitchen cabinets, grills, gates, and light fittings. The number of rental flats was also increased by 25 percent to 500 units per quarter (*The Straits Times* 27 Aug. 1995). This change was reinforced by the HDB's revised CPF Housing Grant Scheme, which made it more attractive to first-time buyers who were willing to buy second-hand resale flats by increasing grants (from S$30,000 to S$40,000) to such buyers, likely to be young couples hoping to marry and settle down in their own home (*The Straits Times* 30 Aug. 1995). The change was intended to encourage earlier marriage and earlier child-bearing, a direct consequence of the government's concern that Singapore's birth rate was below replacement level because Singaporeans were marrying later and bearing less children, or were not marrying at all (see Perry, Kong, and Yeoh 1997).

While the policies hitherto discussed have dealt with singles as unmarried women, in 1994, explicit focus was given to unmarried mothers, who were disallowed from buying their flats directly from the HDB. They could only do so from the open resale market, where flats are more expensive (*The Straits Times* 22 Aug. 1994). The obvious intention was to use the housing policy as a direct means of making things more difficult for and an indirect means of expressing disapproval of unmarried mothers. As Prime Minister Goh argued, allowing unmarried mothers to buy flats directly from the HDB would appear to make unmarried motherhood a respectable part of Singapore society. As he pronounced unequivocally, "This is wrong. By removing the stigma, we may encourage more women to have children without getting married" (quoted in *The Straits Times* 22 Aug. 1994). The same refusal to support another group of single women, namely, those separated or divorced from their husbands, is also evident. These women are treated in much the same way as all other applicants, with no special considerations for their special circumstances in the buying or renting of flats.

Taken together, these housing policies reveal the state's adherence to a particular ideological construct, that of the "normal" family, on the grounds that it forms the basis of a strong, stable society, the substance of a cohesive "nation." However, in making it difficult for singles to own apartments, the state is essentially guided by patriarchal notions of what a family should comprise. Ostensibly, the primary guiding force is pragmatic concerns about land scarcity. While the pragmatic argument is that the island's small size is unable to house all its citizens should singles be allowed to buy their own apartments, it is apparent that, if the concerns were purely pragmatic, then any combination of singles should be able to purchase and occupy HDB flats. Clearly, patriarchal ideals constitute a critical impetus for housing policies and pragmatic reasoning is called upon for justification. The "normal" family, at the end of the day, is ideologically constructed as the basis of the Singapore "nation."

The difficulties posed by the HDB to unmarried women who wish to live apart from their parents or siblings are negotiated in particular ways by such women. For example, they access the private-property market, although doing so is only possible for a small minority whose paychecks allow for it. Some rent rooms in flats in which other families are resident. Yet others enter into legal marriages, but only on the understanding by both parties that the marriage is purely legal and a means by which to obtain a flat.

With regard to policies that frown on single motherhood, negotiations have come from civil society, and in particular, the Association of Women for Action and Research (AWARE). As Constance Singam, former president of AWARE, pointed out, no woman would take on the burden of single motherhood willingly and those who would had resources of their own. Most single mothers, however, were abandoned mothers (*Sunday Times* 28 Aug. 1994). Indeed, the state may, in a sense, be viewed as the "second offender" (Pain 1991), since these unmarried mothers find themselves abandoned first by the men who had fathered their children and then by the state, which through its policies was abandoning them, too. AWARE has attempted to influence HDB policies so that such women may acquire flats, arguing that the HDB should allow separated women to have priority in renting a flat. Such women, AWARE argues, might not want to buy a flat, pending a divorce, because of the possibility of reconciliation (*Sunday Times* 19 Feb. 1995). The HDB, however, has not been forthcoming.

On the other hand, efforts to perpetuate the "normal" family as the fundamental unit of society and the inculcation of extended familial ties through public housing have achieved some measure of success and little resistance. As some measure of the impact, in 1993, 19.5 percent of married children lived with their parents while 45.2 percent lived near their parents, either next door, in the same block, within walking distance, in the same estate, or in a nearby estate. This situation was described as "intimacy at a distance," in which the benefits of an extended family could be enjoyed without sacrificing the independence of a nuclear family (*The Straits Times* 14 July 1995). By living out some of the "ideal" arrangements as defined by the HDB, Singaporeans are in fact endorsing the state's constructions of the "normal" family as the fundamental unit of society.

Conclusion

Singapore has come a long way from 1960, when the HDB was first established to deal with massive problems of overcrowding and unhygienic conditions in slums and squatters. Over the last four decades, the HDB has provided Singaporeans with a living environment that is the envy of many. Home ownership has been achieved to a large extent, and an HDB flat remains, for most Singaporeans, the biggest asset that they have, consuming most of their CPF contributions. At the same time, housing policy has served as one of the state's ideologically hegemonic tools in building consensus and achieving political legitimation. In many ways, housing policy is central to the state's attempt to construct particular versions of "community" and "nation," anchored in particular ideological roots, from pragmatism and developmentalism to multiracialism and modernism. Through the housing landscape, the state has attempted to develop a "sense of place" and a "gracious society," anchored in firm family ties and defined ideologically in terms of a "normal" family. In these constructions, concretized in the everyday taken-for-granted housing landscape, the Singapore "nation" is one that is raced (through its foregrounding) and gendered (through women's expected caregiving roles).

Housing-market regulatory mechanisms can go a long way in achieving and maintaining particular goals, such as ensuring priority to particular types of family structures, particular mixes of races in estates, and particular orientations toward work. However, a high degree of residential mixing does not necessarily imply greater integration and better intercommunal relations. Crevices, albeit minor, in everyday use of space, for example, suggest that fault lines continue to exist in intercommunal ties. Nor do quotidian experiences in housing estates and new towns always bear out the vision of a "gracious society" characterized by consideration for public property and for other denizens, indicating a slippage between desire and reality that stems, not from deliberate resistance, but from routine, unreflective behavior among a people unconcerned about visions and constructions of the "nation." Further evidence of divergence between construct and reality is borne out in the issue of home ownership.

While home ownership is designed to, among other things, confer a sense of stakeholding and sense of place, the "single biggest asset" for many people in fact also facilitates movement out of any particular "place"—be it Queenstown, Toa Payoh, Bishan, or even Singapore—because the asset, once sold, yields significant sums of capital. In sum, while there is little evidence of overt resistance to either the functional or ideological roles accorded to the housing landscape, there are simply multiple reinterpretations and divergent ways of living out everyday lives.

7

Naming the Streets, Inscribing the "Nation"

The Colonial Inheritance of Street Names

One hundred and fifty years of colonial rule in Singapore conferred on its landscape an official network of street and place-names that reflected the mental images and ideological purposes of the dominant culture (Yeoh 1992). As part of a "realized signifying system" (Agnew et al. 1984) embedded in everyday practice, street names provided a tangible (although not necessarily unproblematic) record of colonial imaginations. The predominant pattern of street names, for example, commemorated mainly European city fathers, public servants, and "deserving" citizens (for example, Farrer Road after a municipal president, Onraet Road after an inspector-general of police, and Owen Road after the secretary of the Cricket Club) who were considered to have contributed significantly to public work and urban development as well as governors (for example, Anderson Road and Shenton Way) and British royalty (for example, Victoria Street and Connaught Drive); recalled linkages with other places within the British Empire including Britain itself (for example, Bristol Road and Sussex Garden); and endowed places with racial connotations, reflecting the colonial tendency to order society by separating the colonized into distinct, recognizable containers (for example, China Street in Chinatown; Baghdad Street in the Muslim quarter, and Hindoo Road in Little India). Most street names thus honored the perceptions and priorities of powerful European namers rather than those of the people living in the places so named.

In this chapter, we are concerned with the way in which toponymic inscription in the landscape as inherited from the colonial era is reshaped by broader sociopolitical conditions in postindependence Singapore. In particular, we examine the changing bases underlining the naming of streets as part of the newly created nation-state's bid to foster a sense of "nation" and "national identity" in Singapore. In as much as there is often slippage between the ideological intents of the state and the effects on the people, we are also concerned with the people's reactions to the naming of the city's streets.

"Malayanizing" the Landscape

In mounting a program of "nation-building," one of the projects was a concerted effort to sever colonial apron strings and foster and assert a sense of local identity, a sense of place, through a rewriting of the everyday landscape. Changes in street-naming policies clearly reflected these imperatives. In March 1967, ground rules laid down to guide the decisions of the Street-Naming Advisory Committee instructed the committee to steer clear of "old colonial nuances, British snob names, towns and royalty" and to give priority to local names (*Minutes of Meeting of the Advisory Committee on the Naming of Roads and Streets* 14 Mar. 1967).[1] Preference was to be given to a fuller utilization of Malay names to signal Singapore's allegiance to the Malay as opposed to the colonial world; and where English names were to be used, they should reflect "the historical background of the area," "current affairs of public interest in Singapore," local flora and fauna, and the physical nature of the area (*MMACNRS* 14 Mar. 1967).[2] In addition, as a depar-

1. Appointed by the Minister of Finance in February 1967, the Committee comprised the director of inland revenue (chair); the postmaster-general; the head of Urban Renewal, Housing, and Development Board; a research officer from the Institute of National Language and Culture; and a representative from the History Department of the then University of Singapore (*MMACNRS* 2 Feb. 1967). While the membership composition varies, this committee continues to function today under the Valuation and Assessment Division of the Ministry of Finance's Inland Revenue Department.

2. Malay(an) names have existed on the Singapore landscape since its founding as a British trading post. Despite the overlay of an extensive network of colonial names, names of local origin were not entirely obliterated. Nineteenth-century maps produced by the colonial authorities continued to feature some Malay and Chinese names (albeit in romanized transliterations with irregular spellings), particularly in denoting districts and areas (e.g., "Bedok," "Mandai," "Jurong," and "Ang Mo Kio"); capes (e.g., "Tanjong Pagar," "Tan-

ture from the liberal toponymic "canonization" of prominent public figures, which had preoccupied street-naming decisions in the prewar colonial days, "no person should have a street named after him [*sic*] during his [*sic*] life-time, except where the individual ha[d] performed some outstanding public service" (*MMACNRS* 14 Mar. 1967).

In the wake of these decisions, while the majority of street names of colonial origins remained inscribed in the landscape, the postindependence era spawned a whole generation of indigenous toponyms that not only drew inspiration from local material but also substituted the Malay equivalent *"jalan"* or *"lorong"* for the word "road" or "street" (for example, Jalan Layang-Layang after the Malay name for the swallow and Jalan Silat Gayong after a Malay martial-art form). One of the earliest proposals was to change "colonial" names (such as Queensway, Margaret Drive, and Commonwealth Avenue) in Queenstown (named after the British monarch), the first satellite town built in the 1960s by the Housing and Development Board (HDB), to Malay names (*MMACNRS* 26 June 1967). While this suggestion was "strongly resisted" by the Board to avoid "confusion and inconvenience" and also because "Queenstown [was] well-known throughout the world and should be preserved," the policy to name all streets in new housing estates in the National Language (Bahasa Melayu) took effect in various smaller estates such as the Kallang Airport estate,

---

jong Katong," and "Tanjong Punggol"); beaches (e.g., "Pasir Panjang" and "Pasir Ris"); rivers (e.g., "Sungei Seletar" and "Sungei Kranji"); riverine settlements ("Choa Chu Kang," "Lim Chu Kang," and "Yio Chu Kang"); and islets (e.g., "Pulau Brani," "Pulau Ubin," and "Pulau Ayer Chawan"). Many of these names were later borrowed in christening roads and streets in the vicinity and thus persisted throughout the colonial era. Place-names derived from the Malay vernacular (of which some might have predated British settlement) were thus preserved, although often they had to be transmogrified to fit English-speaking tongues. Thus "Sa-ranggong," an area named after a long-legged water bird called the *"ranggung,"* was gradually transmuted into "Serangoon" while "Kálang Púding" (the latter word referring to the garden croton, a shrub with variegated leaves) evolved into "Kallang Pudding." In the late nineteenth century, the pool of place-names of local and Malayan origin was further augmented by a municipal resolution "to use names of rivers and districts in the Malay Peninsula as being better adapted to the purpose than the names of persons or families" (Yeoh 1996, 238). When names were assigned to new streets laid out on either side of Anson Road near Tanjong Pagar in 1898, names such as "Enggor Street," "Tras Street," "Bernam Street," and "Raub Street" commemorating Malayan places were chosen.

where streets were named using Malay numerals (for example, Jalan Satu, Jalan Dua, and so forth, meaning Street One, Street Two, etc.) (*MMACNRS* 26 June 1967; 6 July 1967). Conversely, street names that perpetuated colonial imagery were avoided at all cost.[3]

The experiment to rework the toponymic text to assert local identity and represent the Malayan vision of independence soon encountered constraints. The available Malay vocabulary relating to Malayan fauna, flora, and material culture was soon exhausted and painstaking scrapping of the bottom of the lexicographical barrel produced names that the deputy prime minister described as "comic and unintelligible" (*MMACNRS* 26 June 1967). The ideological significance of introducing intricate Malay toponyms was also unappreciated by the predominantly Chinese dialect-speaking inhabitants of the housing estates, who found street names such as Pesiaran Keliling (meaning "Circular Drive") "tongue twister[s] of absolute horror" (*MMACNRS* 26 June 1967). Some historically rooted Malay names—those considered too complicated or inauspicious—were also changed by the authorities themselves. For example, Pulau Blakang Mati (literally translated as "the island of those who die behind") was rechristened "Sentosa" (meaning "peace and tranquility") to foreshadow its development as a resort island. Developers of private housing estates and residents also protested against the proliferation of Malay street names (for example, names after birds such as Jalan Chiak Padi, Jalan Chiak Raya, etc. in Clementi Park estate and names after colors such as Jalan Merah Saga, Jalan Hitam Manis, etc. in Chipbee Gardens), describing these concoctions as "confusing," "ridiculous," and "prejudicial to the dignity [of their estates]," and, in turn, appealing for the reinstatement of English names (*MMACNRS* 22 Aug. 1967). Even ostensibly "meaningful" names encapsulating local pride such as Jalan Khairuddin (after a well-known local composer of Bangsawan plays) in Opera Estate (where street names are

3. Twenty years down the road, the debate over the place of "colonial" names in the landscape was resurrected, this time over the naming of the newly built MRT stations. Two stations, originally christened Victoria (after the British monarch) and Maxwell (after a prominent colonial family), were renamed Bugis and Tanjong Pagar (local names), because, to quote the chairman of the MRT Corporation, while "we have no hang-ups about our colonial past, . . .we thought we'd have a few more local names" (*The Straits Times* 23 Nov. 1986).

connected to the operatic world) met with the disapproval of residents, who petitioned for the street to be renamed Fidelio Close (after a character in Western opera) (*MMACNRS* 10 Oct. 1967).[4]

While not all petitions met with success, the case of Mount Sinai, a private housing estate where streets had been named in Malay after various types of cloths (for example, Jalan Kain Limau, Jalan Kain Telepok, and Jalan Kain Matsuli), is illustrative of how residents pressed for the renaming of the streets (as Mount Sinai Drive, Crescent, View, etc.) First, they pointed out that "not everyone [could] pronounce [Malay] names with the correct accent"; few knew the meaning of these names and thus could not remember them; and adjacent estates had "nice-sounding" names such as Moonbeam Walk, Moonbeam Terrace, Holland Grove Drive, and Holland Grove Terrace. Next, they solicited the help of a powerful individual, in this case the education minister who lived within the estate, to support their case and bring it to attention of the authorities (*MMACNRS* 12 July 1968). Apparently, the exercise to use Malay street names to signify independence and provide a common toponymic language that might draw together the plurality of local worlds did not succeed; ironically, people preferred road signage and residential addresses in English, the language of the colonial masters, which they perceived as neutral if not superior.

"Multiracializing" the Landscape

While the failure of street names in one language to be properly understood and pronounced by fellow citizens of different ethnicities was nothing new (indeed, this was the social reality for a long time under the colonial regime, when English was the official toponymic language), it became unacceptable in the newly forged context of multiracialism, where the state must not be seen to privilege any one "ethnic" language but to strike a balance between the interests of "separate but equal" "racial" groups. By early 1968, newly proposed guidelines for street naming specified that street names should "reflect the multi-lingual, multi-racial and multi-cultural context of the society," and "be easily translated or pronounced in

4. Bangsawan plays are old-time Malay operas.

the other official languages [English, Mandarin, Malay, and Tamil]" (*MMACNRS* 17 Jan. 1968). A few months later, the about-face became even more explicit: the Street-Naming Advisory Committee was to "stop naming streets after flowers, fruits, animals etc. in Malay," avoid the use of "Jalan" for "Road," and "carefully review any objection to the existing street names in Malay" (*MMACNRS* 29 May 1968). In short, the attempt to create unity on the basis of a National Language signifying identity with the mainland (Peninsular Malaysia) soon collided with another "nation-building" framework, the political ideal of multiracialism—a contradiction intensified by the painful experience of separation from Malaysia in 1965.

The policy directive to use the National Language for street naming was truncated, and in turn, a new proposal to use "mathematical naming," a strategy with fewer racial overtones, was put on trial (*MMACNRS* 4 July 1967). Because Singapore roads were not laid out in a grid or "cobweb" (radial) fashion, a full-fledged numerical naming system was not feasible. Instead, an adapted version, whereby streets in newly built private and public housing estates were sequentially named Lorong 1, 2, 3, etc., was proposed (*MMACNRS* 10 Oct. 1967). This scheme, however, was censured by the finance minister (under whose purview the Street-Naming Committee came) for "sterility and lack of imagination" (*MMACNRS* 29 Dec. 1967). Under the minister's direction, a number of housing estates that had already acquired numerically inspired street names were brought back to the drawing boards: Lorongs in Goldhill Gardens, a middle-class private estate, for example, were renamed Goldhill Avenue, Rise, Drive, and View (*MMAC-NRS* 2 May 1968). Numerical nomenclature, however, continued to be used for streets and roads in several generations of public-housing estates from Toa Payoh, a new town of the 1970s designed using the ring road system, to new estates of the 1990s such as Pasir Ris.

It was in the industrial rather than residential landscape that the logic of multiracialism and the integral part it played in "nation-building" were most conspicuously inscribed. In naming some thirty new roads in Jurong Industrial Estate, Singapore's pioneer estate developed by the Jurong Town Corporation (JTC) and the lynchpin of the nation-state's fledgling industrialization program, the Street-Naming Committee was tasked to put "special emphasis on names in four official languages . . . to reflect the multi-lingual, multi-racial and multi-cultural content of the society in Singapore" (*MMACNRS* 2 May 1968). In addition, chosen names should suggest "industry" and "progress" to reflect constant striving after economic success, an ingredient critical to the survival of the "nation" (*MMACNRS* 2 May 1968). These two strands of state ideology, multiracialism and an industrial work ethic, were communicated through the toponymic text in a systematic and none-too-subtle manner: permutations of words that suggested "industry" were chosen in turn from the four official lexicographical repositories, resulting in names such as Enterprise Road, Quality Road, Tractor Road, Fan Yoong Road (Mandarin, meaning "prosperity"), Soon Lee Road (Mandarin, meaning "progressing smoothly"), Jalan Tukang (Malay, meaning "skilled craftsman"), Jalan Pesawat (Malay, meaning "machinery"), and Neythal Road (Tamil, meaning "to weave," a reflection of the textile factories located along this road) (*MMACNRS* 29 May 1968; 12 July 1968; 7 Aug. 1968; 6 Sept. 1968).

The process of inscribing the language of multiracialism in the landscape was not straightforward and uncontested. For example, there were differences of opinion about how multiracialism was best represented toponymically. JTC favored creating "districts" of Chinese, Malay, and Indian names as "a means of easy identification" (*MMACNRS* 6 Sept. 1968). In contrast, the Street-Naming Committee felt that such a form of "segregation" was not "in line with the Republic's multi-racial character" and that names in the four official languages should be interspersed throughout the estate (*MMACNRS* 6 Sept. 1968). JTC also preferred a preponderance of Chinese names because "most of the investors [were] Chinese" (*MMACNRS* 12 July 1968; 6 Aug. 1968). It provided an alternative list of mainly Chinese street names and, while the Street-Naming Committee rejected the principles on which this idea was based as being incongruent with the logic of multiracialism, it tacitly acceded to JTC's request by assigning a larger proportion of Chinese street names while still retaining a "multi-racial" mix (*MMACNRS* 6 Aug. 1968). The inscription of hegemonic meanings in landscape text is hence more akin to an uneven, negotiated process of constant mediations rather than a static, consensual once-and-for-all translation of a monolithic ideology into material form.

Standardization, "Pinyinization," and Bilingualism

The power of landscape text to render ideology more concrete and therefore more real and unquestioned will only have maximum effects if people actively encounter and draw upon the text in daily practice. Up to the late 1960s, while "multiracializing" the landscape required assigning street names using the four official languages, only romanized script was used in road signs and street directories. For the majority of the population unschooled in English, romanized street names were not comprehended and in fact often transliterated beyond recognition.[5] In order for the multiracial toponymic text to move from an ideological statement of intent to an internalized social reality in the lives of the citizens of the "nation," the people must be able to understand and make use of the available repertory of street names. It was towards this end that in 1967 the state appointed a committee to provide and disseminate an authorized Chinese translation of street names (*Report of the Committee on the Standardization of Street Names in Chinese* 1970). The Committee on the Standardization of Street Names in Chinese was charged with the responsibility of systematizing and simplifying "existing renderings of street names in Chinese so as to avoid confusions and unhappy transliterations" and ensuring that translations were not only "faithful rendering[s] by sound but should also be elegant and meaningful" (*The Straits Times* 13 June 1970). The arduous task of translating more than 500 street names, particularly given the various practical and linguistic difficulties such as transliterating multisyllabic Malay street names into monosyllabic Chinese characters, took a full three years to complete (*RCSSNC* 1970, 5).

While the Committee achieved a measure of standardization in Chinese street names, this success did not close the debate concerning how street names could be made more meaningful within a multilingual society. In the 1980s, the state's attempt to apply the *"hanyu pinyin"* system (a universally accepted Mandarin system of romanizing Chinese characters) to street and place-names triggered heated discussions in Parliament and on

---

5. Apparently, one Chinese transliteration of Raffles Place means "Raffles was impolite," while Woodbridge Hospital, a mental hospital, was transmogrified into "the House of Devils" (*The Straits Times* 13 June 1970).

the streets. Those who supported the *"pinyin* revolution" pointed out that, apart from the advantages of standardization, *"pinyinized"* names were more acceptable than the old romanized dialect names because the latter were no more than haphazard translations bequeathed by the British colonial administration (*The Straits Times* 27 Dec. 1991). Those who appealed against the move argued that the old, familiar dialect place-names were "part of our heritage" and "of strong historical meaning for Singapore," while the new *pinyin* code of pronunciation would "baffle" older-generation Singaporeans and even "come across as insensitive to minority race[s]" (*The Straits Times* 19 Mar. 1987; 20 Mar. 1987; 25 June 1988; 27 Dec. 1991). Tek Kah Market, a Hokkien name that meant "market under the shade of the bamboo trees," when *pinyinized* to become Zhujiao market sounded like "pigs' legs market"; the Nee Soon Road area, named after Lim Nee Soon, a well-known Chinese rubber magnate and "pineapple king" who owned large stretches of land, would be transformed into the dialect version, Yishun, and bore no obvious etymological relation to the illustrious pioneer (*The Straits Times* 19 Mar. 1987; 25 June 1988).[6] The debate drew strong views from a number of public figures, who entered the fray to oppose the use of *"hanyu pinyin"* for street names. As prominent architect Tay Kheng Soon (quoted in *The Straits Times* 18 Feb. 2000) recalled,

> [I] asked the street-naming committee: "When the day comes to name a boulevard or a street after one of our famous leaders and important public figures, will we use *hanyu pinyin* names or will we use their Singaporean names? Certainly a street will have to be named after Dr Goh Keng Swee [former deputy prime minister]. And his *hanyu pinyin* name is Wu Qing Rui. Who in Singapore would know who Wu Qing Rui is?"

In March 1987, a compromise was reached: the national development minister announced that old place-names including Chinese dialect ones would be kept, although the changes (including Zhujiao and Yishun) that had already been effected would not be overturned (*The Straits Times* 19 Mar.

6. "Nee Soon Road" was officially named in 1950 by the Rural Board to facilitate postal services not only because Lim Nee Soon served on the Rural Board from 1913 to 1921 but also because he owned a large plot of land in the area.

1987). As such, a number of incongruities remain etched on the landscape: for example, while Lim Nee Soon's name has effectively been erased from the landscape because there is nothing to connect it to the transmogrified "Yishun" in the popular imagination, other road names in the area named after Nee Soon's business concerns and family members include "Chong Kuo Road" (named after Nee Soon's eldest son), "Peck Hay Road" (named after Nee Soon's wife), "Thong Aik Road" (named after Nee Soon's rubber factory), and "Thong Bee Road" (named after Nee Soon's shop in Beach Road) that escaped *pinyinization* continue to persist.

The respite from the state's attempt to couple street-naming policy to the nation's language policy was a temporary one. In the 1990s, the debate over street names was resurrected once more, this time in the wake of the prime minister's suggestion that road names and public signs in "historic districts" such as Chinatown, Little India, and Geylang Serai (a Malay heartland) should carry two languages (*The Straits Times* 3 Apr. 1992). More than sixty bilingual signs embellished with "appropriate" ethnic motifs (the lotus for signs in Little India, the pagoda in Chinatown, and the Minangkabau house in Geylang Serai) were put up in a pilot scheme to gauge public response (*The Straits Times* 11 Apr. 1992). With this action the state aimed to "remind Singaporeans of the historical significance of these areas," to underscore the multiracial character of the city, and to give it "an Asian feel" (*The Straits Times* 11 Apr. 1992). Akin to an exercise in "salvage toponymy," these road signifiers were intended as reminders of lost heritage in a modern city, where much of the original cultural practices had already been eroded (Yeoh and Kong 1994; Yeoh and Lau 1995; see also chapter 8). This time around, however, these street names attracted little public response and the one comment expressed in the main paper's forum page indicated disappointment that romanized and not Jawi script was used alongside English names in the signs erected in Geylang Serai (in contrast, Chinese and Tamil characters were used in Chinatown and Little India respectively) (*The Straits Times* 21 Apr. 1992).

Evidently, while the state invested much ideological weight in Singapore's toponymics and constantly tried to configure and reshape landscape text to both systematize and popularize its usage, this process is not without negotiated encounters as people questioned, challenged, or came up with alternative readings of both the forms and meanings of street names. The "web of signification" (Ley and Olds 1988, 195) spun by the state is not totally hegemonic or compelling because landscape contains a "duplicity" (Daniels 1989, 206), being illusory and at the same time impervious.

Conclusion

> They called it, the Pied Piper's Street—
> where any one playing on pipe or tabor,
> Was sure for the future to lose his labour.
> —from Robert Browning's
> *The Pied Piper of Hamelin*

> One of the first things done in Hobbiton . . . was . . . the restoration of Bagshot Row . . . There was some discussion of the name that the new row should be given. *Battle Gardens* was thought of, or *Better Smials*. But after a while in sensible hobbit-fashion it was just called *New Row*. It was a purely Bywater joke to refer to it as Sharkey's End.
> —from J. R. R. Tolkien's *The Lord of the Rings*

The salience of place-names in the first instance lies in the sites they occupy in the everyday landscape and the roles they play in the everyday world. Signposted streets and places are necessary as markers of "place" for the practical purposes of communication and travel, the delivery of services from home catering to fire-fighting. In the words of Raja-Singam (1939, 12) in his pioneering work on Malayan street names, street names are "on the lip [sic] of thousands everyday. Postal employees have their eyes on them. Ambulance and fire-engine drivers take their direction from them as they rush by. Taxi-drivers and rickshawallas [rickshaw pullers] know them all." Place-names assist in the construction of social maps, providing cues and clues to social position and practice, activity and ambience. They are an integral part of place meanings; not only do they mark out a place and delineate its boundaries, but they also provide clues to its distinctive identity and social status, recall (albeit in a condensed and not necessarily unproblematic fashion) its history, and ultimately contribute to people's engagement with their own heritage in the everyday landscape. Like the evocative

7.1. A littered landscape of different street-naming systems.

"Pied Piper's Street" and "Sharkey's End" inscribed in fictional landscapes, street names recall place memories—sometimes of legendary proportions—in the minds of inhabitants.

Beyond their practical significance, however, street names may also be fashioned to carry ideological intent. In as much as the Singapore landscape under colonial rule was racialized (Yeoh 1992), the landscape of nationhood also bore the imprint of equally salient ideologies such as multiracialism because all systems of authority draw on some form of landscape text to legitimize their rule (Duncan 1985). The multiracial landscape of independence was as much a social construct as was the racialized landscape of colonial rule. At the same time, in as much as "landscape serves as a vast repository out of which symbols of . . . ideology can be fashioned" (Duncan 1985, 182), the process of naming streets is one in which hegemonic meanings are inscribed in a manner of a "moving equilibrium," which is "always contested, always changing" (Warren 1993, 183). The mapping of nationalist ideologies onto Singapore's street names was an uneven process, reflecting the contradictions and swings in the policies of "nation-building" and at the same time incorporating to some extent the reactions and resistances of its citizens. In harnessing the power of names inscribed in the landscape to construct a "nation," the state was driven to both topocidal maneuvers—after all, erasing the name of a place is sometimes as powerful as the "annihilation of place," what Porteous (1988) termed "topocide"—and more consultative modes such as using pilot street-naming projects to gauge public reaction. Some of these measures to change the signification of place in everyday material space as a means to reshape the national imaginary have attracted strong responses from individuals and groups who have countered these street-naming schemes; others have essentially met them with a level of tacit acceptance. The result is a "littered" landscape, one reflecting the coexistence of different systems of signification (colonial names, Malayanized names, numerical names, names in different languages, dialect names, *pinyinized* names, bilingual names) in the body of the "nation," each with its own onomastic pattern, serving to underline the view that the "tapestry" of a landscape is constituted by an "unglamorous di-shevelled tangle [of] threads" (Eagleton, quoted in Baker 1992, 9).

8

Re-creating the Past, Reconstructing the "Nation"

Heritage Landscapes: The "Nation's" Psyche, Tourism Resource

In this chapter, we first outline the state's engagement with issues of heritage conservation at a specific juncture of its development. With the view that heritagized landscapes constitute particularly salient sites at which to interrogate the way the past is being reclaimed and fashioned to produce identity and meaning for the collective self, we turn to specific examples of such landscapes, which have either been subject to state intervention or commercial bowdlerization or both. With each of these cases, we also attempt to clarify the politics of memory at work in rendering heritage landscapes into contested spaces in producing and destabilizing the nation.

In the immediate postindependence period and for at least two decades, the Singapore landscape was dominated by a demolish-and-rebuild philosophy to excise urban slums and rural *"kampungs,"* to etch into the city the lineaments of technological progress, and to optimize scarce land resources for economic development. The construction of a new nation-state based on a vision of modernity required first the erasure of traces of the past on the urban palimpsest that seem to impede the work of the new order (Kwok et al. 1999, 6). In Janadas Devan's (1999, 22) words, "Singapore, in many ways, is a product of forgettings," where "forgetting" is not an accidental or ignorant act but a "structural necessity." Part of this exercise in forgetting involved making deep and thorough excisions in the landscape to remove all that is thought to be obsolete or retrogressive and to make way for embedding "new" memories appropriate to the state's construction of the national self. The construction of heritage in a postcolonial "nation" constituted by overlapping diasporas attempting to decisively break from its multiple pasts is, as Janadas Devan (1999, 21, 33) reminds us, "potentially dangerous": "But precisely because our history forgets, it is peculiarly prone to radical simplifications. . . . Precisely because the past cannot be contained within a limited geographical, cultural and political space, we are tempted to confer upon it an ideal history, a proper genealogy."

If the first two decades of the "nation's" development was dictated by systematic amnesia and the erasure of the past, the next two saw a more concerted attempt to recover memory loss and in so doing fashion an appropriate genealogy that would constitute the nation's legitimacy and that is clearly marked, signposted, and concretized in the landscape. "Remembering" emerged at a specific time and place in the nation's development—both as an inevitable condition of the cycle of progress and loss and as a deliberate strategy of forging the nation's future. Chua (1995b) argues that "nostalgia" and a harking back to the past—a past portrayed as a "foreign country" where "they do things differently" (Hartley, quoted in Lowenthal 1995, xvi)—during the 1980s and 1990s were rooted in the wider critique of and resistance to the relentless drive toward economic development, the frenetic pace of life, high stress levels, the corruption of new-found materialism, and the consequent "industrialisation of everyday life." It is a critique of the *historic moment* when the "nation" has "arrived" in an economic and material sense but lost the meaning of leisure and time to stand and stare. It is also a critique of the *place* in which Singaporeans find themselves, a city bristling with efficiency and productivity but without a certain intangible spirit and soul.

Nostalgia is hence not only a construction of the past but also a condition of the present. Such a groundswell of public opinion in favor of the past coincided with state evaluations of the dangers of "forgetting to remember." In the 1980s, the governing elites noted with great apprehension the increasing Westernization of Singapore society. Although Westernization had served Singapore well in its quest for industrialization, it had also brought in train values that were perceived to be incompatible with traditional Asian values. This unease over what Kwok (1993, 7) calls "the complexity of our cultural condition" took the form of pronouncements and debates in both official and public discourse on a number of themes urging the preservation of "Asian" and "traditional" values and the maintenance of "local" cultural identity and heritage. It also led to the search for "Shared Values," as discussed in chapter 3, which would bind Singaporeans together and provide direction and identity. According to George Yeo (1989, 48), then minister of state (finance and foreign affairs), "To be great, a nation must have a sense of its destiny. As we trace our ancestries, as we sift through the artifacts which give us a better understanding of how we got here, as we study and modify the traditions we have inherited, we form a clearer vision of what our future can be."

The perceived need to reclaim Singapore's Asian roots as a bulwark against Westernization and the search for core values emphasized the importance of heritage and traditions because it was argued that these provide "the substance of social and psychological defence" (*The Committee on Heritage Report* 1988, 26). Thus, Lee Hsien Loong (1989, 33), then minister for trade and industry and second minister for defense, noted that Singaporeans should "retain our heritage but examine them for values which need to be modified, and scrutinise foreign traditions for ideas which can be incorporated but do so cautiously. Our roots are important. We should not be root-bound, but neither should we abandon our roots. They anchor us, and will help us grow."

A Committee on Heritage was set up in April 1988 to "assess the progress made in identifying, preserving and disseminating awareness of our heritage" and to "propose measures which will encourage Singaporeans to be more widely informed and appreciative of our multi-cultural heritage" (*The Committee on Heritage Report* 1988, 12). Singapore's "unique heritage," reported the committee, "can play a vital part in nation building" for an understanding of one's roots and the lessons of history can help younger Singaporeans "balance our Asian values and western influences," appreciate and "draw inspiration" from the city's multicultural diversity, and "constantly renew work values and maintain the adaptiveness which underlies our economic success" (*The Committee on Heritage Report* 1988, 6–8).

According to the committee, Singapore's "heritage" comprises five categories: nation-building heritage derived from and including the "experience of living under, and [the people's] response to, the British colonial administration; the Japanese Occupation; the post-war struggle for independence; and the struggle against Communism"; heritage of economic success, which focuses on "the values of our migrant predecessors who came to Singapore and their economic achievements"; multicultural heritage "expressed in the lifestyles, customs and traditions of the different ethnic communities"; heritage of the man-made environment comprising buildings, landmarks, and other "visible and tangible links to our past [in] the physical landscape"; and heritage of the natural environment, "which defines our territorial identity and our location within the Southeast Asian ecological region" (*The Committee on Heritage Report* 1988, 27–29). Heritage thus does not stem solely from British colonial imprint nor is it of purely local import but consists of both tangible and intangible forms bequeathed by the past, which are perceived to contribute to "our shared experience of becoming a nation" (*The Committee on Heritage Report* 1988, 22). Of these various categories, it was often argued that heritage inscribed in the built environment is of particular significance because, without "visual landmarks," "all other records of the past remain abstract notions, difficult to understand and link to the present" (*The Committee on Heritage Report* 1988, 46). "It is clear therefore," continued the report, "that the conservation of buildings, structures and other districts which provide the sign posts from the past to the present is critical to the psyche of a nation" (*The Committee on Heritage Report* 1988, 46).

The Urban Redevelopment Authority (URA) publicly announced its Conservation Master Plan in December 1986 (*MND Annual Report 1987*, 35). The plan covered more than 100 hectares, including Chinatown, Kampong Glam (identified as a traditional Malay enclave), Little India, the Singapore River, Emerald Hill (a residential street distinguished for Peranakan architecture), and the Civic and Cultural District (a precinct comprising museums and other civic and cultural buildings).[1] In 1989, the Planning Act was substantially amended and the URA was made the national conservation and central planning authority. The amended Planning Act formalized the URA's main tasks with regard to conservation—in effect, what the URA had already been doing for the last three to four years. These tasks included identifying buildings and areas of historical interest

1. "Peranakan," or "Nonya and Baba," culture is a local hybrid comprising Chinese, Malay, and colonial British elements.

for conservation, preparing a conservation master plan, and guiding the implementation of conservation by the public and private sectors (Planning Act 1990, Sections 10(6)(c), 13, 14, and 15). With the URA's responsibilities with respect to conservation established, official designation of ten areas as "conservation areas" quickly followed. These areas are Kreta Ayer, Bukit Pasoh, Telok Ayer, Tanjong Pagar, Little India, Kampong Glam, Boat Quay, Emerald Hill, Cairnhill, and Clarke Quay (*Republic of Singapore Government Gazette* Mar. 1989, No. 1154, 2343). In September 1991, the number of designated conservation areas was doubled by the addition of Joo Chiat, Geylang, Jalan Besar, Blair Plain, River Valley, Beach Road, Bukit Pasoh Extension, Desker Road, Petain Road/Tyrwhitt Road, and Race Course Road/Owen Road (*Republic of Singapore Government Gazette* Sept. 1991, No. 3867, 7025–26).

The creation of heritage landscapes not only provides the nation with a sense of historical continuity but also confers on its city visual identity to rise above the homogenization exerted by forces of technology, modernity, and globalization:

> For our city to be truly great, we cannot rely only on modern architecture, which is restrained by the economics of efficient construction, the use of new technology, and the pervasive international architectural style of the 20th Century. It is inevitable that our new developments suffer the fate of looking like the new buildings in other cities of the world. The only way that gives our city a distinct personality is our historic past through the selective conservation of old districts and buildings. (*Conservation Within the Central Area with the Plan for Chinatown* 1985, 1)

Indeed, the "heritage question" became more and not less important as Singapore aspired to become a "cosmopolitan city" (in the words of Prime Minister Goh Chok Tong, quoted in *The Straits Times* 30 Aug. 1997) and to position itself strategically in the superleague of globalizing cities. This move already began in the mid-1980s, when new economic diversification strategies were needed in response to a slowdown in manufacturing, shifts in the international division of labor, and the erosion of Singapore's competitiveness in labor-intensive operations. As part of the city's strategy to carve out a specialized niche as an international business and service center, strengthening the tourist industry played an important role. During the 1985 recession, the expansion of tourism projects, for example, was recommended by a ministerial committee as a means of reviving the flagging construction sector and absorbing the country's high level of savings (Chang et al. 1996). The recession also came in the wake of a sharp 3.5 percent fall in tourist arrivals in 1983. Part of the remedy to these economic ills gave impetus to preservation as a means to repair the ravages of development and to enrich the cityscape because the fall was blamed in part on "the lack of color in the increasingly antiseptic city-state" (Burton 1993, 36). In 1984, one of the three main problems for the tourism industry identified by the Tourism Task Force was the attrition of tourist attractions because Singapore had lost its "Oriental mystique and charm best symbolized in old buildings, traditional activities and bustling road activities" in its effort to construct a "modern metropolis" (Wong et al. 1984, 6).

The recommendations of the Task Force included the conservation of cultural areas and historical sites; these were later incorporated in the Tourism Product Development Plan of 1986 (Pannell, Kerr, and Forster 1986). This plan included the expenditure of US$223 million for the redevelopment of, among other things, ethnic enclaves such as Chinatown, Little India, and Kampong Glam; the Singapore River, a Heritage Link which encompasses all historic buildings in the city area of colonial origin; as well as specific projects such as the upgrading of Raffles Hotel (the *grande dame* of colonial hotels in Singapore), the redevelopment of Fort Canning (a fort turned park, museum, and arts center), the restoration of Emerald Hill, and the re-creation of Bugis Street (formerly an open-air site famous for its raucous street life and local food). Thus, in the words of Teo (1994), "tourism played a very significant role in the rethinking process" where Singapore's urban conservation is concerned. Conversely, "heritage conservation constituted one element of multi-faceted redevelopment strategies designed to cater to tourist demands for uniqueness on the one hand, while providing an opportunity to improve urban aesthetics on the other" (Chang et al. 1996). The interest in reclaiming heritage is prompted as much by pragmatic as by purely aesthetic or psychological reasons. Heritage, as the Committee on

Heritage noted, is a "valuable tourism asset" for "it makes us different and interesting for visitors" (*The Committee on Heritage Report* 1988, 30).

As Zukin (1991, 27) has noted, landscapes subject to the forces of globalization are constantly undergoing a process of "creative destruction" (borrowing Schumpeter's term) whereby the "longevity" and "cultural layers" of the landscape are constantly fragmented, reworked, and recycled in tandem with market forces. As Singapore takes on globalizing aspirations, its heritage landscapes, as marketable landscapes for a global audience, become subject to further annihilation and re-invention. Tourism 21, a new national tourism planning exercise mounted in 1996 to prepare for the challenges of the twenty-first century, charted the way to further reconfigure heritage and cultural spaces from inward-looking "Instant Asia" to a global-looking New Asia (Chang 1997). Fashioning Singapore as the "Tourism Capital" of the region, this blueprint attempts to capitalize on the theme "New Asia-Singapore" to convey the fusion between modernity and dynamism on the one hand and a traditional "Asian soul" on the other. This sense of paradox is, for example, well captured by slogans proffered in posters, postcards, and magazine layouts such as "I saw a city with its head in the future and its soul in the past," "Can a city of the future still let you sleep in the past?" and "Can a global business centre also be a gourmet's paradise?" The view is to portray Singapore as a nation that has achieved the "right" synergy between past and present, the local and the global, a fitting symbol of a newly emerging Asia, highly modern yet richly Asian at the same time—"progressive and sophisticated, yet still a unique expression of the Asian soul" (*Singapore Tourist Promotion Board Annual Report* 1996, 5).

In Tourism 21 the STPB, renamed the Singapore Tourism Board (STB) in 1997, recommended eleven zones of "thematic development" ranging from "Ethnic Singapore" and "Mall of Singapore" to "Rustic Charm." In this tourism blueprint, the thematic approach based on "targeting opportunity areas around suitable existing attractions and sites, and transforming them into "thematic zones" with a unifying character or theme" (*STPB Annual Report* 1996, 27) forms the main strategy to reformulate the city's cultural products to make Singapore "a destination for memorable experiences," thereby encouraging return visits even among "time-strapped visitors." By integrating "activity clusters, services, facilities, and even street furniture" in historic areas into a single themed development (*STPB Annual Report* 1996, 28) and by creating "cultural trails" and furnishing storyboards, information plaques, and signs, local culture is rendered more transparent and digestible for tourist consumption.

The main strategy in the (re)packaging of cultural landscapes thus involves the invention and superimposition of distinct themes as tools to help tourists interpret and make sense of local lived cultures. As one of the "cultural strategies of visual consumption" in producing "landscapes of power" (Zukin 1991, 206), "theming" involves compressing, collapsing, and disciplining time and place, history and culture, into a single organizing leitmotif. Themed landscapes are thus primarily preoccupied with "reproductions," "semiotics," and "image-ability" at the expense of "the human ecologies that produce and inhabit them" (Sorkin 1992, xiv). Through this process, time and place are "falsified" (Shaw and Williams 1994, 168). The differences between past, present, and future are therefore erased, time is "flattened . . . into a continuously presented present" (Pemberton 1994, 245) while place is transformed by the masking of the everyday and the elaboration of the spectacular. The strategy involves repackaging landscapes by weaving new "narratives" into existing cultural spaces, thereby infusing them with "stories" to intrigue visitors. In short, a new *text* dictated by the organizing theme (and therefore usually simplified, linear, and unitary for easy consumption) overrides the apparent disorder and unconnectedness of the everyday *context*, resulting in what Crang (1994, 314) describes as the selective mapping of experience into a "virtual object," "places [that] exist by inscription," and "itineraries [that] organise history."

In Singapore, the imperatives behind both "nation-building" and tourism are strongly productive of, and have powerful effects on, the shape of heritage landscapes. These landscapes are expected to draw on the coalescence of both sets of forces and, Janus-faced, they become an identifiable emblem for the collective psyche of the "nation" as they represent and market the "nation" to the rest of the world. We turn to three specific examples to illustrate the dynamics and politics at work in the shaping of heritage landscapes in Singapore.

Chinatown: The Politics of Re-invention

As one of the "Historic Districts" (in the Urban Conservation Master Plan) and "Ethnic Quarters" (themed under the "Ethnic Singapore" thematic zone under Tourism 21), Chinatown has been accorded high priority in the state's creation of heritage landscapes.[2] Within the frame envisioned by the new agenda, traditional buildings such as Chinatown's shophouse landscape are no longer viewed as obsolete structures incompatible with the image of a modern, dynamic city. Instead, from this perspective, shophouses "create a sense of human scale, rhythm and charm not found in much of our modern architecture" while "the variety of building facades exhibit . . . creative use of the multi-cultural resources," providing relief from "the monotony of a high-rise environment" (*URA Annual Report* 1985, 13, 15). Traditional Chinatown is no more merely the territorial domain of a community of Chinese in decline but is elevated to national importance as a civic asset, "a common bond place" for "Singaporeans living in outlying new towns" (*URA Annual Report* 1985, 15). Conserving Chinatown as a veritable repository of tradition, history, and culture can thus be understood not simply as a means of upgrading the built environment but, by rendering heritage in material form, the conserved Chinatown landscape serves the sociopolitical purpose of binding Singaporeans to place, to the city, and, ultimately and vicariously, to the "nation."

Chinatown, alongside other "ethnic quarters," is also central to the state's attempt to bolster the tourist industry by selling Singapore as first "instant Asia," then "new Asia"—"a city of many colours and contrasts, cul-

2. The Chinatown conservation area covers approximately twenty-three hectares accommodating a total of about 12,000 structures, of which about 700 are privately owned. It is subdivided into four smaller districts: Kreta Ayer (a commercial area centered at Trengganu and Pagoda Streets where the largest day and night street market used to be held until the early 1980s and the site of the Jamae Mosque and Sri Mariamman Temple, both gazetted national monuments); Telok Ayer (the main landing point for nineteenth-century immigrant laborers and distinctive for the number of Chinese trading companies set up here as well as prominent landmarks such as the Thian Hock Keng Temple, the Nagore Durgha Shrine, and the Hokkien Huay Kuan); Tanjong Pagar (formerly a residential area for laborers working in the port nearby); and Bukit Pasoh (formerly a residential area and also the site of the Ee Hoe Hean Club, a recreational club for wealthy Chinese).

tures and cuisines" (Chang and Yeoh 1999). While the colonial state had racialized the Chinatown landscape using negative Chinese stereotypes, the contemporary state has inverted this image and capitalized on what it deems to be positive Chinese cultural traits. Chinatown is now identified with the pioneering spirit and enterprise of early Chinese immigrants to Singapore and is showcased as a distinctively Chinese cultural area, which "brims over with life, capturing the essence of the old Chinese lifestyle in its temples and shophouses and nurturing a handful of traditional trades [such as] herbalists, temple idol carvers, calligraphers and effigy makers . . . in the face of progress" (*STPB Annual Report* 1991, 28–29). Against a backcloth of shophouses and temples, large-scale festival activities, fairs, *wayangs* (Chinese opera), puppetry, and trishaw rides can be "staged" to provide both locals and tourists with "a different kind of experience" (*URA Annual Report* 1985, 15). Particularly during Chinese festivals, lion and dragon dances are brought in, national Chinese calligraphy competitions and exhibitions are held, ancient Chinese lantern quizzes are hosted, and Cantonese operas are performed (*The Straits Times* 19 Feb. 1985). Conserved Chinatown is conceived as an oasis of difference—both for the tourist gaze and for locals in search of the vanished past.

In order to harness market forces to heritage conservation, rent control was lifted in 1988–89 under the Controlled Premises (Special Provisions) Act to allow for the recovery of premises for redevelopment in accordance with conservation guidelines (*URA Annual Report* 1990, 2, 6). To encourage private owners to restore their buildings, the URA made available various incentives such as waiving development charges, eliminating car-parking requirements, and assisting owners needing to relocate their old-single person tenants (*URA Annual Report* 1988–89, 21). At the same time, restoration has to adhere to stringent guidelines pertaining to the facade design, internal structure, signage, materials used, and any other forms of alteration or addition with a view to retaining historical continuity and the architectural distinctiveness of the place (*URA Annual Report* 1988, 52).

Following these guidelines, property owners and developers have seized the opportunity to evict former tenants; refurbish the visual and structural quality of shophouse units including their wall openings, five-foot ways, columns, pilasters, window shutters, balconies, and ornamenta-

8.1. Chinatown refurbished shophouses.

tion; and sell them on the market as "heritage" properties of particular interest to retailers wishing to "capture the shopping and gourmet traffic right in the traditional retail heart of Singapore" (*The Straits Times* 23 Sept. 1991). In determining the type of building use, approved trades—usually those identified as symbolic of Chinese tradition—are encouraged while certain pollutive or incompatible trades are proscribed (URA 1988, 72–73).[3] Within these broad parameters, however, URA's underlying philosophy stresses that market forces should be left to decide what types of trades exist in conservation areas because successful purchasers of conserved buildings have to make economic returns in order to continue to restore and maintain them. Thus, while meticulous attention is paid to preserving buildings and other structures "for the past they represent," lifestyles and trades are left to the vagaries of free competition (*The Straits Times* 23 Oct. 1991).

Thus as it is implemented in Chinatown, conservation does not go

3. Approved trades include herbal tea shops, religious paraphernalia shops, Chinese medical halls, clog makers, *mahjong* makers, calligraphers, and fortune tellers. Pollutive trades include engineering workshops, tire and battery shops, Western fast-food restaurants, supermarkets, and laundrettes.

against the grain of the earlier phase of urban renewal but shares similar ideological emphases such as the commitment to public-private partnership in renewing the urban fabric, the focus on upgrading the physical environment and visual cityscape, and the importance of controlling types of land use, rooting out incompatible use and disciplining the urban form. While the stress is on "difference" exhibited by traditional motifs as opposed to the monotony of tower blocks, such "difference" is to be achieved within the ambit of modernist planning and goals. This situation is not at all unanticipated given that the national conservation authority appointed in 1989 is synonymous with the URA, created in 1974.

In the latest round in the re-invention of the Chinatown landscape in line with the "new Asia" vision, the STB unveiled a S$97.5 million plan to "revitalise" and "enhance the Chinatown experience." The proposed "facelift," which aims "to bring out the full flavour of the place's sights, sounds and smells," includes an interpretive center to provide a "gateway" for visitors entering Chinatown, a new theater for *wayang* performances, street performances from puppet-making demonstrations to martial-arts shows, five "themed" gardens, a food street with open-air cooking and dining, and a new market square selling fresh produce (*The Straits Times* 29 Sept. 1998; 22 Nov. 1998). This latest strategy draws heavily on the idea of "theming" and the creation of "narratives," or "storylines which connect places and experiences in visitors' *minds* out of the raw material of local history" (*STB Annual Report* 1996, 63). The key principle is to represent the history of the place as a linearized history, an "ideal geneaology." The STB (1996, 28), for example, makes it clear that "the final product [after being repackaged as a single themed narrative] should be able to allow any visitor, whether in a packaged tour or in a free and independent format, to understand how and why Chinatown came to be—covering for example the Chinese diaspora, Sir Stamford Raffles' town plan which led to the creation of ethnic zones in Singapore, the trades of yesteryears, present conservation efforts and future developments." The history of Chinatown, as mapped onto both "real" (on the ground) and "representational" landscapes (on brochures, maps, storyboards, and tourist guides), is yet another version of the history of the nation as a unidirectional history of progress, moving inexorably from the past to the present and into the future.

Like urban renewal before it, the incessant process of reworking the Chinatown landscape through urban conservation and subsequent "facelifts" is state-driven, conceived as part of the need to refurbish the built environment as well as to serve sociopolitical purposes of forging the nation. It is implemented in a way that reifies a particular version of the visual past and of Chinese culture. These meanings and purposes invested by the state in the conserved landscape pervade people's everyday encounters with the place. However, in the Chinatown landscape as lived, these ideological designs are neither entirely hegemonic nor totally transparent. Alternative readings have emerged. To illustrate this last point, we will examine how people living and working in Chinatown have come to terms with two sets of landscape meanings ascribed by the state: first, the revitalization and embodiment of a quintessential Chinese culture in the conserved Chinatown and, second, the role of the conserved landscape as "a common bond place" for Singaporeans. We also argue that recently there have been clear signs that non-governmental groups have been able to tap local sentiments and galvanize a more concerted response to the state's reconfiguration of the Chinatown landscape.

In conserving Chinatown as a testimony to the vibrance of Chinese culture, state strategies focus mainly on refurbishing the traditional architectural facades of Chinatown buildings. Where market forces do not preclude, resurrecting "vanishing trades" that are perceived to epitomize the Chinese past is also encouraged. For many Singaporean Chinese who live and work in Chinatown, however, the Chinese cultural life of the place does not reside simply in the architectural form but also in the full range of trades and lifestyles, from "the traditional makers of paper houses and cars for ancestor prayer offerings, the barber who cuts hair in the backlane, the old coffeeshops where residents gather to chit chat," and so forth (*The Straits Times* 16 Oct. 1991). Notwithstanding URA's stance that traditional Chinese trades would be given every encouragement, many retailers fear that an open-tender system would inevitably squeeze out the small, traditional businesses, which would have to make way for more upmarket shops. Temporary structures housing shopkeepers selling shoes and knick-knacks, stalls at shop fronts selling seasonal fruits like mangoes and durians, small family-run businesses selling food and daily necessities, and myriad other enterprises that cannot afford the post-conservation hike in rentals have in fact faded out (*The Straits Times* 29 Apr. 1988). Other business that have survived conservation such as small Chinese tea houses and herbal medicine halls have been upgraded into *dim sum* (a light Chinese meal comprising assorted dumplings) *cum* herbal tea restaurants (*The Straits Times* 21 Jan. 1990).

While conservation has fostered a state-envisioned "Chineseness" embodied in distinctive architecture, a scattering of unique "dying trades" to represent the Chinese past, and a variety of "Chinese" festive activities, it has also led to the demise of much more prosaic elements that go into the making of a Chinese lived culture. Shopkeepers, families, and street vendors lament the rapid attrition of longstanding small businesses that have been part and parcel of the familiar landscape where the retailer-client relationship goes back a long way. This situation is contrasted to the cautious way in which they view the sudden influx of gentrified shops managed by new people. They are far from persuaded that what the URA promotes as "adaptive reuse" of traditional buildings has revitalized the "traditional Chinese way of life." In coming to terms with the rapid changes of the landscape, old-time residents see themselves as the generation that marks the passing of the old way of life: the future is uncertain and all one can do is, in the words of a long-term resident, to live "a day at a time." The state's rewritten version of the Chinese cultural landscape is hence one that ignores "the inner workings of culture" (Wagner and Mikesell 1962, 5), choosing instead to identify culture solely with architecture and a few "representative" trades. The Singaporean Chinese in Chinatown have, however, remained aloof to such a version of the landscape and are not entirely oblivious to the irony that, in its attempt to refurbish Chinese architecture and revive Chinese "dying trades," the state's conservation efforts have essentially damaged the day-to-day cultural life of the place.

The state also sees no contradiction in its claim that the conservation of Chinatown serves both tourists who wish to savor the sights and sounds of the old Chinese lifestyle and locals who need a tangible reminder of their roots. While most agree that conservation has led to an improvement in the physical environment in Chinatown, those who live, work, or shop there are less convinced that conservation is "for the people." Many think of the conserved shophouses as being "nice and charming" but add that "they are not for us anymore," that "locals do not carry out purchases there [the conserved block] but go there simply to look," and that "the wares there are sold at tourist prices." While the spanking cleanliness and bright hues of the conserved rows of shophouses are generally seen as attractive, some feel that they "somehow don't look right," that they are "inauthentic," and that, with the emphasis on the picturesque, they are suitably tailored to appeal to the "tourist's way of seeing" (Relph 1976, 85). Indeed, the fact that conserved Chinatown is a landscape made for tourist consumption is particularly evident when dusk approaches and tourists are bussed off: Chinatown residents assert that the place takes on the "silence of a ghost town without a soul in sight," compared to pre-conservation when it "can be said to be a place with no night." Thus, in contradistinction to the state's aims of creating a conserved landscape imbued with historical and cultural meaning for Singaporeans, locals reinterpret this landscape as another promotional effort for the tourists, far removed from the practicalities of their own daily lives. Other than the brief excursion to gaze upon the architectural beauty of the place when locals too become tourists in their own land, conserved Chinatown has become for the ordinary Singaporean something "like an antique" (*The Straits Times* 4 Jan. 1987)—distinctively charming but impractical and unaffordable.

The distancing of conserved Chinatown from lived culture has also formed the crux of the Singapore Heritage Society's (a local nonprofit interest group for the promotion of heritage consciousness) criticism. In a proposal submitted in December 1996 as part of the "Enhancement of Chinatown" tender for STB (and ultimately rejected by the authorities), the society cautioned against turning the conservation area into an "ethnic theme park" using "the simplistic formula of capitalist profit criteria" (Singapore Heritage Society and Associated Consultants 1997). Instead, the society argued that "to be vibrant," an ethnic thematic zone such as Chinatown needs "above all to be meaningful to Singaporeans." The society has also contributed articles to the local press, arguing that the STB's "freeze-frame" approach would reduce Chinatown to a "simplistic," "exoticized," "Orientalist caricature of itself," and a "sanitized" product "stripped of complexity" and embellished by "inapplicable cultural ideas" (*The Straits Times* 22 Nov. 1998; 12 Dec. 1998; 16 Mar. 1999). A major bone of contention here is whether ethnic areas in the Central Area should function as residential or tourist landscapes. In the flurry of exchanges involving members of the public as well as spokespersons for STB, critics argued that the makeover betrays the individual and collective memories of those who have grown up with the place. A member of the public, for example, lamented that "we are caught in a frenzy to develop land, property, festivals and nightlife for the tourist and investor. I beg those in charge to have mercy on us common people. When I am old and dull, let me have something to look at to tell me that I once belonged here" (*The Straits Times* 16 Mar. 1999). Similarly, the Singapore Heritage Society maintains that, if Chinatown is to keep its life and memory, priority must be given to incorporating into the landscape the "residential community"—"the people who lived there and will live there" (*The Straits Times* 22 Nov. 1998). In turn, STB has proclaimed that the intention of conservation is to restore "residential living" to Chinatown, although thus far it has provided few details as to how this will be accomplished apart from indicating a few sites for new homes to be built.

Kampong Glam: The Politics of Exclusion

One prime area of disagreement where the conservation of whole areas is concerned is the drawing of boundaries demarcating what is worthy of conservation and what remains exposed to the threat of the redevelopment juggernaut. Urban conservation is necessarily a selective scheme, but the politics of selection is often exacerbated by planners who betray their ignorance of the past by producing plans "directly at odds with the historical development of the town plan and its natural divisions" (Slater 1984, 333). Lines staking out the conservation area conceived on the planner's drawing board often have material effects when translated into practice. They serve as "picket fences [which imply] that the things outside the fence are not historical" (Lewis, quoted in Handler 1987, 138). The designation of the Kampong Glam Historic District as a conservation area in July 1989 provides an illustration of the politics of being inside/outside the conservation project.

Probably named after the *gelam* tree,[4] Kampong Glam was "the historic seat of Malay Royalty in Singapore" where both the Sultan's Palace (or "*istana*") and the Sultan Mosque are located (*Kampong Glam Historic District 1995*, 15).[5] In Stamford Raffles's 1822 town plan for Singapore, Kampong Glam was officially allocated to the Malays and other Muslim traders and merchants from the Malay Peninsula, the Indonesian islands, and Arabia. In the second half of the nineteenth century, the area was characterized by the rapid growth of immigrant communities, leading to the mushrooming of "*kampungs*" (urban villages) such as Kampong Java, Kampong Malacca, and Kampong Bugis in the vicinity. A small but influential part of the Muslim community during this era were the Arab traders who achieved much success in both trade and property development. Wealthy Arab families established Muslim charitable endowments for the maintenance of mosques and religious schools (or "*madrasahs*"), the most prominent being the Alsagoff Arab School and the Madrasah Aljunied Al-Islamiah (or the Aljunied Arab School). "Steeped in Islamic tradition," Kampong Glam survived into the postindependence era as an area known for "tight streetscapes" and "traditional businesses" including textile wholesalers; frame makers, tombstone carvers; sandal making; Muslim eating houses; and shops selling rattan handicrafts, gems, and religious paraphernalia such as praying mats (*A Manual for Kampong Glam Conservation Area* 1988, 20–22).

The parceling out of the Kampong Glam Historic District involves the targeting of about nine hectares of land within the larger region, primarily "based on existing roads [Victoria Street, Jalan Sultan, Ophir Road, and Beach Road] serving the area" (*A Manual for Kampong Glam Conservation Area* 1988, 30). It is argued that the "unique characteristic of Kampong Glam is

4. This is a native tree that grows up to 30 meters tall with a papery bark. In the past, it provided both durable timber and medicinal oils pressed from its leaves. Its bark was used by the areas's seafaring people to caulk their boats.

5. When the East India Company set up a trading base in Singapore in 1819, it built a palace for the Sultan Hussein of the Johore Empire (which included Singapore). This palace was rebuilt in the 1840s for Sultan Ali Iskandar Shah, son of Sultan Hussein, and continues to be inhabited by descendants of the royal family.

The original Masjid Sultan (Sultan's mosque) was completed in 1824 to serve the Muslim community in the area, although the present structure, a gazetted national monument, dates from a 1928 reconstruction.

8.2. Istana Kampong Glam.

the contrast between the streetscape, with its low and uniform scale, and the large open spaces of the palace grounds" (*Kampong Glam Historic District* 1995, 77), so that the conservation landscape is centered on the area's "historic hub" comprising a proposed show house featuring Malay heritage and culture at the site of the Sultan's Palace; a proposed teahouse at No. 73 Sultan Gate, the former residence of the *"bendahara"* (one of the Sultan's officials); a proposed community house at the former Pondok Java; a "festival street" (Bussorah Street) and a "trading spine" (Arab Street); as well as the Alsagoff Arab School (*A Manual for Kampong Glam Conservation Area* 1988, 25–26). Recognizing the need to exercise sensitivity and conscience "in handling the District's historic fabric" because buildings "once destroyed . . . are lost forever" (*Kampong Glam Historic District* 1995, 77), the planners have also extended their conservation plans to include the Malabar Muslim Jama-Ath, a charming and aesthetically appealing mosque occupying a site just outside a corner of the conservation area.

While many of these intentions have not yet been translated into effects, conservation of the Historic District has proceeded with the pedestrianization of Bussorah Street and landscaping with palm streets and old-style lamp shades to "create a Middle-Eastern ambience" (*The Straits Times* 14 Apr. 1992) as well as the meticulous restoration of several rows of shophouses along Arab Street and Kandahar Street. Signboards and street furniture signifying the historicity of the district have been erected and plans are afoot to "consolidate and enhance ethnic-based activities which contribute to the overall charm, character and identity of the Historic District" (*Kampong Glam Historic District* 1995, 80). Within the borders of the conservation project, a state-envisioned "Malay heritage" is being fostered and reinterpreted, if not invented, as "pieces of life and landscape . . . are objectified—isolated and displayed as bounded heritage objects—according to aesthetic and political standards . . . which . . . will be dependent on current tastes and assumptions" (Handler 1987, 138). While the objectification of heritage artifacts in the bounded landscape defines and reifies a particular version of heritage, the legal codification and subsequent naturalization of the entire Historic District further serve to police the boundary between what is and what is not heritage.

Immediately outside the conservation boundaries, a different ethos pervades. The principle and spirit of conservation does not transcend artificially demarcated lines. Just north of the Historic District, on the other side of Victoria Street, the Madrasah Aljunied Al-Islamiah, the other notable *madrasah* with deep roots in Kampong Glam, was slated for demolition in mid-1996 to make way for an urban park (*A Manual for Kampong Glam Conservation Area* 1988, 11). Built in 1927 in commemoration of Syed Omar bin Ali Aljunied, one of the earliest Arab traders to arrive when Singapore was established as a British trading post and an illustrious leader and philanthropist looked upon as a "prince" by the Malays (Pearson, 1955, 92), the *madrasah* was built on *"wakaf"* land consecrated by Syed Omar himself.[6] Surrounded by a Muslim cemetery, which houses the resting places of Syed Omar and his family members (Buckley 1984, 563), the school has played a sustained and active role in Islamic education, nurturing prominent Islamic leaders including legislators of Islam, religious heads, and preachers.

6. An act of *"wakaf"* in the Islamic faith refers to the transference in perpetuity of proprietorship of a piece of property from the legal owner to Allah (God). The object ceases forever to be subjected to the right of private ownership and is instead consecrated for the use of Muslims and the advancement of Islam.

The exclusion of the Madrasah Aljunied Al-Islamiah from the Kampong Glam Historic District and its consequent exposure to the wrecker's ball have raised some disquiet among staff and students of the *madrasah*. The paradox of conservation boundaries as lines that divide an inside space where Malay heritage is sanctified and elevated and an outside space where similar arguments for historic and cultural significance are discounted is not lost on them. Several issues relating to the conservation-redevelopment divide were raised. Some felt that the exclusion of the *madrasah* was a mere trick of cartography and the road system: the neat rectangular area bounded by Ophir Road, Victoria Street, Jalan Sultan, and Beach Road was simply not elastic enough from a planning perspective to accommodate the area around the *madrasah*, which would have featured as an untidy protrusion from the conservation area. As one informer puts it, "luck has a lot to do with [conservation issues] as far as state intentions are concerned . . . One cannot just depend on logic and facts." Another informant felt that it was ironic that the compact rectangular conservation boundary had been extended to accommodate the Malabar Muslim Jama-Ath, but that it would not be "misshapened" for the sake of the *madrasah*, because the latter cannot aspire to the architectural merits of the former.[7] Yet another informer, however, argued that the *madrasah* was built with an architectural style and facade similar to those of the Sultan's Palace within the gazetted area and that the former's exclusion is "nothing but pure politics." Another contention raised by informers was the fact that "the other *madrasah*" in the area—the Madrasah Alsagoff, which is historically associated with another prominent Arab family, the Alsagoffs—enjoys conservation status because it was "fortunate" enough to lie within the rectangular boundaries. The enforced disparity of status between the two *madrasahs* is detrimental; according to one informant, "Both of these two *wakaf* lands are very different, despite being *madrasahs*. They point to different legacies and heritage of a similar era. They were built by two of the most prominent Arabs in Singapore at

---

7. Ironically, rather than "misshaping" the conservation area, extending the conservation boundaries to include the *"wakaf"* land on which the Madrasah Aljunied Al-Islamiah and the Malabar Muslim Jama-Ath are sited would prevent the latter from being an awkward protrusion.

that time and to destroy one at the expense of the other is to consider one as more important than the other, which is inconsistent with the Islamic decree." According to the principal of the school, the reason given by the state as to why the *madrasah* would be demolished was to make way for a bigger structure to house the increasing intake of students. However, informers also felt that this explanation would only appear convincing if the state were not in the process of acquiring much of the land where the present building sits. From the present 4.4 hectares belonging to the trustee of the land (a descendant of Syed Omar Aljunied), only a mere 0.52 hectares would be awarded to the building of the new school. What caused even more controversy was the fact that consecrated *wakaf* land acquired was slated to be turned into a park, an act tantamount to sacrilege for some. As one informant explained, "Taking the *wakaf* land is synonymous with treating the Malays and the Islamic faith with disrespect. How can they just destroy the legacy of our forefathers like this without even considering the sentiments of the people whose lives would be affected dramatically?" Furthermore, the Muslim cemetery housing the tombs of the Aljunieds is widely perceived within the Malay community as a *"keramat"* (holy shrine), thus further confirming the "sacredness" of the site under threat.

Indeed, the spatial politics surrounding the Madrasah Aljunied is interpreted by some (with a touch of hyperbole) as being part of a more generalized state politics against the Malays as a minority community. From this perspective, by selectively choosing which area or history to propagate and which should remain hidden, state conservation-redevelopment practices are complicit in simultaneously erasing and inventing heritage, even within a given (as opposed to across) cultural hearth(s). In spite of the larger and noble aim of conservation as a means by which Singapore's heritage can be transmitted to the ordinary citizen, it is clear that designating boundaries based on the vagaries of the existing street network and without consultation with the occupants of the area ultimately defeats this purpose. While the URA publishes draft manuals describing the proposed conservation to be undertaken for each historic district, the information is intended "for purposes of inviting feedback from professionals" (*A Manual for Kampong Glam Conservation Area* 1988, inside cover) but not the general populace.

Singapore's heritage landscapes are expected to conform to the politi-

cal ideal of "multiracialism," the social formula that attempts to forge a Singaporean identity out of separate but "equal" "races." In managing multiethnic heritage, the state aims to be "even-handed," that is, to ensure there is
equal representation of the major ethnic groups in the choice of historic
monuments and districts (Tay 1991, 39). Rather than sharpen social cleav-
ages along ethnic lines, the state argues that conserving historic places of
various ethnic groups in Singapore provides a new "glue" that could bind
together a multiethnic, multicultural society (Tay 1991, 41). However, providing each major ethnic group with a historically conserved site is not a
solution without problems. The decision to demolish the Madrasah Alsagoff Al-Islamiah and to convert the existing *wakaf* land into a park
demonstrates a lack of sensitivity to the cultural practices of the
Malay/Muslim community in Singapore. Clearly, the state's conservation
strategies based on the management of multiethnic heritage have not entirely resolved the redevelopment-conservation dilemma in Singapore.
Conflict arises because gazetted monuments and conservation areas often
slice up the organic form and texture of cultural hearths in an arbitrary fashion, legislating boundaries between a defended zone perceived to be of historical value and an excluded landscape that is threatened with excision. By
privileging the "inside," conservation projects divert attention from whole-
sale destruction of "other" heritages "outside." While ethnically appor-
tioned heritage landscapes are intended as testimony to the forging of a
multiethnic "nation," spatial definitions of what constitutes sanctioned, legitimate (and therefore unsanctioned, illegitimate) landscapes of such a nation could equally become politicized notions, rendering every heritage
site, by dint of its very presence, a contested and exclusionary space.

The Merlion: Monument and Myth [8]

The recovery of heritage, the establishment of national symbols, and the
revival of traditions are key to asserting a sense of the "nation," and as
Featherstone (1993, 178) noted, symbols, ceremonies, and rites often need
not be invented *ex nihilo* because they can draw on traditions and ethnic cul-

---

8. The phrase "monument and myth" is taken from Harvey (1979).

tures that possessed plausibility. Singapore's quest for national symbols has produced what is undoubtedly the most highly visible and widely promoted iconographic feature of the Singapore landscape—the Merlion, a "half-beast, half-fish" form conceived in 1964 as the emblem of the Singapore Tourism Promotion Board (STPB) in an attempt to create an internationally recognizable symbol synonymous with Singapore.[9] Chosen from a logo competition organized by the STPB, the Merlion was recommended for use as the STPB's corporate crest on 26 March 1964. It was thought to be "appropriate because it incorporated fact and legend" (*The Straits Times* 9 Apr. 1999); while the lion head signifies the story of how Sang Nila Utama sighted a beast he thought was a lion on his first visit to the island in the eleventh century, the fish symbolizes Singapore's beginnings as a fishing village. Compared to other recognizable symbols such as the orchid or the traveler's palm, it was felt the Merlion embodied "rich historical symbolism" (*The Straits Times* 22 Mar. 1999). The registration of the Merlion logo as a trademark of the STPB was finalized on 20 July 1966. The Merlion is the quintessential product of a hybridity of signs scissored out from a number of different contexts. Its provenance is a case of prodigious (but not unproblematic) cutting and pasting from a range of sources including a vague historical trajectory, Malay literature (the *Sejarah Melayu*),[10] the etymology of place, speculations about the fauna profile in early Singapore, animal symbolisms, and the practical considerations of Singapore's role as a port city standing at the intersection of land and sea, as seen in the following blurb, which often accompanies Merlion mementos:

> Singapore traces its earliest history to the 4th century A.D. It was then known as Temasek or Sea Town, situated, as it still is, at the converging point of trade routes between the East and the West. At the end of the

9. The Singapore Tourist Promotion Board (STPB) officially changed its corporate name to the Singapore Tourism Board (STB) in 1997.

10. The *Sejara Melayu*, or *Malay Annals*, is considered one of the greatest literary works in Malay. Based on both traditional and Islamic moral and ethical values, it is centered on the theme of the rise and fall of the Great Melakan Empire. Most scholars consider it as both a literary work of fiction and a form of moral discourse in which historicity is a secondary element rather than the ruling logic (Cheah 1999).

11th century A.D., Prince Nila Utama of the Sri Vijaya empire arrived with a party on the island. Legend has it that he encountered a strange and wild beast on landing and further enquiry established the beast to be a lion (although in all probability it was a tiger). Hence the name Singapore or SINGAPURA, which in Sanskrit means Lion (SINGA) City (PURA). The Merlion—with the head of a lion and the body of the fish—represents both the ancient and the modern names of the Republic. The lion alluding to the fabled beast that once roamed the island and the body of the fish symbolising Singapore's origins as a sea town.

After eight years of consistent use by the STPB, the Merlion, the authorities felt, not only deserved greater publicity as a tourism icon but should be elevated to "a distinctive symbol with which [Singapore] can be identified" (STPB 1971–72, 12). This led to the idea of a 26-foot Merlion at the mouth of the Singapore River. Constructed by Lim Nang Seng and his two sons Lim Pee Nee and Lim Pee Boon, and conceived under the STPB's Special Committee for Conversion of Selective Historic Sites into Tourist Attractions (formed in December 1970), the Merlion project began in November 1971, with the statue being installed at the river mouth in July 1972. Prime Minister Lee Kuan Yew officiated in the installation ceremony on 15 September 1972, declaring his hope that the symbol will in time be identified with Singapore "just as the Eiffel Tower is identified with Paris" (STPB 1972–73, 12).

Throughout the 1970s, Merlion Park and the adjacent Elizabeth Walk proved to be popular leisure sites for tourists and Singaporeans. With its panoramic view of the Singapore Harbor and the highly photogenic Supreme Court and the ever-popular Satay Club (now expunged) within walking distance, the Merlion unofficially assumed the role as the leading attraction and most photographed site in the Colonial District.

Over the years, the mutual reinforcing ties between the Merlion and Singapore's tourism industry have been strengthened in different ways. Just as the tourism industry benefits from an instantly recognizable icon that is unique to the country, so the Merlion confers to members of the industry a badge with which tourists can easily identify. For example, the STB recognizes "good retailers" by conferring a Merlion label, which shopowners proudly display to attract shoppers. In 1985, the STPB also devised the Merlion Week. A single week in the month of December (the peak month of tourist visitation) was devoted to publicizing Singapore overseas; educating the public on the importance of tourism to the economy; and fun-filled activities such as shopping sales, food fests, entertainment events, fashion shows featuring local designs, and a "Merlion Fest" in Orchard Road complete with cultural dances, games, and competitions.

As an associational icon, the Merlion is part of a rarefied group of objects in Singapore (others include the Raffles Hotel and the national orchid) that tourists insist on seeing, photographing, and, where possible, purchasing related products as proof of their having "experienced" Singapore. The commercialization of the Merlion is best witnessed through the variety of goods it has spawned such as Merlion dolls, key chains, carvings, pens, and other artifacts. The STPB certainly encourages the Merlion's commercialization as a way of drawing attention to the country. In 1989 alone, the board approved forty-nine applications for the use of the Merlion. These uses include everything from the deployment of the Merlion overseas in promotional campaigns and festivals to a wide range of souvenirs. The STPB also makes an effort to celebrate the Merlion's birthday each September. On its twenty-first birthday in 1993, for example, commemorative Merlion telephone cards were commissioned and varied activities were organized throughout town. Most notable was the baking of Singapore's largest-ever birthday cake, with the birthday celebrations held, strangely enough, a distance away from the Singapore River at Takashimaya Square in Orchard Road (STPB 1993–94). Such ongoing efforts indicate the STPB/STB's proactive approach in deploying the Merlion for tourist ends.

The most ambitious Merlion project to date was launched in 1993 by the Sentosa Development Corporation in its plans to build a 37-meter-high Merlion (equivalent to a 11-story building and said to be the tallest freeform tower in Asia) atop a 23-meter-high ridge in the island of Sentosa. Conceived as an opportunity to add a focal point to Sentosa while creating a new "storyline" to enthrall tourists and visitors, this S$13 million project was completed in mid-1996. Apart from their vastly different sizes, the Sentosa Merlion is distinct from its predecessor at the Singapore River in

other ways. The Sentosa version comes equipped with a storyline by courtesy of the Merlion Walk, in which plaques and storyboards about the "Rise
of the Merlion" are included. The story goes that, as the legendary guardian
of Singapore, the Merlion visits Sentosa each year to watch over the isle
previously known as Temasek to ensure that all is fine before returning to
the sea. One day when Temasek was threatened with destruction by a fero-
cious storm, the Merlion with its magical powers subdued the storm and
preserved the land. The path of the Merlion to its throne on Sentosa (i.e.,
the Merlion Walk), filled with water pools and water-spouting sea creatures, tells of the self-sacrifice by thousands of sea creatures laying their
bodies down for their majestic master. By night, the Merlion awakens during a light, sound, and water show extravaganza at the Musical Fountain,
with the Merlion lit with 16,000 fiber-optic lights and lasers shooting from
its eyes. The Merlion attraction is complete with a Merlion Shoppe (selling
all forms of Merlion paraphernalia), a restaurant, and a themed shipwreck
scene at the basement. Unlike the Merlion Park at the river, an entrance fee
is charged at the Sentosa Merlion.

While the Merlion has been successfully deployed as Singapore's key
tourism icon in a number of ways, its reception on home ground appears
more ambivalent and mixed. First, it should be noted that the distinction
between the notion of a tourism icon and that of a national symbol is often
elided. STB, for example, often uses the term "tourism icon" and "national
emblem" in the same text, as if they were interchangeable, or conflate the
two as in "national tourism icon" (*The Straits Times* 22 Mar. 1999). Representations of "self" projected for the consumption of significant "others" may
return to define the possibilities and parameters of self identities in the end-
less dialogic play and interpenetrations between "self" and "other."

In this vein, the Merlion as a national icon takes pride of place on the
poetic landscape of the nation, most prominently transposed there in
Edwin Thumboo's *Ulysses by the Merlion* (1979), in which the poet, envision-
ing himself as "chief bard of the tribe," assumes the persona of "the wander-
ing Ulysses, [linking] him on the one hand to [the poet's] own past history
and poetic development, and on the other, to the history and circumstances of his island nation, of which the merlion is a fitting symbol" (Ee
1997, 46–47). The work has been hailed a "visionary and hopeful poem on

8.3. The Sentosa Merlion.

... the reality and meaning of change" (Gooneratne 1986, 15), in which Thumboo accepts the Merlion, "this powerful creature of land and sea," as Singapore's "invention of a new symbol, an "image of themselves, represent[ing] the collective yearning for a soul" (Ee 1997, 49). There are, of course, other interpretations of Thumboo's poem (e.g., Lee Tzu Pheng's *Merlion to Ulysses* and Ban [1985]), but the point here is that the Merlion has gained literary currency as a symbol around which, or at least a counterpoint against which, to write the Singapore story.[11]

Beyond the literary sphere, and among those to whom the Merlion is not so much a poetic device as a concrete node in the Singapore landscape whose image is also ubiquitously encountered in forms ranging from chocolates to bus tours, there is an uneasiness borne of ambivalence toward the notion of the Merlion as national symbol. In Heng's (1993, 94) study of the Civic and Cultural District, a survey of 146 local respondents revealed that, while 34 percent endorsed the Raffles Statue and 22 percent agreed

11. Ban (1992, 23) argues that the poem is about both the repressive nature of the historical template and the need to "yearn again for images" (in Thumboo's words), the Merlion being symbolic of gaining the power of imagination to "re-write the boundaries of its own existence and meaning."

that the Singapore River embodied the heritage of Singaporeans, only 4 percent had similar opinions of the Merlion. A possible explanation is that the Merlion is perceived to be a decorative "work of art" aimed at tourists, rather than an icon of local identity in the way the Raffles statue or the City Hall are (Heng 1993, 73). Adopting Boorstin's (1992, 103) cynical description of "tourist attractions" as places "of little significance for the inward life of a people, but wonderfully saleable as tourist commodity," one can perhaps say that the Merlion's entrenched status as a tourist attraction works against its role as a national symbol.

Another reason for the Merlion's failure is what is perceived as its limited genealogy and contrived origins. For a place to be claimed as "Singaporean," some would argue that it needs to evolve organically. In his assessment of tourism development in Singapore, Pannell Kerr Forster (1986, V–26) reminds us that "people create their own people places, not planners or "producers." Hence, unlike the original Chinatown or Kampong Glam, for example, which have evolved over decades and thus lay stronger claims to heritage status, the Merlion is a self-consciously styled attraction created for the express purpose of forging a tourism image. Measured against animal symbols well entrenched in the canons of Asian tradition and mythology such as the dragon, the phoenix, the *garuda*, the *naga*, and the horse (animal images mentioned in *Ulysses*), the Merlion fails to evoke the same sense of historical depth and cultural creativity. In this regard, Lee Tzu Pheng's (1997) description of the Merlion in her poem *The Merlion to Ulysses* (written in reaction to Thumboo's *Ulysses by the Merlion*) as "the instant brainchild of a practical people" is very apt and alludes to the authorities' mechanical approach to churning out national symbols and the often dismal results of such endeavors. This is also probably what a particular member of Parliament had in mind when criticizing the Merlion as "tacky," "totally unconvincing," and unbefitting of being a national icon, causing considerable consternation among tourism planners and operators who, according to newspaper reports, "defended the Merlion stoutly, saying that it was a national icon and an important tourism draw" (thereby implying that such national stature should insulate it from criticism) (*The Straits Times* 22 Mar. 1999).

This conflict does not mean that the Merlion is totally incapable of evoking strong local affinity. Boorstin (1992) has argued that, over time and prolonged contact, even "pseudo events" such as staged dances and cultural practices take on a veneer of authenticity and permanence. In the context of the Merlion, several possibilities of mythmaking have been suggested. For example, one commentator who wrote in to the press argued that the important issue was not so much whether the Merlion is founded on "historical facts and accounts" as claimed by the STB (*The Straits Times* 9 Apr. 1999) but how the legend is "scripted." He advocated keeping faith with the "really respectable legend" of the Sang Nila Utama's lion sighting on the shores of the island as being the lynchpin in sustaining a consistent legend, rather than constant re-invention and embroidery of the myth in different incarnations of the Merlion story (such as during a particular National Day celebration, when a "new" legend woven around how mythical creatures went in search of a fair land was launched; or in the Merlion inscriptions in Sentosa, which centered on how the Merlion acquired a gleaming tail of phosphorescent, sacrificial sea creatures). If depth of time is a crucial ingredient in the work of mythologizing, stressing the Merlion's roots in antiquity and keeping the storyline consistent may help anchor and perpetuate the myth of Singapore's Merlion-founding in the popular imagination. However, this requirement contradicts the logic of the tourist marketplace, which needs recurrent innovation and re-creation, where landscape needs to be constantly fragmented and reworked in response to market forces (Zukin 1991, 27). It is hence unclear to what extent tourism-driven icons can gain currency as national emblems because the former privilege incessant annihilation and recycling while the latter require stability and rootedness.

Conclusion

> Not surprisingly, this city created out of nothing—with no tradition of a shared past or common language and culture—has relied as much on symbols and similes to instill pride in its citizens as on boosting its gross domestic product and standard of living.
>
> —Journalist Chua Mui Hoong
> (*The Straits Times* 29 Aug. 1992)

Not only has Singapore been called "a nation born of imagination," it is said to be one in which "destiny . . . remains very much a rewriting and a re-imagining by each generation of what is possible" (Ban 1992, 23). The need to "create the psychological space that will make up for the lack of those luxuries of physical environment, of historical complexities that provide advantage for others" (Ban 1992, 23), is particularly strong at this moment of its history, when the state strives to remind the nation's citizens that Singapore is still "the best home" worthy of their commitment even as it urges them to respond to regional and global opportunities with entrepreneurial verve (Goh 1999). As argued in this chapter, the creation of heritage landscapes, ranging from the conservation and re-imaging of ethnic areas (such as Chinatown and Kampong Glam) to the manufacture of monumental symbols whose iconography draws on and combines myth and reality (such as the Merlion), forms part of the "process of cultural and geographical imagining" (Gruffudd 1994, 61) integral to the work of nation-building.

While heritage landscapes provide convenient and visually effective means of translating the "history" of the "nation" for public consumption, it should be remembered that "space, place and geography" are often also "sources of fragmentation" that resist the homogeneity of events and negotiate "the snares of totalisation" (Philo 1992, 144). This idea points to Danielss's (1989) "duplicity of landscape" (as discussed in chapter 2). In responding to state-envisioned heritage landscapes and symbols, there are clearly alternative readings and resistances against such hegemonic intentions, although rarely expressed in confrontational style. Some have clearly found state-propelled conservation and preservation efforts to be superficial, with little penetrating beneath the veneer of commercialization to creatively connect with the past. As such, so-called heritage landscapes designed by state agencies have been dismissed by some as "a piece of kitsch . . . some kind of feeble confection" (architect Tay Kheng Soon, *The Straits Times* 18 Feb. 2000) and by others as being somewhat bland and disengaged from the development of a sense of national identity. As one former journalist (Irene Ng, *The Straits Times* 18 Feb. 2000) puts it, "Something which struck me when I watched how the countries celebrated the new millennium was the distinctive buildings where their citizens gathered. In Australia, it was the Sydney Opera House. In Washington, it was the Abraham Lincoln Memorial. When it came to Singapore, it was Orchard Road, with shopping centres. Why is there no one building here that could be a focus of national pride?" While many of these counter-opinions are articulated by individuals in disparate fields, and while there is yet insufficient coalescence of views and strategies to constitute an effective mobilization of the ground on heritage issues alone, it is clear that what Daniels (1989) calls the "manipulative" aspects of landscape are not entirely compelling—at least not to segments of the people who constitute the body of the nation.

9

Arts (f)or Survival

Making Spaces for the Arts

Documenting Performing Arts Spaces in Singapore

At the opening of a local conference titled *Art versus Art: Conflict and Convergence* in 1993, Ho Kwon Ping, chairman of the Practice Performing Arts Center, a private arts school, made the following observation about the increased attention paid to the arts in Singapore in the late 1980s and 1990s:

> We are moving so very rapidly in a national effort to change this underdeveloped state in the Arts. It was only in 1988 when the Ong Teng Cheong Advisory Council on Art and Culture completed its extended study. The change that has taken place in the last five years has been phenomenal: We now have a Cabinet Minister for the Arts, a National Arts Council, half a dozen professional performing companies, a National Gallery under renovation, arts major degree programmes in both universities and as much as $500 million set aside to build a world class arts centre scheduled to open before the year 2000.[1] (*Art versus Art* 1995, 7)

Indeed, the Singapore government desires to make the city-state a "global city of the arts" and has stepped up efforts to achieve this. What has brought on this vigor in cultural policy and action, which was lacking before? As Liu Kang, one of Singapore's pioneer artists, noted, the lack of support for the arts in the post-World War Two and early postindependence

---

1. The center, now named the Esplanade—Theatres on the Bay was officially opened in October 2002.

years was stark; the government spent tens of millions on secondary and primary schools, but nothing on an arts academy (the Nanyang Academy of Fine Arts, then the only arts academy in Singapore). It spent huge sums building structures like the National Stadium but did little to channel the funds to developing the arts. Perhaps, Liu reckoned, it was because the government was very good "when it came to things related to business (the airport, the harbor), but negligent when it comes to the arts" (*Art versus Art* 1995, 13).

What was the situation with respect to facilities for the arts in Singapore at independence and how has it evolved through the last three and one-half decades? In this chapter, we will focus on performing arts and, in particular, two key types of facilities for their use: performance spaces and housing for arts groups. We will begin by outlining the evolution of both types of spaces before proceeding to analyze the ideological meanings invested in these spaces by the state and arts practitioners. We will not provide a detailed exposition of the development of the arts in Singapore but we will leave that to emerge from the subsequent analysis. Suffice to say at this point that the opening paragraph of this chapter captures succinctly the trajectory of the arts in Singapore—from initial underdevelopment to more recent enthusiasm for development.

Tables 9.1 to 9.3 document the development of performance venues in Singapore. They illustrate how, at independence in 1965, there was an appalling lack of venues. There were only three venues: the National Theatre, Victoria Concert Hall, and Victoria Theatre. By the 1970s, the situation had not improved much. The most popular concert hall in the 1970s was the Singapore Conference Hall. While it was ideal for orchestral and choral performances as well as instrumental recitals, the Singapore Conference Hall had difficulty in attracting foreign orchestras, which needed a concert capacity of at least 2,000 before a performance was commercially viable (the Conference Hall only had 1,024 seats). In spite of its good acoustics, it was also built more for conferences and seminars and was a poor choice for dance and drama performances because of the small stage, absence of curtains, and inadequate lighting (*The Straits Times* 16 Oct. 1979). Other venues posed different problems: Victoria Theatre had mediocre acoustics while the National Theatre, a semi-open structure, had poor

Table 9.1
Performance Venues

Auditorium/Theater	Year Completed	Seating Capacity	Remarks
Victoria Concert Hall	1905	883	PA system, piano available. Rehearsal space available.
Victoria Theatre	Built in 1862 as a Town Hall; converted into a theater and memorial hall in 1905.	904	Proscenium stage. PA system, sound reinforcement equipment, stage lighting, grand piano, orchestra pit, optical effect attachment. Rehearsal space available.
National Theatre	Completed in 1964; demolished in 1986		
Singapore Conference Hall	1965	1,024	For conferences, conventions, seminars, meetings, ceremonies, concerts, cultural performances, and film shows. Rehearsal space available.
Golden Theatre	c 1968	1,393	Suitable for performances, entertainment shows, and film shows. Rehearsal space available.
RELC Auditorium	1972	350	Sound system, projection equipment and screen, theater only large enough for talks, screening movies, and minimum instrumental shows. No rehearsal space available.

Table 9.1
Performance Venues (cont.)

Auditorium/Theater	Year Completed	Seating Capacity	Remarks
Singapore Power Auditorium (PUB Auditorium)	(original) 1978	511	Microphones, overhead projector, audio with taping facilities, dimmer controlled lighting. Rehearsal space available.
Drama Centre	Built for the Singapore Council for Adult Education in 1955; converted into a theater in 1980.	326	Sound and lighting equipment, and grand piano available. Rehearsal space available.
World Trade Centre Auditorium	1982	988	Stage lighting and equipment, electro audio system, broadcasting facilities, project equipment, sound system. Rehearsal space available.
Kallang Theatre	Constructed in 1970 as a commercial cinema; refurbished as a theater in 1986	1,744	Stage lighting and sound reinforcement system; sound control room, communication and stage production system, grand piano. Rehearsal space available.

Table 9.1
Performance Venues (*cont.*)

Auditorium/Theater	Year Completed	Seating Capacity	Remarks
SLF Auditorium	1986	918	Piano, stage lights, sound system. Rehearsal space available.
Black Box	1988	120	Sound and lighting system. Theater only available for rent if co-presented with Theatreworks. No rehearsal space available.
Singapore Indoor Stadium	1989	8,137 (permanent seats); 2,660 retractable seats	Multipurpose hall. Rehearsal space available.
Guinness Theatre: The Substation	1990	118 to 146	Multipurpose hall. Film projector, lighting, sound system, semi-grand piano, smoke machine, PA system. Rehearsal space available.
Haw Par Villa (Tiger Balm Gardens) amphitheater	1990	2,000	Amphitheater for both wet and dry weather. Rehearsal space available.
Jubilee Hall	1992	388	Stage lighting and sound system available. Rehearsal space available.
WTC Harbour Pavilion	1992	5,000	Stage rigging, sound system, broadcasting facilities, stage lighting. Rehearsal space available.
Asian Village Theatre	1993	1,000 to 1,500	Amphitheater-style performance venue, Balinese-styled terrace seating area. Rehearsal space available.
Act 3 Theatre	1994	200	Theatre has no fixed seating. Especially ideal as children's theater. Rehearsal space available.
Paradigm Theatre	1994	150–200	Stage lighting, PA system, microphones, projector and screen, surround-sound system. Rehearsal space available.

Table 9.1
Performance Venues (cont.)

Auditorium/Theater	Year Completed	Seating Capacity	Remarks
Suntec City Auditorium	1996	596	
Revenue House Auditorium	1996	215	Proscenium stage. Sophisticated audio-visual presentation system. Rehearsal space available.
Alliance Francaise de Singapore Multi-purpose theatre	1997	240	Suitable for screening films, drama, concerts, and theater productions. No rehearsal space.
DBS Auditorium	Information unavailable	556	Film and slide projector, grand and upright piano, spot and stage lights available. Rehearsal space available.
MND Auditorium	Information unavailable	242	May not be suitable for stage performances due to the size and elevation of the stage. Only available to government departments and statutory boards. No rehearsal space.

Source: Directories: Arts Facilities (National Arts Council 1996); Edwards and Keys (1988); individual venues.

Table 9.2
Performance Venues At Community Centers

Auditorium/Theater	Year Completed	Seating Capacity	Remarks
Boon Lay CC	1980	129	PA system. Available for rehearsals.
Siglap CC	1988	450	Grand piano, blackout curtains, stage curtains, sound system, stage lighting. Available for rehearsals.
Mountbatten CC	1992	176	PA system. Available for rehearsals.
Tampines Cultural Centre	1994	285	Stage lights, sound equipment, video system, electronic dimmer, communication system, draperies. Available for rehearsals.
Nanyang CC	1996	108	Available for rehearsals.
Marine Parade Community Club	1999	Not available	Applications open to arts groups in 1999.

Source: Directories: Arts Facilities (National Arts Council 1996); individual venues.

acoustics; carried noise from passing traffic and insects; was not air conditioned; and was open to rain, insects, bats, birds, lightning, and clinking bottles (from canteen boys stacking the crates after intermission) (*The Straits Times* 16 Oct. 1979; 4 Dec. 1982; 9 Jan. 1984). By the 1980s, the facilities had deteriorated further, and a Committee on Performing Arts was appointed by the Advisory Council on Culture and the Arts (see later discussion) in 1988 "to examine the present status of performing arts in Singapore and to recommend strategies which could lead to the integration of the performing arts as a permanent and visible manifestation of Singapore's cultural lifestyle" (*Report of the Committee on Performing Arts* 1988, 2). The committee did not hesitate to point out further problems. Besides the fact that Victoria Theatre and the Drama Centre were suitable only for small to medium-sized performances, leaving no possibility for large professional companies, their stage equipment was also out of date and the environment was "decidedly aged." The Victoria Concert Hall suffered the same prob-

Table 9.3
Performance Venues in Schools/Institutions

Auditorium/Theater	Year Completed	Seating Capacity	Remarks
ACS Auditorium	1992	1800	Piano
ACS Centre of Performing Arts	1992	650	Piano
NUS Theatrette	1993	300	Babygrand and upright pianos. Sound equipment.
Chinese High School Drama Centre	1994	392	Stage lighting, sound reinforcement, choral riser, conductor stand, projection screen.
LaSalle SIA	1995	600	Cultural hall and studio theater (black box).
MGS Auditorium	1992	650	Microphones, channel mixer, amplifier system, projectors.
RGS School	1992	500 (multipurpose hall) 250 (Drama Theatre) 1000 (Amphitheater)	
NUS Cultural Centre	2000	1700 (main hall) 400 (theatre)	

Source: Respective institutions.

lem of a lack of audience and stage capacities while the Kallang Theatre inherited the limitations arising from the fact that it was built for another purpose (*Report of the Committee on Performing Arts* 1988, 26). Given these limitations, it was difficult to present creative works that called for differences in ambience to achieve optimal effect (*Report of the Committee on Performing Arts* 1988, 50). The same committee also highlighted the fact that total performances had increased in the 1980s from 789 in 1982 to 1,539 in 1987 (see Table 9.4). Hence, apart from the inadequacy of venues, there was also a general insufficiency of venues: with an average utilization rate of 70 per-

Table 9.4

Total Number of Indoor and Outdoor Cultural Performances, 1982–87

	1982	*1983*	*1984*	*1985*	*1986*	*1987*	*Total*
Music	277	301	290	318	516	461	2163
% increase/decrease over preceding year		+8.66	-3.65	+9.66	+62.26	-10.66	
Drama	218	250	305	269	362	560	1964
% increase/decrease over preceding year		+14.68	+22	-11.8	+34.57	+54.7	
Dance	47	60	45	68	96	94	410
% increase/decrease over preceding year		+27.66	-25	+51.1	+41.18	-2.08	
Others	247	264	353	364	652	424	2304
% increase/decrease over preceding year		+6.88	+33.71	+3.12	+79.12	-34.97	
TOTAL	789	875	993	1019	1626	1539	6841
% increase/decrease over preceding year		+10.9	+13.49	+2.62	+59.57		

Source: Report of the Committee on Performing Arts 1988, liii

Note: 1982, 1984, and 1986 were Festival of Arts years and therefore saw a high number of performances. However, because of the closure of the National Theatre in 1984, a number of performances had to be canceled, explaining the lower rate of increase in that year.

cent in 1987, performing-arts groups found increasing difficulty in booking venues on preferred dates and during certain periods of the year (*Report of the Committee on Performing Arts* 1988, 36). During the Festival of Arts, venues that had not been designed for performances (such as conference auditoria) had to be used (*Report of the Committee on Performing Arts* 1988, 50). Given all these constraints, the committee recommended the construction of a performing arts center, a call that the government heeded. It led to the formation of the Singapore Arts Centre in 1992 (now the Esplanade Company Limited), which was to build the Esplanade-Theatres on the Bay. It would include a 2,000-seat concert hall and a 1,800-seat Lyric Theatre.

Providing space for the performing arts, however, does not involve merely providing performance venues. Each production entails months of preparatory work, which may include rehearsals, sectional practices, building of props and sets, as well as administrative activities such as fundraising and repertory planning. Appropriate rehearsal spaces are needed, as are workshops, storerooms, and office space. As importantly, if not more so, "performing arts groups also have a psychological need for a place they can call 'home' to give members a sense of permanency and security and to build group loyalty and support" (*Report of the Committee on Performing Arts* 1988, 27). Two surveys conducted in 1983 and 1985 by the Cultural Affairs Division of the former Ministry of Culture and the Ministry of Community Development respectively revealed the dire need for such accommodation. Few groups had fixed locations for rehearsals and work. Most rented space on a sessional basis at theaters, schools, and community centers. Some operated from private homes of members, a highly unsatisfactory circumstance given that the high-density housing situation in Singapore generally meant constrained spaces and noise disturbances. A few groups were fortunate to have purchased suburban premises in the past, but these were few and far between (*Report of the Committee on Performing Arts* 1988, 28).

In recognition of the needs of arts groups, an Arts Housing Scheme, a subsidized housing scheme for arts groups, was introduced in 1985 under the purview of the Ministry of Community Development; it provides practice and administrative space to arts groups at subsidized rent. Its main purpose is to give arts groups a home within which they can develop their activities and thereby help to foster a culturally vibrant society. It is open to all registered arts organizations. The criteria for the selection of the groups include a good track record, managerial strength, artistic standard, level of activity, and growth potential. In addition, groups are assessed on their need for housing, merit of planned activities, and commitment to organizational and artistic developments. These spaces are generally converted from unused government buildings (see Table 9.5). In 1988, however, the committee reported that the Arts Housing Scheme only partially met the needs of performance groups for proper working and rehearsal facilities. The buildings were old and deteriorated. The period of tenancy was short (three years) with no certainty of renewal, which made it difficult for performing arts groups to undertake the high costs of refurbishment. The buildings made available were unsuitable in that rehearsals held concur-

Table 9.5
Arts Housing Scheme

Building/ Location	Year Completed	Art Form Housed/Facilities	Arts Group Allocated to
Telok Ayer Performing Arts Centre	1985	Drama, Chinese opera, music, multidisciplinary	Multi-tenanted (17 arts groups)
Stamford Arts Centre	1988	Drama, music, dance, Chinese opera, multidisciplinary	Multi-tenanted (10 arts groups)
Substation	1990	Exhibition hall, theaterette, studios	The Substation Ltd
Former Selegie Primary School	1990	Arts institution	Nanyang Academy of Fine Arts—Short Street campus
One-Two-Six Cairnhill Arts Centre	1992	Drama, multidisciplinary	Multi-tenanted (6 arts groups)
Former Tun Sri Lanang Secondary School	1992	Arts institution	LaSalle—SIA College of the Arts
Former Rangoon Road Primary School	1993	Dance, music	Singapore Indian Fine Arts Society
48 Waterloo St	1995	Visual arts/exhibition hall	Calligraphy Society of Singapore
60 Waterloo St	1995	Dance/dance studios	Dance Ensemble Singapore
30 Selegie Road	1996	Visual arts/exhibition hall	Photographic Society of Singapore
Former Kampong Eunos Community Centre	1996	Visual arts	Federation of Art Societies

Table 9.5
Arts Housing Scheme (*cont.*)

Building/ Location	Year Completed	Art Form Housed/Facilities	Arts Group Allocated to
Former St Anthony's Convent	1996	Arts institution	Nanyang Academy of Fine Arts—Middle Road Campus Chinese Opera Institute
54, 56, 58 Waterloo Street	1996	Music/Auditorium, music studios	Young Musicians' Society S'pore Youth Choir S'pore Youth Chinese Orchestra
Smith Street and Trengganu Street	1998	Chinese opera, drama, literary writing, music, multidisciplinary	Chinese Theatre Circle Ltd; Ping Sheh; Xin Sheng Poets Society; S'pore Assoc of Writers; Toy Factory Theatre Ensemble; Er Woo Amateur Musical & Dramatic Society; Harmonica Afficionados Society (S'pore); TAS Theatre Co (S) Ltd; Drama Box
42 Waterloo Street	Dec 1998	Drama	Action Theatre
155 and 161 Middle Road	Mar 1999	Visual arts/exhibition gallery/artist studio/art bookshop/sculpture park	Sculpture Square Ltd
19 and 20 Merbau Road	2000	210-seat auditorium/ black box	Singapore Repertory Theatre
63 Caseen Street 72–3 Mohd Sultan Road 41,42 Robertson Quay	2000	Mixed-use; gallery, theaterette, dance studios	Applications open to arts groups in July 1997

Source: Directories: Arts Facilities (National Arts Council 1996); National Arts Council (official correspondence 1998).

rently by different groups became a source of irritation to one another. The simple solution of air conditioning to filter out noise pollution was not possible because the old buildings did not have sufficient utility supply and risked electrical overload (*Report of the Committee on Performing Arts* 1988, 37–38). In spite of these problems, some housing was better than none, and yet there were not enough buildings to house groups looking for accommodation. Since 1988, many more buildings have been refurbished and the National Arts Council (NAC) now looks after the program. However, in spite of the large increase in the number of facilities, it was reported in 1995, when the economic situation was good, that even while sponsorship for the arts had gone up, sponsors were more willing to support concerts and plays than the arts housing program, which they saw to be less high-profile. This fact posed problems for arts groups that needed sponsorship for the customization costs of renovations to suit the interiors of buildings to their own needs (*The Straits Times* 4 Nov. 1995). Needless to say, with the Asian economic crisis in the late 1990s, housing the arts is not a top priority for many potential sponsors.

Pragmatism and Developmentalism: The Arts (f)or "Survival"

What does such a trajectory in the development of performing arts facilities reveal about ideological thinking in Singapore? For one thing, it clearly reflects the movement of the state's cultural policy since independence, from one of relative neglect to a discovery of the economic potential of the arts and renewed emphasis on its nation-building potential. The consequence is that greater state effort has been put into supporting and developing the arts, via, among other things, providing arts facilities—especially during the 1990s. Indeed, the development of landscapes and spaces for the performing arts in Singapore parallels closely the trajectory of the state's involvement in the arts. Specifically, from independence until the late 1970s (and some would argue into the mid-1980s), landscapes of the arts were conspicuous by their absence because the arts were accorded low priority, given the view that scarce national resources should be diverted to develop Singapore's fledgling economy, reflecting the ideology of pragmatism and survival. It was only in 1978 that some attention began to be focused on culture and the arts with the establishment of the Cultural Affairs Division of the former Ministry of Culture and the Singapore Cultural Foundation. The former organizes art exhibitions, concerts, literary activities, dramas, and dances to "stimulate a love for and appreciation of the arts among the young thereby helping to raise the cultural standards of the republic" (*Singapore Facts and Pictures* 1978). The latter's objectives were wide-ranging:

• To finance cultural projects and activities organized by the Ministry of Culture and subsequently, Ministry of Community Development, private individuals, or organizations;

• To assist in developing the talents and skills of Singaporean and arts personnel through the award of scholarships, training grants, or study loans, and in financing training courses;

• To assist in the establishment of new cultural organizations through grants or loans for the purchase of arts equipment;

• To assist in preserving and building up a body of Singaporean artist creations through the purchase of fine arts and documentation of Singaporean literature, art and craft, music, dance, and drama;

• To assist in increasing and upgrading the range of arts facilities in Singapore;

• To assist artists and arts organizations in undertaking cultural exchange programs; and

• To finance such other cultural projects and activities as may be approved by the Board of Trustees.

Despite the establishment of these bodies, as Koh (1989, 736) pointed out, in the mid-1980s the government still held the view that "material and social welfare, earning a living, and economic survival have always been Singapore's mostly immigrant community's primary concerns, and the arts have never been seen as a 'basic need.'"

Quoting in 1985 Prime Minister Lee Kuan Yew, who praised France's "high cultural achievements in the arts and literature" but went on to promptly proclaim that "Singaporeans can aspire to no such heights" because "we are a small young society struggling to achieve some measure of security in our basic needs" (*The Straits Times* 6 Apr. 1985), Koh illustrated the thinking that led to the insignificant support for the arts (including arts facilities) until then. This fact is further evidenced in the proclamation from

Minister for Culture S. Dhanabalan (1983, 16) that "we often talk of improving the quality of life in Singapore as distinct from improving the standard of living. We have concentrated, and rightly so, on improving the standard of living of Singaporeans. . . . Without better standards of living—more jobs, more housing, more education, better health—one cannot hope to improve the quality of life."What then prompted the increased attention to the arts beginning in the mid-1980s? In part, it was the economic recession then, which led to the establishment of a high-level Economic Committee, tasked to chart future directions for growth. The committee proposed diversification strategies, and among the host of measures it recommended was to harness the arts as a potential growth area as part of the "service sector," albeit a relatively minor part. Specifically, cultural and entertainment services were given brief attention as one of seventeen service categories that could be further developed.[2] Several recommendations were made as to the role of the cultural and entertainment services, defined to include the performing arts (popular music, symphony, drama), film production (for theaters and television), museums and art galleries, and entertainment centers and theme parks. These recommendations were made in recognition of the fact that such services were economic activities in their own right, that they enhanced Singapore as a tourism destination, improved the quality of life and helped people to be more productive, and contributed to a vibrant cultural and entertainment scene that would make Singapore more interesting for foreign professionals and skilled workers and could help attract them to work and develop their careers in Singapore (*Report of the Sub-Committee on the Service Sector* 1985, 211). The specific recommendations made by the sub-committee on the service sector were to develop arts festivals along the lines of the successful Hong Kong Arts Festival and the Festival of Asian Arts; to harness the potential of television in promoting variety shows, music and singing competitions, and popular drama; to develop a more extensive range of museum and art galleries with richer and more interesting selections that would be more attractive to foreigners; and to develop high-quality theme parks with local historical and

2. The others were classified under six divisions: transport and communications, business services, financial services, commerce, personal and social services, and others.

cultural flavor. These recommendations represented the first explicit, albeit somewhat ad hoc, acknowledgment of the economic potential of artistic and cultural activities, and although there were few clear signs that the recommendations were systematically taken up in the three to five years following the report, many of these ideas have since been given serious attention and been carefully developed. As Koh (1989, 720) articulated, because Singapore is a democratic socialist state that eclectically combines a socialist spirit with capitalist practices, it is no surprise that cultural values and development are "consistently, even insistently, linked to economic development and productivity."

However, in spite of the belated growth in attention to the arts and the progressive emergence of more performance venues and some initial arts housing facilities by the mid-1980s (see Tables 9.1, 9.2, 9.3, and 9.5), critics were not satisfied with what they saw to be "half-heartedness and halfway measures," described critically as "a disabling lack of conviction and lack of nerve" (Koh 1989, 737). As one example, the decision to demolish the National Theatre has been cited to demonstrate the instrumental rationality of the state. The decision was made in spite of professional opinion that the problems associated with its open-air nature could be solved by enclosing it, while structural concerns could be allayed by strengthening the roof structure. Indeed, it was the ideological weight of pragmatism that led the state to opt for demolition in the face of significant public sentiment and despite the fact that the theater had been built to be a "permanent memorial" (*National Theatre Trust Annual Report, 1961–62* 1962, 1). The appeal to historic value, fond memory, and personal attachment cut little ice in the face of one of the key deciding factors: the demolition of the theater would allow for the development of a proposed new expressway. By 1984, an announcement was made that the theater would be demolished, and about two years later it was totally leveled.

Another example of the pragmatism of the state was the construction of the Singapore Indoor Stadium. Koh's (1989, 737) analysis is instructive:

> Expectations were high when after the National Theatre Trust had been relocated to Kallang Theatre, plans were announced for another big auditorium in Kallang as "one way of bringing about the vision of Singapore,

1999." Singapore already has four open sports stadia, the largest being the National Stadium (with a seating capacity of 55,000); yet this new, covered, 14,000-seat facility was to be used primarily as a stadium for sports at national and international levels. Announcing the plan, the Minister of State (Community Development) said, almost as an afterthought: "It could also be used for musicals, circuses, cultural shows, and other family-type entertainment." (Wong Kan Seng, speech at Kuo Chuan Community Centre, 24 Aug. 1985)

Like the National Theatre before it, and like the multipurpose halls to be found everywhere in schools, community centers, and tertiary institutions built merely on cost-effective grounds, this new venue was built pragmatically to serve every activity—but to serve none particularly well.

Even as practitioners of the performing arts strained to find their own solutions, in 1988 the arts received a further government boost when an Advisory Council on Culture and the Arts (ACCA) was appointed to review and chart out a new direction for Singapore's arts development. Two of the most significant recommendations for institutional support that have been implemented are the formation of the NAC in 1991 and the National Heritage Board in 1993.[3] The former, in particular, has since played a significant role in promoting the performing arts in Singapore. A third crucial recommendation, and one which has also been taken up, is the establishment of the Esplanade-Theatres on the Bay. Among the multiple symbolic meanings that may be read into this complex, one insistent reading must be rooted in the economic role it is expected to play in generating revenue. In

3. According to its mission statement, the NAC's functions are to support and promote the practice of the arts by nurturing local artistic and creative talent; to actively promote Singaporean arts and artists both in Singapore and abroad; to provide and manage a number of different performance- and exhibition-related facilities for the arts, and to constantly strive to attract to Singapore a wide range of international artistic talent and events (http://www.nac.gov.sg). The NAC falls under the purview of the Ministry of Information and the Arts.

The National Heritage Board seeks to "explore and present the culture and heritage of Singapore through the collection, preservation, interpretation and display of objects and records so as to promote a better understanding of our roots and instill a sense of national identity in Singaporeans" (http://www.nhb.gov.sg).

many ways, the Esplanade represents the state's latest and, to date, most ambitious and expensive venture into the production of landscapes for the arts, and it represents what Singapore hopes to achieve: the vision of a global city, acting as a hub not only for banking, finance, manufacturing, and commerce but also for the arts—thus helping to "create new ideas, opportunities and wealth" (George Yeo, minister for information and the arts, quoted in *Singapore: Global City for the Arts* 1995, 5).

To elaborate, evidence of the state's appropriation of the arts for economic gain may be found in the pronouncements that were emanating from no less than Minister for Information and the Arts George Yeo, as well as from other government members of Parliament and leaders of government bodies. Yeo was most active among ministers in publicly suggesting that, "to be competitive in the next phase of our national development, we need to promote the arts" (Yeo 1991, 56) and that, while Singapore had been "an international market for rubber, for spices, for oil, for Asian Currency Units, for gold futures, and for many other things," it also hoped to be "an international market for the arts" (Yeo 1993, 66). He explained this expectation:

> We should see the arts not as luxury or mere consumption but as investment in people and the environment. We need a strong development of the arts to help make Singapore one of the major hub cities of the world. . . . We also need the arts to help us produce goods and services which are competitive in the world market. We need an artistic culture . . . we also need taste. With taste, we will be able to produce goods and services of far greater value. (Yeo 1991, 54)

Some of these views were echoed by government Member of Parliament Heng Chiang Meng, who used economic arguments to ask for better financial support of cultural activities. He suggested that "such funding can be viewed as supporting an infant industry. Looking at the arts industry in London and New York, I see no reason why Singapore cannot be a major arts centre if we put our minds to it . . . all the necessary ingredients for the promotion of arts as an exportable industry are here" (*Parliamentary Debates* 21 Mar. 1991). Heng cited for support the view that a wide range of industrial products needed not only to be functional and durable, but that increasingly, there was demand that they were also well designed and aesthetically pleasing. Hence an artistic base was crucial for industrial progress. Executive director of the NAC, Foo Meng Liang, also expressed economic reasons for arts promotion, citing figures to show how the arts in the United Kingdom provided one-half million jobs and accounted for 27 percent of the earnings from tourism in 1987, and how the arts created about 110,000 jobs in the New York-New Jersey area and generated an annual turnover of US$9.8 billion (*Art versus Art* 1995, 29). The chairman of the NAC, Liu Thai Ker, also articulated the view that there was nothing wrong in the arts being "aligned with economic impetuses." He argued that, while the arts were traditionally associated with the need to be subsidized, the government now recognized that the economic gains were potentially far greater than the expenditure, which made government spending on the arts justifiable. His view was that investment in the arts was the act of a "responsible government" (personal interview, 12 May 1997).

The 1990s have therefore seen more rigorous pursuance of policies and strategies to harness the economic potential of the arts. All three types of cultural economic policies that Frith (1991) identified are evident: an industrial cultural policy (focused on electronic goods and the media for the purveyance of arts and culture), a cultural tourism policy (where consumers are brought in as imports), and an urban cosmetics policy to help make Singapore look attractive to tourists and visitors who might end up staying, bringing in investments with them (Kong 2000c). The huge amount of state funding—S$1 billion (Brady 1995)—that is being injected into the development of new and the upgrading of old cultural facilities is evidence of the state's commitment to making Singapore a regional hub, if not global, for the arts. In particular, the Esplanade, funded to the tune of S$667 million, is expected to bring in monetary returns. As its former Executive Director Robert Iau articulated, the Esplanade was designed to comprise sufficient facilities to cater to the needs of the "240 million people in the region"—not just the 3 million people in Singapore (personal interview, 20 May 1997)—evidence of the strong cultural tourism policy undergirding the decision to construct it.

The pragmatism and developmentalism that form the foundation of

Arts (f)or Survival   181

9.1. The Esplanade.

the state's support for the arts in the 1990s, encapsulated in the vision to develop a global city for the arts and symbolized in the commitment to build the Esplanade and make it work, have received less than enthusiastic response from the artistic community in Singapore. Practitioners are critical of the state's interpretation of Singapore as a regional center for the arts. This mistrust is because they read into the state's strategy purely economic intents:

I think it's quite clear that what the government means by developing the arts is for a very economic kind of reason. Big touring groups that come in, big musicals, pop concerts. Michael Jackson is the arts to them. And that's the truth, this newfound interest in the arts and the SAC, a lot of it is economic . . . I know a lot of people will be dazzled. You just see all this analysis of how much money the Michael Jackson concert alone generated in the economy. And you get these cash registers ringing in everybody's mind. (Simon, playwright, director, and actor)[4]

However, providing the "hardware" (infrastructure and facilities) without concomitant attention to the "software" (creative development) is deemed regressive for the development of local or indigenous arts, and Tim (artistic director, arts company) argues that the only outcome will be that

With all the sophisticated and well-developed infrastructure, Singapore will be a good magnet for tourists, travellers, convention goers and other people who are involved in international conferences to stop over and savour international culture in Singapore but there will be little place for local communities to develop their own art forms. . . . Exhibitions like the Guggenheim will be quite happy to come to Singapore. Cats and Les Miserables will be quite happy to show in Singapore, given all the incentives and help. And I think given the kind of commercial development we have in film, we'll have some of the most up-to-date Hollywood movies or movies from all over the world being shown in Singapore. So we will be a kind of place where top-rate acts from all over the world will be available at all times. . . . It's also the same for the visual arts, in terms of art fairs like Tresors and big auctions like Sotheby's and Christie's. There will be this global flavour that takes place, but there will not be anything indigenous worth talking about. This is a serious problem.

Tim goes on to argue that this situation would make Singapore "a kind of emporium for the arts . . . another retail space in Singapore."

Why do practitioners hold this negative view of state initiatives, which ostensibly will serve the arts well? As David (playwright) articulates, it is

4. All practitioners have been given pseudonyms unless their views already appear in published form.

because, with such heavy financial investment in the Esplanade, there is a need to "go for surefire successes" that will cover the cost of renting the spaces and eventually recovering the investment. He, along with other practitioners like Simon and Tim, all recognize that few local groups can afford to use the spaces. Certainly, as Edwin (playwright) articulates, "profit-making theatre" will be favored above "exploratory, indigenous forms," with the result that "people who are still exploring new forms feel the pressure to have to abandon more of those projects and go for more audience determined plays so that they can economically justify [their work], so that they can feel that there is an audience to their theatre."

Apart from the inability to compete on financial grounds, artistically, local groups are still experimenting and finding a distinctively Singapore idiom, and are of the opinion that they will not yet be able to draw the crowds in the same way that foreign acts will. As architect and critic Tay Kheng Soon put it, "What is the [Esplanade]? It's primarily a number of big concert halls to host, under very salubrious conditions, the top performing groups from the developed world as they cycle through Asia. What will that do in terms of taste for Singapore experimental art? Zero! Because the Singaporean who has seen these tremendous shows will look down upon local productions" (*Commentary* 1993, 66). For that reason, Simon is of the opinion that the Esplanade is "a huge mistake" because it signals the decision to "push back the schedule for developing the small performing spaces in favour of bringing forward the large facilities."

Practitioners also held an unequivocal view about the need for local artistic development. As Tim highlighted, no regional or global hub for the arts "whether it was London or Paris in the past, whether it's New York today or Tokyo, can ever hope to achieve that kind of status without having at least as strong a basis of indigenous works as it does for international platforms." Across the different art forms, practitioners called for the opportunity to develop "something unique to us" (Henry, film organizer and music critic) or "real local arts . . . from the locals and related to local things . . . something that people are familiar with and can understand" (Irene, dancer). Playwright and director Kuo Pao Kun asked pointedly, "Can we have a Singapore Arts Centre by just bringing all the arts of the world to Singapore without our own education, without our own creativity?" (*Art versus Art* 1995, 145) In effect, such practitioners subscribe to a view of the arts as "rooted in an understanding of local cultural resources" (Bianchini 1993b, 212). As Arun Mahizhnan (*Art versus Art* 1995, 34) points out, articulating the views of many practitioners, economic returns should not be the fundamental reason for supporting the arts. They should be the by-product. However, the developmentalist ideology, which emphasizes the primacy of economic growth and development, has placed the needs and growth of local artists below the presence of large-scale, often imported, cultural industries that will turn the wheels of economy.

Minister George Yeo is clearly unpersuaded by the practitioners' arguments, and has spoken unequivocally about the state's continued intention to provide opportunities for foreign acts to perform in Singapore and, indeed, to facilitate such opportunities: "Nothing is more inimical to the development of the arts than a false nationalism which tries to protect a market under the guise of safeguarding some misconceived national essence. We offer Singapore as a venue and as a stage for artists and those who enjoy the Arts from all over the world" (Yeo 1992, 114). From this perspective, he is committed to keeping the doors open to "foreign talent," as in "every other aspect of our national life," because "if the arts in Singapore are only by Singaporeans for Singaporeans, we will get nowhere for we are too small . . . Singapore is Singapore only because our national spirit is a cosmopolitan one" (Yeo 1994, 36). Indeed, Yeo has turned the argument on its head. While local artistic practitioners argue that supporting local artistic development contributes to "nation-building," he argues that it becomes a form of "protectionism" that is a "false nationalism." Using another tack, the state has also countered that it has not neglected the development of local arts, pointing out that it channels significant funding to local groups and offers old buildings to house them in the Arts Housing Scheme (Brady 1995). However, scrutiny of the budget makes a poignant point: while S$1.65 million was channeled (in 1996) to the provision of housing for forty-one local arts groups, two art institutions, and twenty-six individual artists, S$667 million is expended on the construction of the Esplanade (*National Arts Council Annual Report* 1996).

Given the clear signals from the state, practitioners and critics have sought to negotiate their preferred sociocultural agendas within the constraints of the state's economic agenda in a number of ways. First, and probably the most effective strategy, is the deliberate but difficult process of developing "alternative arts spaces" in Singapore. Chief among these is the Substation, an arts center established in 1990, which its artistic director, T. Sasitharan, defines as serving to

• Nurture and develop promising young Singapore artists;

• Encourage Singapore artists to be innovative and bold in thought and work;

• Facilitate arts appreciation among as wide an audience as possible;

• Promote interaction among artists and art lovers of different national, cultural, and linguistic backgrounds;

• Raise the level of critical and intellectual discourse on arts and foster research, study, and rigor in artistic practice; and

• Be a center for an emerging Southeast Asian aesthetic, incorporating the rich visual, musical, performance, and literary traditions of the region. The Substation houses a 120-seat theaterette, an art gallery, a dance studio, two multipurpose rooms, a garden courtyard for performances and other arts events, an art shop, and a box office, and has become a central place for young local artists, providing a space for rehearsals, installations, workshops, and performances, offering a "home to cultivate and foster imaginations, *particularly those that find other spaces inhospitable*" (Sasitharan n.d., emphasis added). The opportunities it affords new artists and new styles has rendered the Substation "an alternative space for the arts" by default, in Sasitharan's view:

> In Singapore, so much of the established spaces and companies happen to be working with what is considered very mainstream or middle-of-the-road work, so any company which tends to do anything a little off-centre is considered alternative. And that is the position of the Substation. . . . When we do an experimental theatre presentation, or when we do something about experimental music or contemporary music, contemporary visual arts, which no one else happens to be doing, that is what we become identified with.

The Substation provided one of the first Black Boxes in Singapore, in contrast to the prosceniums of large theaters such as the NAC-run Victoria Theatre. This addition "empowered new actors and new groups and incorporated them even though they had no voice training and no technology" and therefore "allowed more people access into theatre" (Edwin). Simon articulates the view that the Substation and other alternative spaces have been important for the development of Singapore arts; they are "sanctuaries of experimentation where one can learn from failure" because the pressure to fill audience spaces is not as great and "a culture of development" is evident. In other words, the imperatives of economic gain driven by ideologies of developmentalism are not as apparent in this "alternative" space. This fact is particularly important, in Simon's view, because the Singaporean "has this intense fear of failing, of being deemed a flop. That is sort of very troublesome and counter-productive when it comes to the arts, in particular, theatre, when you realise that the moment you dare not fail, any sort of development is impossible because you are constantly going in this circumscribed circle rather than expanding the circle."

A second strategy of negotiation that practitioners have adopted is to work within the parameters set up by the state. This technique has primarily taken the form of a call for space within the Esplanade, and even a more open call for the Esplanade to support local groups. Simon expresses this idea most pointedly when he argues that the Esplanade should be a "dedicated space for performing arts in Singapore by Singaporean artists." He nevertheless acknowledges the need to bring in foreign performances so that there could be "synergy, opportunities for linkages and for learning," and so suggested that, if the Esplanade could not be a space for Singaporean artists alone, it could at least have a resident local group. Otherwise, he argued, "it cannot be the Singapore Arts Centre."

Finally, critics and practitioners seek their own ideological spaces by (re)interpreting the state's cultural policy, focusing particularly on the Esplanade as the site of (re)interpretation. The most strident, perhaps, among those leading the ideological charge is writer and critic Janadas Devan, who takes the view that the state is interested in developing the Esplanade only as a symbol of its "power and glory." He argues that, if the needs of the practitioners are for small drama centers, small performance stages in community centers in various parts of the island and arts housing facilities, for example, the fact that the state was spending so much money on the one location suggests that the Esplanade was really intended to serve a purpose other than local cultural development (*Art versus Art* 1995, 63). Janadas interprets the situation as an attempt to embody power and glory, citing other examples around the world—such as the Taj Mahal and Versailles—of the construction of monuments for the same ends, be it for king, emperor, or state (*Art versus Art* 1995, 54). He argues that "it is precisely because art has always been about power that we are going to build for ourselves an Arts Centre. It is not an accident that the state's involvement in the arts has taken the form of a commitment to build a monument to art" (*Art versus Art* 1995, 63). Without the wherewithal to reverse or forestall the direction of cultural policy, Janadas resorts to ideological criticism of the state, claiming that as a monument, the Esplanade will be damning for the development of the arts precisely because it is a monument, because "by definition, monuments commemorate the dead. There is a kind of reciprocal structure: when you go before a monument you not only commemorate the dead, you are struck dumb. This is the general effect of government intervention in the arts" (*Art versus Art* 1995, 63). Artistic space in Singapore is thus literally and metaphorically debated and negotiated between the state (with its cultural economic policy and driven by its ideology of pragmatism and developmentalism) and practitioners (with their socially and culturally driven agendas).

"Asian" Roots: "Nation"-building Through the Arts

One of the key ideological tropes that has pervaded state discourse and policy is that of the role of the arts in Singapore in contributing to "nation"-building, not least through the need to recall the "Asian" roots of Singapore arts. As illustrated in detail elsewhere (Kong 2000c), the lack of attention to the arts in the 1960s and 1970s was only punctured by the reminder that artistic and cultural activities should counter the negative influences associated with "yellow culture" of the "decadent West" and remind Singaporeans instead of Asian traditions and roots. This goal is evident, for instance, in the parliamentary arguments of government MP Tay Boon Too, who championed the view that "the various orchestras, dance troupes and choirs in the National Theatre should be regarded as a cultural army representative of Singapore" (*Parliamentary Debates* 22 Mar. 1971) and the assertions of the parliamentary secretary to the minister for culture, Inche Sha'ari Tadin, that "the arts can play a vital role in nation-building through the inculcation of correct values," especially because, "more than ever," Singapore was faced with "the threats from the aggressive culture of the West" (*Singapore Government Press Release* 30 Nov. 1974). By the mid- to late 1970s, this took active form with the government encouraging the composition of songs by Singaporeans to help "develop a sense of national identity and instill a sense of patriotism in our young people" (*Parliamentary Debates* 16 Mar. 1977). Engagement in the arts, it was hoped, would also "redeem us from the ill-effects of a materialistic, money-oriented existence" (Inche Sha'ari Tadin, *Singapore Government Press Release* 30 Nov. 1974)—especially important given the emphasis on economic development in the newly independent state. As part of this drive, space for the arts was created out of parks in the busy central business district, even if performance venues were scarce. Significant, for example, was the attempt to bring music to the ordinary person, with the police, Singapore Armoured Regiment, navy, and People's Association Bands playing at Empress Place and Raffles Square (*The Straits Times* 7 Sept. 1979).

At the same time that "healthy" artistic and cultural pursuits were deemed to have a role in "nation-building," throughout the 1960s and 1970s, as intimated earlier, the government also held the view that cultural products, particularly popular cultural products from the West, constituted "unhealthy" "yellow" culture that "destroy[ed] [young people's] sense of value, and corrode[d] their willingness to pay attention to serious thought" (Lee 1967). As Inche Sha'ari Tadin argued,

> It is important to have a rich, established cultural tradition particularly at this time of Singapore's development. This is because there is the danger of our Republic being inundated by undesirable influences from the outside world. Already many young people are mindlessly aping foreign mannerism. They think that the process of modernisation simply means drug-taking, a-go-go dancing and pornography. Once our youths have adequate cultural anchorage, they will be less prone to these modern excesses (*Singapore Government Press Release* 26 Apr. 1973).

The values and lifestyles that were associated with the "decadent West" included the keeping of long hair, hippism, and drugs, and it was believed that these values were purveyed through cultural products such as rock music, foreign films, and television programs. Night spots such as night clubs with live bands and discos were closed down and bans and censorship were introduced and tightened in a bid to control the insidious dangers. The definition of "artistic" pursuits was thus closely policed, as were the spaces in which they took place.

The ideologically hegemonic attempts to root Singaporeans and Singapore arts in Asian culture are not confined to the 1960s and 1970s. As we illustrated in chapter 3, the call on "Asian" values has permeated the decades since independence and has found renewed vigor in the 1990s. The design and construction of the Esplanade provides abundant grist for the analytical mill in this respect. Prime Minister Goh Chok Tong, for example, articulated the view that the Esplanade, together with the various museums being developed, should "evoke in Singaporeans an appreciation and understanding of the old civilisations they all belonged to, and the part of the world they were in." In addition, he argued that, "as Singapore developed and became more open to the external cultures and influences, and as Singaporeans traveled and absorbed different values, they should be even more aware of their ancient roots." Heritage and culture, he said, "held a people together, made them a distinct society and gave them moral strength" (*Sunday Times* 21 Jan. 1996). This belief is reinforced unequivocally in the vision statement of the Esplanade Company Limited, expressed in an early corporate brochure, in which it was proclaimed that the Esplanade would be "among the first of a generation of new arts centres in Asia ushering the Asian renaissance." This commitment to Asia is translated into the design process and architectural form: seven Asian arts experts were invited to advise the design team (*The Straits Times* 23 July 1994), and the final outcome was said to be "inspired by Asian architecture," with the auditoria "encased in a translucent cladding which will glow as a cluster of lanterns at night," reflecting the "tranquil living spaces of Southeast Asian architecture" (Corporate brochure).

The claims to "Asianness," however, were refuted vehemently by the general public and by architects in particular. The British-Singapore team Michael Wilford and partners and DP Architects won the contract to design the center based on "its flexibility, creativity and good working relationship with other firms involved in the project." The selection process was, however, followed by "a flurry of passionate exchanges in the press . . . on issues of open competitions, prequalification, selection criteria, home-grown talent, risk-taking, Asian identity and the proposed centre's suitability for Asian art forms" (*The Straits Times* 27 July 1994). One of the strongest critics was architect Tay Kheng Soon, who argued that the Esplanade represented a quest for a new Asian identity but that its potential had been lost. His lengthy exposition of the important symbolism of the Esplanade bears repeating here:

> The project focuses on the dilemma of being Asian and Modern at the same time . . . What it takes culturally to achieve a modern Asian identity in the context of a closely networked globalised world is . . . the essence of the challenge of today, and the building of the [Esplanade] is the symbol of this. . . . The concept and the design of the [Esplanade] represents, as I see it, an important step in the quest for a new Asian identity for us. The dilemma is made all the more stark when, with available money, it is easier to obey the dictates of the international arts circuit than to persist in clarifying our history, nurturing fresh sensibilities and inspiring latent fires of creativity. It is easier with money to buy a show, employ an architect, hire consultants. It is more difficult to use money and resources to build cultural confidence. The building of the Esplanade [Singapore Arts Centre] represents all those issues to me. Dramatist Kuo Pao Kun's call a year ago when he said "this art centre should not be the last of the great western arts centre, but be the first of a series of new Asian ones" drove the point home. (*The Straits Times* 30 July 1994)

In actual design terms, he argued that the hall structures were dominant, a fact which symbolized

> an implicit acceptance of the dominance of western arts in the consciousness. That the huge structures were allowed to overshadow actually and symbolically the diminutive Asian arts performances spaces and received no effective correction in the design is demonstrative of either a timidity and/or an insufficient consciousness of the importance of this as a cultural issue. I fear that the historic moment that this project presents to Singapore to interject at this juncture of Asia's new age is drifting away.

He also argued that the design reflected the reality of the arts scene in Singapore, which is that "the western blockbuster shows will, willy-nilly, dominate the arts scene" (*The Straits Times* 30 July 1994). Certainly, he recognized that Asian performances were not excluded from the "great halls," but he argued nevertheless that "the few occasions when Asian arts will perform in these halls will not alter the perception of the disproportionate relationship of the arts as represented in the design concept . . . and visible every day on the Esplanade by the Bay" (*The Straits Times* 30 July 1994).

Like him, Richard Ho, another architect in private practice, argued that the design had no precedence in Asian architecture (*Business Times* 10–11 Sept. 1994). Even non-Singaporeans joined in the debate, with an Italian visitor writing to say that "your populace may be shortchanged by a design that says nothing about your country being a microcosm of the rich Asian cultural heritage. . . . the proposed design of your Arts Centre ignores totally the rich architectural traditions of Asia" (*Business Times* 6–7 Aug. 1994).

While the Esplanade represented for some the opportunity to capture Asia in microcosm and symbolize an "Asian age," others argued that it was the moment to create a distinctively *Singaporean* symbol that would be distinguished even from other Asian forms. A member of the public expressed this well, arguing that the design of the Esplanade was so lacking in distinctiveness that it could well be on the banks of Tokyo Bay, "the Wayang pavilion re-labelled as a Kabuki pavilion and the Satay club as an Udon club and presented as the Tokyo Arts Centre." How, then, could it manifest a "nation's psyche" and "be on display for the rest of the world to scrutinise" (*The Straits Times* 12 Aug. 1994)? Indeed, how could it overtake the Merlion as Singapore's national symbol, in the same way that some felt the Sydney Opera House had superseded the kangaroo as a symbol of Australia (*The Straits Times* 1 Aug. 1994)?

The Arts as Embodiment of Multiculturalism

Among those members of the public who were critical of the Esplanade because of its lack of Singaporean distinctiveness, there were some who argued that the four main cultures in Singapore should have been represented in some way in the actual shape of the buildings (*The Straits Times* 1 Aug. 1994). Although there were no specific suggestions on what form this could take, the call reflected the way in which multiracialism and multiculturalism have been imbibed by Singaporeans. This commitment to the 4Ms ideology is also reflected in the Substation's express mission, translated into everyday practice. In its marketing brochure, the Substation hails diversity as one of its key characteristics, interpreting diversity to mean an undertaking to develop that which is "multi-disciplinary, multi-media, multicultural and multi-lingual" (*A Home for the Arts* 1996). In practice, the Substation encourages and promotes artistic endeavors involving various races, languages, and cultural styles. Music Space, for example, a series of concerts featuring the original works of Singaporean composers to serve as a regular platform for aspiring composers, has featured, in one session, as diverse forms as a piano solo in Western tradition, a popular song sung by Malays accompanied by the Hokkien flute, and "xinyao."[5] As artist and poet Tan Swie Hian highlighted, "It is timely. The Chinese, Indians and Malays in the arts just don't mix. Now, the Substation will break these barriers. . . . The Substation will be a place where artists of the different races can discover each other," thus facilitating a "cross-pollination of ideas" (*The Straits Times* 24 Feb. 1990).

While practitioners seek a multiculturalism that entails cross-cultural fertilization of ideas and forms, the state interprets support for multiculturalism in different ways. First, in providing a larger number of performance venues, it argues that different cultures may take advantage of available space to meet their cultural needs. Thus, the Esplanade, for example, is said to "help meet the cultural needs of different segments of Singapore society—Chinese, Malay, Indian or Eurasian, Eastern or Western, young or old" (*The Straits Times* 22 July 1994). This ostensible even-handedness re-

---

5. *Xinyao* is a shorthand Mandarin term for "*xin jia po nian qing ren chuang zuo de ge yao*" ("the songs composed by Singapore youths"), an extraction of the first and last words of the longer term. Their compositions generally consist of simple melody lines using basic chords and, particularly in the early stages of *xinyao* development, it would be common to find that "two guitars at most provided the rhythm" (*The Straits Times* 22 Dec. 1985). Occasionally, there would be some supplementary piano, flute, or violin accompaniment. The Mandarin lyrics usually focus on feelings of youth and growing up.

mains just that—an apparent equality of treatment that does not necessarily translate into an actual equality of opportunity. This situation is because groups engaging in different cultural and linguistic media have varying levels of sponsorship and audience support, and therefore varying degrees of likelihood to have access to certain spaces. For example, given the predominance of English-language theater performances over performances in other languages (*Sunday Times* 20 Dec. 1998), certainly in terms of audience base, it would be far more likely for English-language theater to hold commercially viable performances in larger halls for longer periods. Given the seating capacity of the Esplanade auditoria, for example, it would be difficult for some cultural groups to stage performances there, thus refuting the argument of equal treatment translating into equal opportunity.

A similar argument may be applied to the NAC's Arts Housing Scheme, which uses as its criteria for selection a good track record, managerial strength, artistic standard, level of activity, and growth potential. Herein lies evidence of the ideological interweaving of multiracialism and meritocracy that was discussed in chapter 3. Because the ideology of multiracialism and the related 3Ms lead to the suspension of race, language, culture, and religion as the basis of resource distribution, access to such resources can only be gained through merit, defined in terms of achievement. The resources at stake here for the arts groups are subsidies and access to housing facilities, making concrete the ideology of meritocracy, borne on the chariots of multiculturalism.

Even as multiculturalism and the related ideology of meritocracy are intended to lend support to art forms and groups that have a good track record, defined not least in terms of strength of audience base, it ironically has led to the demise of at least one particular form of street theater, Chinese (dialect) opera. Part of the policy and practice that derived from the 4Ms ideology in Singapore, as indicated in chapter 2, was the reduction of Singapore's multifarious population into the "clear-cut" "CMIO" categories, with Mandarin being encouraged over the use of other Chinese dialects as one measure of reducing the complexity of the Chinese population. Together with the onset of modernist living associated with the introduction of Housing and Development Board (HDB) estates (chapter 6), former patterns of life and cultural associations had to be abandoned or modified while new ones were created. Certainly, the racial enclaves of old and the ways of life and traditional arts associated with them were eroded—among them Chinese puppet theater and Chinese opera performed in dialect as popular street *"wayang."* As Koh (1989, 721) pointed out, they became part of a "dying breed" until enthusiastic amateur groups sought to revive them through talks and demonstrations in schools and community centers as well as a Hong Lim Park Chinese Opera Series, which sought to reach the younger, English-educated audience. A certain degree of success was achieved in the eight-year history of the series, conducted in the open air in Chinatown to replicate the conditions of the old street *wayang.* There were increasing audience numbers. In 1986, however, the series was discontinued, ironically because the ideology of multiculturalism brought it indoors to merge with the multicultural Traditional Theatre Festival held that year, which was touted as bringing the benefit of "the end of *wayang,* the birth of an art" (Sng 1986). Multiculturalism as ideology and practice therefore did not offer as much support and opportunity for development of the arts as state rhetoric declared and perhaps intended.

The Arts and Community-building in Singapore

As with any "nation-building" effort, considerable attention has been paid to the development of a community—real and imagined—in which constituents feel a sense of belonging and attachment. The arts have been appropriated in various ways to play a role in this community-building, as we will illustrate using three examples: the National Theatre, the Esplanade, and the use of public spaces for artistic activity.

The manifest role of the National Theatre in "nation-building" was unabashedly declared in 1959, when Minister for Culture S. Rajaratnam announced the decision to build "a permanent memorial to mark the attainment of self-government" and a symbol to affirm the people's faith in their ability to create a Malayan "nation" and culture (*The Straits Times* 8 Jan. 1984). Unlike the case with the Esplanade, five practicing architects in Singapore were invited in 1960 to submit designs for the National Theatre. The winning proposal was submitted by Alfred Wong and was designed with the national flag in mind, with its five red-brick and white diamond-shaped lofty spires representing the five stars and symbolizing a dynamic "nation" aspiring for greater heights, and a fountain in the front of the courtyard of the theater to echo the crescent moon. With such flagrant expression of "nation-building" intent, it is of little surprise that this "cathedral to nationalistic ideals" (*The Straits Times* 13 Jan. 1984) sought to become a focal point in community-building. The chief effort in this direction was the "dollar-a-brick" drive, which saw donations from Singaporeans of all walks of life contributing to the construction of the theater. Rajaratnam made capital of this fact, proclaiming that "the completion of the theatre was an example of the co-operation of a variety of people" and provided "a good example of how the success of any effort depend[ed] ultimately on the cooperation and dedication of people from all walks of life" (*The Straits Times* 16 May 1964). This "community" effort, which made possible the National Theatre, also known as the "People's Theatre," was replicated in 1967 when plans for conversion of sections of the building for the use of its newly formed National Theatre Club relied on appeals to the public for donations (*The Straits Times* 10 June 1967). Similarly, air conditioning of the dressing, reception, and conference rooms depended on community contributions (*The Straits Times* 1 Mar. 1967). In another vein, the National Theatre Club, once set up, held lectures, demonstrations, and regular cultural programs for its members at a deliberately low subscription fee so that "as many of the poorer section of the population can join" (*The Straits Times* 10 June 1967), indicative of the effort to reach out to the "community" that supported it.

Like the National Theatre, the Esplanade has similarly been upheld as a symbol of community ownership and participation. The corporate brochure proclaims the fact that "Singaporeans from all sectors of society" had helped to develop it. Indeed, as part of the design process, various sectors of the community were consulted: the Users Advisory Group, which comprised fifty-eight performers and artists; the Design and Aesthetics Advisory Group, made up of nine Singaporean architects and architecture lecturers; and the Commercial Advisory Group, whose six members are property developers and businessmen who advise on the optimal level of commercial activity required to keep the arts center a hub of activity (*The Straits Times* 22, 23 July 1994). In addition, a special lottery was organized to raise funds needed to build the center, and that too has been heralded as symbolic of Singaporean ownership. As Minister for Information and the Arts George Yeo said, his hope was that "Singaporeans would feel a collective sense of ownership and participation in building the centre and develop an enduring emotional attachment for it" (*The Straits Times* 22 July 1994), a view similarly expressed by then President Ong Teng Cheong (*The Straits Times* 22 July 1994). Yet again, not all Singaporeans agreed that the community had been involved, arguing that "a building as significant and as close to the psyche of Singapore should have more input by ordinary people" (*The Straits Times* 12 Aug. 1994).

In more general terms, the state's cultural agencies also have sought to build "community" through engaging all sectors of the community in artistic pursuits, thus breaking down barriers between different groups and correcting any sense that the arts might be only for the elites. This effort has been pursued rigorously through the NAC's outreach program, which has used a spatial strategy to bring arts to the masses. Specifically, it has organized a "Concert in the Park" series, with concerts in parks located in housing estate heartlands, such as Bishan, East Coast, and Pasir Ris; central city parks such as Orchard MRT Park, Fort Canning, and Bras Basah; and in the Botanic Gardens. In conjunction with the National Parks Board, it also jointly organized the Asian Performing Arts Festival at the Fort Canning Park (*The Straits Times* 26 Apr. 1997). The NAC has worked with shopping-center management and community centers in housing estates to bring the arts to easily accessible and highly frequented places for the population. Public libraries and commercial buildings have also been approached for the possibility of locating facilities for the arts in these places (*The Straits Times* 10 Oct. 1997). In these efforts, the state finds support from arts groups, which agree ideologically and practically, evident in similar outreach programs by drama groups such as The Necessary Stage and the Substation.

The Arts as Manifestation of a Modernist City and Gracious Society

In addition to the various ideological uses to which landscapes of the arts have been put as outlined above, they have also been pressed into service as a showcase to Singaporeans and the rest of the world that the city-state is a modernist city and a "gracious society." In chapter 3, we outlined the government's plans to develop a "world-class city" as encapsulated in the document *Living the Next Lap*, intended to guide the city's development and covering all the key areas of life from housing and education to leisure and defense. The vision was translated into a planning blueprint in the form of the Revised Concept Plan, which explicitly acknowledged and addressed the need to retain a quality foreign workforce and the need to give increasing consideration to the preferences of professional and skilled workers, be it in housing, leisure, or other facilities. Part of these perceived preferences were for a city that was throbbing with intellectual and cultural life and characterized by vibrance. One of the strategies has therefore been to enhance the level and quality of artistic and cultural activities in Singapore. It is with this goal that the various forms of support for the arts have been implemented. Whether it is the arts housing scheme or the construction of the Esplanade, or other support schemes such as the "semi-residential status in theatre scheme" (which grants concessionary rental rates of performing venues to groups in the scheme), the intention is to contribute to the development of a culturally vibrant society that is necessary if Singapore is to become a "world-class city." This effort is, of course, provision of the "hardware," which artists have argued is, at best, necessary though insufficient and, at worst (in the case of the Esplanade) detrimental to the development of local arts.

At the same time that the discourse and rhetoric, as well as the policy and practice, of developing a "world-class city" has proceeded, the state has also developed, particularly from the mid-1990s, a public rhetoric that emphasizes the development of a "gracious society," an apparent shift from the earlier emphasis on economic development, per se. For example, in a speech addressing youth leaders in 1996, Prime Minister Goh Chok Tong outlined his vision for Singapore's sociocultural development whereby the country is characterized by a civic-conscious and gracious people, and an intellectual, cultivated, compassionate, and caring society. It is one in which universities will be throbbing with ideas and where there is a thriving arts scene. As we illustrated in chapter 3, there is no serious suggestion that economic growth should be halted, but the idea that the "non-tangible aspects of life" need greater priority has indeed gained wider currency, as expressed in the prime minister's view that there is more to being a successful country than having lots of money. Rather, a successful country is one in which its people are able to appreciate the finer things in life and are concerned for one another and for public property (*The Straits Times* 22 Apr. 1996). One measure of a more gracious and cultivated people, he suggested, was the ability to enjoy good music. He used such enjoyment as a metaphor for the finer things in life, which reflected his larger statement that the arts were important to Singapore because they made for a more thinking, gracious, and sophisticated society. This view is reflected in his statement that it was now time for Singaporeans' senses to be "touched and stimulated by aesthetics and creative works" (*Sunday Times* 21 Jan. 1996) after the initial years of preoccupation with economic development. It is against this ideological construction of the "nation" that efforts to develop the arts, reflected in the development of arts facilities and the appropriation of public spaces for the arts, must be understood.

While there is little disagreement with the vision, some have cautioned against the inculcation of a superficial appreciation of the arts without a concomitant instillation of values. Then Minister of Information and the Arts George Yeo, for example, foregrounded the need to imbue the right values in young children as a key to developing a keener appreciation of culture and heritage and a more gracious society. Only then would graciousness and a true artistic sense emerge from within. As he so pointedly articulated, "If we are gracious, if we excite interest in the arts purely for economic reasons, if we smile in order to sell a few more trinkets to visiting tourists, then we have not succeeded and that is not really what we want. We want whatever graciousness we have, whatever artistic sense we have, to emanate from within. Otherwise it is all superficial" (*The Straits Times* 16 Mar. 1996). Indeed, the minister touches on an issue that has drawn criticism from Singaporeans. As one commentator argued,

> In reality, does knowing the difference between Bach and Beethoven, or having the skills to tickle both the ivories and the erhu,[6] make one the em-

6. A Chinese musical instrument.

bodiment of consideration, tact and humility—in short, the qualities which add up to graciousness? Even taking the view that the more cultured one becomes, the better behaved one will be—at least in public—is it not more difficult to coat the population with this veneer of civility, than to use fines and campaigns to keep the beast in check? (*The Straits Times* 16 Mar. 1996)

Conclusion

The varied contours of landscapes catering to the performing arts as discussed in this chapter illustrate pointedly how these arts and their landscapes have been called to service in Singapore to contribute to the construction of "nation." Whether it is through contribution to economic development, to the realization of a "world-class city" and gracious society, through reinforcement and reflection of commitment to "Asian roots" or multiculturalism, or through insistent involvement of the "community," landscapes for the arts are an integral part of the state's ideologically hegemonic endeavor and the process of "nation"-building. Policies and programs pertaining to the use of space for the arts are therefore a crucial part of the state's larger cultural policy and complement other dimensions of arts development. Whether it is tax incentives to attract arts enterprises, more liberal rules for permanent residence in Singapore for arts-related personnel, or enhancement of arts education (see Kong 2000b), each effort relies ultimately on the "reach" of performances, unachievable if facilities are unavailable. Landscapes for the arts therefore remain an important strategy through which the state's vision of a "Singapore nation" is to be met.

The specific forms that such landscapes of aesthetics take and the kinds of performing arts that they support are, however, the subject of differing views. Whereas the state's vision of a "gracious" society and "world-class city" necessitates the construction of a "world-class" performing arts center (the Esplanade) and the invitation to "world-class" acts to perform in Singapore, for Singaporean practitioners these actions risk snuffing out local cultural identity. Such erosion of local cultural spaces (both literally and metaphorically) is renegotiated in a variety of ways: through the reassertion of "alternative arts spaces" such as the Substation, the negotiation for space within the Esplanade for Singaporean artists, and at the ideological level, debate in the discursive realm.

The state's vision to develop Singapore into a global city for the arts, rooted mainly in pragmatic concerns about economic generation, finds alternative expression in the practitioners' concern that the arts should be about "community self-development and self-expression" (Bassett 1993, 1785). In seeking to develop a Singapore idiom and an indigenous voice in their cultural products, practitioners endeavor to draw from local cultural resources as well as to contribute to community life, so much so that artistic and cultural activities may become part of the warp and woof of daily life, generating a pulse and rhythm in the city. The cultural spaces that practitioners seek are those in which "[a]rt, artists and art-lovers mingle, muse and meditate," and where there is room "for eloquent failures as for resounding successes" (Sasitharan n.d.). As practitioners recognize, economic imperatives emphasize "growth and property development and find expression in prestige projects and place marketing" (Bassett 1993, 1785) and may not necessarily contribute to cultural regeneration. There is a danger that urban cultural entrepreneurialism will create a city in which economic spectacle replaces cultural substance and "aesthetics replaces ethics" (Harvey 1989, 102). What practitioners argue for is the city as a cultural entity, with "places where people meet, talk, share ideas and desires, and where identities and lifestyles are formed" (Bianchini 1993, 212). Their alternative vision is one in which the arts is a part of people's daily lives, a part of the wider community rather than an appendage to it (Wynne 1992, x). While this idea finds a certain resonance with recent state visions, there remains some distance to cover to achieve a rapprochement between the parties with regards to these landscapes of aesthetics.

10

Conclusions

Power Relations and the Social Constructedness of "Nation"

The central issue in this book is the social constructedness of "nation." As our starting point, we accepted the notion that "nations" are not natural, pre-given collectivities. They are invented in order that a group of people with divergent orientations may develop into a populace of loyal citizens. Various writers have argued and illustrated that this process of constructing a "nation" has entailed the "invention of a common history; the introduction of official languages; the creation of national symbols, such as currencies, stamps, flags and anthems; the staging of ceremonies and rituals; and the deployment of a wide variety of other cultural forms such as monuments, music and paintings" (Leitner and Kang 1999, 216). Much of the literature has tended to emphasize the role of history over geography in the construction of "nations," although recent work in anthropology, philosophy, and geography has put the accent on the importance of both history and geography: "Any one national identity is always characterized by both a historical and geographical heritage. . . . [it is] the symbolic activation of time and space . . . [that] gives shape to the 'imagined community' of the nation" (Daniels 1993, 4–5).

In the invention of "nation," the employment of both history and geography entails pressing particular ideologies as preeminent, because a "nation" derives in part from a people who subscribe to particular shared ideologies. If these ideologies are the ideologies propagated by the state, that "imagined community" will be a powerful resource for the state to mobilize in its myriad projects, the success of which will reinforce the legitimacy of the political leaders. In working toward achieving this condition of

successful ideological hegemony and a widespread acceptance of its construction of "nation," the state must adopt multiple material and discursive
strategies. Landscapes play a critical role. In the particular case of Singapore, the work of "nation" construction is certainly tied intimately to the
state's projects in ideological hegemony, and we have shown how landscapes play a critical role in this effort, not least by concretizing and natu-
ralizing particular preferred ideologies. Landscapes, in this sense, are far
from neutral.

The study of landscapes is grounded in an analysis of tangible, material
structures, which are simultaneously medium and outcome of ideological
systems. Such analysis allows a recovery of the ideological underpinnings
that go into both their making and their undoing. Emphasis must thus be
paid to the construction and demolition of material forms, as well as the
(redefined) use of existing ones, for in these ways landscapes are vested
with latent meanings beyond their manifest functions. For one, the state articulates nationalist discourses and identities through landscapes. But other
alternative ideologies, as we have shown, also seek to compete for authority to assert their meanings and values. The purveyors of alternative ideologies seek the right to define landscape meanings for themselves. This
domination and resistance illustrates how power is neither entirely
arrogated to the state or political system nor identified with particular individuals. It is a power that emerges from "local arenas of action," "a 'microprocess' of social life or pervasive feature of concrete, local transaction"
(Foucault, quoted in Agnew 1987, 23). It is in this sense that there exist
competing discourses and ideologies among different social groups, articulated through the creation, appropriation, redefinition, and contestation of
landscape meanings. We have sought to illustrate the veracity of these theoretical statements in our empirical work.

Our detailed analyses of various landscapes in Singapore also suggest
that the state's ideological work bears out Shils's (1968) theoretical assertions that ideologies are intimately connected with a quest for order, a
movement towards totalization and an assertion of authority. First, ideologies give form and structure to the socially constructed "nation"—indeed,
what is often an idealized and utopianized "nation." In so doing, ideologies
offer "ordered, simplified visions of the world" (Baker 1992, 4). The world

thus ordered (in the case of Singapore, as "Asian," communitarian, multiracial, developmental, gracious), sidesteps ambiguities and streamlines the
role of the individual in it. Second, ideologies are totalizing in that they insist on a total transformation of society. The "nation" constructed on the
basis of such ideologies is one that offers an "overall representation of a society, its past, present and future, integrated into a complete *Weltanschaung*"
(Duby 1985, 153). Third, ideologies also involve the assertion of authority,
in this case, the authority of the state (to rewrite landscapes through a
process of "discursive naturalization" that legitimizes existing social hierar-
chies and power relations [Rose 1994]). However, authority does not reside
with the powerful alone, because other groups attempt to assert their own
voices in defining their landscapes and meanings. In other words, representations and meanings of landscapes are contested (Agnew and Duncan
1989; Anderson and Gale 1992; Barnes and Duncan 1992); multilayered
struggles over domination and subordination are inscribed in landscapes.

The combined framework of social construction theory and notions of
ideology and hegemony have informed our analyses of Singapore's "nation-
building" project in a postcolonial era of political independence. We sum-
marize below our analyses of how landscapes have been pressed to service
by the state to naturalize its constructions of the "nation." We also articulate
briefly the ways in which alternative uses and meanings of the same landscapes are apparent, alongside the making of alternative landscapes in some
situations. This is true of landscapes of everyday life as well as those less
quotidian; and of those serving a public and civic function, alongside those
more intimate and personal. Taken together, they offer evidence of the social constructedness of the Singapore "nation," as well as the "duplicity of
landscape" in its endorsement and reinforcement of, but also divergence
from, state ideologies.

Singapore: A "Nation" Constructed?

When Singapore was forced into independence in 1965 after being ejected
from Malaysia, it inherited the basic infrastructure of a state but not a nation. The government therefore set about the process of nation-building,
central to which was the construction of a national identity. As we illus-

trated in chapter 2, in the construction of "nation" the state intends the trope of "Asian" to represent values and practices that are "traditional," as set up against the Western "Other," which is, in turn, represented as nega- tively—harmfully—erosive. That which is "Asian" is also anchored in com- munitarian values, in contrast to the individualism of the "West." The "nation" is also one that is constructed as multiracial, multilingual, multicul- tural, and multireligious, managed through an abiding commitment to mer- itocracy. To succeed in such a meritocracy, citizens must subscribe to the state's ideologies of discipline and pragmatism, thus oiling the wheels of economic development, which in turn legitimize the state's continued rule.

Landscapes are critical to the Singapore state's project of "nation- building." They are invested with multiple meanings that naturalize the ideologies that produced them in the first place. Sometimes these ideolog- ical meanings are left implicit, while at other times the state makes explicit its desired readings and displays the ideological capital derived from land- scapes. This is true of the landscapes of sentiment (places of worship and places of final rest, whether cemetery or columbaria), of quotidian land- scapes (housing and streets), and landscapes of aesthetics (performance places) and heritage. These landscapes may also be understood as intimate and private (home, worship, and final rest), or shared and public (streets, heritage landscapes, and performance places).

In chapter 4, we drew inspiration from Henry James's observation that "when life was framed in death that the picture was hung up" (quoted in Warren 1994); here we began our analysis of the way landscapes enter into the construction of the living body of the "nation" by first focusing on land- scapes of death. Regarded as sterile wastelands to be remade for more useful development purposes to serve the "nation," Chinese burial grounds (the predominant "space-wasters") occupying large tracts of land in and around the city were rapidly acquired by the state and cleared, primarily for resur- rection as high-rise, high-density housing estates to accommodate the liv- ing. At the same time, the state strongly discouraged burial as a means of disposal of the dead and instead advocated cremation, replacing the exten- sive clan-based burial landscapes in Singapore with centralized state-run crematorium and columbarium complexes as the main landscape of repose for the dead. In doing so (and along with state provision of other "cradle-to-grave" services), the state attempted to break down traditional clan-based ties and affinities and replace these with social relationships that derived their meaning from "the nation-state framework" (Benjamin 1988, 36).

For those who subscribe to particular religions, places of worship are often centers of meaning—"fields of care," as Tuan (1974) characterizes them. For the state, the construction of a "nation" that is progressive and modernist is undergirded by "pragmatic" and "rational" ideologies, characterized by efficiency in the use of space, and thus, often, demolition and urban renewal (chapter 5). Religious places, like other places that stand in the path of renewal, come under the wrecker's ball, sacred meanings notwithstanding. In this, the state appeals to communitarian values of putting the "nation" before self. However, where such places continue to stand, they become part of the stable of meanings drawn upon by the state in its hegemonic construction of the "nation." They become held up as beacons of multiculturalism and multireligiosity.

In chapter 6, we showed how public housing in Singapore reflects and reinforces the state's ideologies of multiracialism through its policy of mixing people of different "races" in desired proportions. It is an arena through which a gracious society within a developmentalist frame is to be developed, as citizens work to service their mortgages, thus learning and living out the value and virtues of hard work while simultaneously understanding the need for public consideration—particularly when living in close proximity in high-density housing. Public housing fulfills the state's vision of a "nation" characterized by modernity, with its vastly improved conditions from the slums and squatters that characterized the city not too long ago. Through its various strategies, the Housing and Development Board also attempts to develop among residents a sense of place, first to the neighborhood and then, by extension and vicariously, to the "nation." Similarly, through the HDB's policies of allocation, the "normal" family structure is also endorsed and encouraged, while others (e.g., single-parent families or unmarried singles with siblings) are delegitimized. The ubiquity of public-housing landscapes in Singapore ensures that the ideological messages infuse society.

Street names are also highly visible aspects of our landscapes, and ordinarily, are highly functional. However, their everyday use and functionality mask the structures of power and legitimacy that underlie their construction and use. As we illustrated in chapter 7, the postindependence state was quick to harness the power of names inscribed in the social materiality of everyday life to serve ideological purposes. Reflecting changing ideologies in the life cycle of the postcolonial "nation," the vast repository of street names were strategically drawn upon at different points to express a severance of colonial ties and unity with the Malay hinterland (a "Malayanizing" of street names); to reflect the four official "races" as equal but separate categories (a "multiracializing" of street names); and to articulate the intricacies of language policies to promote standardization and bilingualism.

As efficient means to translate the "history of the nation" into visible forms for public consumption, heritage landscapes are part of the process of imagining the "nation" (chapter 8). The landscapes of Chinatown and Kampong Glam, for example, are marked out as physical manifestations of Singapore's "Asian" roots, bulwarks against Westernization. In the various incarnations of the Merlion, myth and reality were prodigiously combined to produce a monumental form with which Singapore could be identified for the consumption of both citizens and tourists. Simultaneously, heritage landscapes and symbolic icons allow the state to claim Singapore's distinctiveness amidst the homogenization that is assumed to come with modernity and globalization. This distinctiveness, in turn, becomes part of the city's strategy to expand tourism, thus contributing to Singapore's continuing economic development and the state's legitimacy.

As a final example, we illustrated in chapter 9 how the development and nature of landscapes for a very particular purpose—the performing arts—have been appropriated to serve the state's multiple ideologies in nation-building. While a conspicuous absence of such landscapes in the 1960s to mid-1980s reflects the view that the arts was a luxury, subsequent state injection of funds for the construction of massive performing-arts spaces was evidence of the fact that the arts had become important in the "survival" and development of Singapore's economy in a new globalized world. At the same time, particular art forms, thought to constitute cultural defense against the "yellow culture" of the West, are endorsed while other "less healthy" forms are rejected. In the design of the arts center, the Esplanade, too, claims to "Asianness" are made with abundant sound and fury.

Similarly, support for the arts, through housing for arts groups, reflects a self-conscious commitment to "multiculturalism." In the construction of two key spaces for the arts, the National Theatre and the Esplanade, and in the use of public spaces for artistic activity, the state, in both material and discursive terms, seeks to build community, drawing Singaporeans in as contributors, stakeholders, and involved audiences. Through such involvement, Singapore and Singaporeans are showcased to the world as constituting a modernist city and a gracious society.

It would be remiss, however, to suggest that the state's hegemonic construction of the "nation" represents a homogeneous imaginary that Singaporeans accept unfailingly. While there are clear evidences of state success in the ways in which Singaporeans applaud the material fruits of state policy and action—and even accept the state's ideological arguments—there are also signs of fragmentation.

In response to the state's remaking of landscapes of death and repose, the citizenry did not remain completely passive in the face of the state's attempt to reach into and intervene with what are some of the most fundamental of human values. While the traditional discourse on Chinese geomancy and ancestor worship, which used to render burial landscapes immune from external intervention, had to a large extent weakened its hold in postindependence Singapore, collective and individual agencies asserting particular claims over the control of death matters continue to surface. Clan-based organizations attempt to negotiate for and wrest concessions from the state to maintain much-reduced plots for the repose of "their" dead. Some of these measures have reaped a degree of success, although it must be noted that these remnant plots are no longer open for burial and serve mainly as memorials of past practices and landscapes. While collective negotiations are rather muted, individuals continue to express their subjectivities through drawing on strategies that allow them to exercise a degree of choice of mode of disposal within the constraints. While most Chinese Singaporeans have accepted the idea that earthly remains will reside in columbaria rather than in cemeteries as an inevitability, individualizing strategies continue to be played out to conserve what is seen as a loss of "meaning" as a result of the shift from burial to cremation.

While there are those among religious adherents who accept the mate-

rial and discursive efforts of the state to explain away the demolition of sacred places in the name of development, others have sought to resist state
hegemony, both materially and ideologically. We have also observed fault
lines among the citizenry who dispute the claims of the state's evenhandedness in multireligious matters. However, it is perhaps in the realm of the religious that the state has been most successful; despite the existence of
counter-hegemonic interpretations of landscapes, by and large, religious
adherents have sought to renegotiate their conceptions of sacredness and
have avoided bloody sacred-secular conflicts (see Kong 1993b), as have oc-
curred in other contexts.

Life in the Housing and Development Board "heartlands" sometimes
negates the state's vision of the "nation" as a gracious community as frac-
tures appear between neighbors living in close proximity and high density.
The appropriation of the upgrading exercise for political purposes, even
while fulfilling modernist visions, is rejected by some as being unconscionable. The sense of place desired by residents, particularly in new estates, is not always apparent. Conflict over use of public space in HDB
estates also runs counter to the image of multiracial harmony.

While the state has harnessed street names to inscribe ideological intents, such a complex "web of signification" (Ley and Olds 1988, 195) does
not always go unchallenged. Most of the time, people respond "locally" to
particular street names that they encounter in the quotidian stream of life
rather than more generally to the entire street-naming text. This response
can range from a strategic apathy—refusing to engage with the ideological
meaning behind the names—to a questioning of the suitability of particular
names. In the specific instance of the *pinyinization* of street names, the reaction against the imposition of a new system of naming was strong enough
to force the state to reverse its policy.

Heritage landscapes are similarly infused with multiple resistant voices
and have resulted in some Singaporeans keeping distance from the state's
constructed version of the "nation." Primarily, residents of Chinatown
frown upon the state's rewriting of their landscape, viewing it as a promotional effort for tourists rather than a conservation effort suited to the
practicalities of their daily lives, despite claims to the contrary. A non-
governmental group, the Singapore Heritage Society, which is concerned

with the promotion of heritage consciousness similarly, cautions against capitalistic concerns that might turn the area into a theme park. In turn, the carving out of the Kampong Glam conservation area marks out, in an artificial way, that which is "inside" and therefore sanctified as Malay heritage, and that which is "outside," subject to demolition. The fact that hegemony is never complete is evident in that such state constructions have been interpreted by some as insensitive and even anti-Malay. Despite an existence of more than twenty-five years, the Merlion continues to be the subject of much debate as Singaporeans wrestle with whether "the lion with the fishy tail" (or tale?) really constitutes a Singapore icon, notwithstanding the fact that it appears to be well-received by tourists.

In making more physical performance spaces and housing for arts groups available, the state is providing the "hardware" necessary to achieve the vision of a "gracious society" that is steeped in culture and the arts. However, we have illustrated how the state's emphasis on the arts as an economic resource may be detrimental to the cultivation of local cultural resources and the development of indigenous artistic voices, because small experimental groups find it difficult to compete with the large foreign performances that are brought in to generate revenue. Alternative spaces for the arts—those which give free rein to local groups to experiment, fail, succeed, and grow—have thus persisted as a conscious counter to the state's cultural strategy. The state's claim that the design of its largest and most prominent performance space (the Esplanade) celebrates "Asianness" is also disputed, while its attempts to encourage multicultural performances actually take performances out of the social context from which they derive meaning, and end up destroying them. In these various ways, then, the state's hegemonic vision of the nation is either actively resisted or simply plays itself out in divergent ways, often through the very landscapes that were meant to naturalize the state's preferred ideologies in the first place.

The social and the spatial, as many writers have argued, are dialectically related. At the same time, it is crucial to remember that the social and the geographical can also be mutually reinforcing. It is thus important to flag the alternative social acts that parallel the investment of divergent landscape meanings and the perpetuation of alternative landscape uses. Each reinforces the other, albeit in (often) uncoordinated ways.

While we have focused on the counter-hegemonic use of landscapes as a channel to express alternative versions of the nation and as a means of diverging from, even if not directly inverting, the ideological stances of the state, we will end by citing two examples of everyday acts to illustrate the parallels in the arena of the social. As Chua (1998, 199) illustrates, such alternative expressions, evident in the unstructured realm of everyday lives, have been articulated in the sphere of language and the arts, and in consumption, for example. While the state insists on a multiracial, multilingual "nation" that simultaneously excludes Chinese dialects, the staging of multilingual plays that include prevalently Chinese dialects represents "a hybridity of tongues" that "protests the eraser [*sic*] of collective memories effected by the elimination of Chinese dialects from the public sphere" (Chua 1998, 199). At the same time, the state's insistence on developmentalism includes a view that economic growth is served by high monetary savings among the people, given the country's lack of natural resources. However, particularly among the young, consumerism has been facilitated by credit facilities, and the body as the site of consumption has become conspicuous, with, among other things, the purchase of designer goods on loans (Chua 1998, 201). Alternative expressions are thus evident in the messy, everyday lived-out experiences of ordinary people. Such alterities, however, do not necessarily amount to a lack of affinity for and affiliation to the "nation," which, at a larger level, appears promising. This fact is borne out in a survey carried out by the Institute of Policy Studies in early 2000, which revealed that 76 percent of a representative sample of 1,451 citizens of Singapore would defend the country, no matter what the personal cost. This identification with the nation is further evidenced in that 73 percent indicated that they would not leave the country in the event of war and the same proportion viewed it wrong for people to give up citizenship to avoid national service (*The Straits Times* 22 Feb. 2000).

In brief, in Singapore the preeminence of the state in the construction of the "nation" is apparent. In many senses, it is literally everywhere—apparent as it is in its material, tangible landscapes. Yet, as Chua (1998, 201) points out, "daily life is, without conscious organization, seeping constantly out of the monolithic ideological and managerial structure of the Singapore state." Alongside the social activities in everyday life that Chua

cites, landscapes similarly offer the same fracture lines along which alternative values may be expressed. While they may not "add up to an inversion
of society over state . . . they certainly create more civic and political space
than is commonly assumed" (Chua 1998, 201).

The Singapore "nation" is socially and spatially constructed, reinforced, and challenged. Through discursive and material naturalization, a
"nation" is made, heralded, and lived, but multiple interpretations and alternative discourses also intersect with preferred state visions. Such is the dynamic stability that characterizes Singapore as a "nation."

References

Adorno, Theodor. 1992. *Quasi Una Fantasia*. Translated by R. Livingstone. London and New York: Verso.

Agnew, John. 1987. *Place and Politics: The Geographical Mediation of State and Society*. London: Allen and Unwin.

Agnew, John A., and James S. Duncan. 1989. Introduction to *The Power of Place: Bringing Together Geographical and Sociological Imaginations*, edited by J. A. Agnew and J. S. Duncan, 1–8. Boston: Unwin Hyman.

Agnew, John A., John Mercer, and David E. Sopher, eds. 1984. *The City in Cultural Context*. Boston: Allen and Unwin.

Anderson, Benedict. 1983. *Imagined Communities: Reflections on the Origin and Spread of Nationalism*. London: Verso.

Anderson, Kay, and Fay Gale, eds. 1992. *Inventing Places: Studies in Cultural Geography*. Melbourne: Longman Cheshire.

Appadurai, Arjun. 1990. "Disjuncture and Difference in the Global Cultural Economy." In *Global Culture, Nationalism, Globalization, and Modernity*, edited by M. Featherstone, 295–310. London: Sage.

Art versus Art: Conflict and Convergence: The Substation Conference. 1995. Singapore: The Substation.

Ayabe, T., ed. 1998. *Nation-State, Identity, and Religion in Southeast Asia*. Singapore: Singapore Society of Asian Studies.

Azaryahu, M., and A. Kellerman. 1999. "Symbolic Places of National History and Revival: A Study of Zionist Mythical Geography." *Transactions, Institute of British Geographers* 24: 109–23.

Baker, Alan R. H. 1992. "Introduction: On Ideology and Landscape." In *Ideology and Landscape in Historical Perspective*, edited by Alan R. H. Baker and Gideon Biger, 1–14. Cambridge: Cambridge Univ. Press.

Ban, Kah Choon. 1992. "Narrating Imagination." In *Imagining Singapore*, edited by

Kah Choon Ban, Anne Pakir, and Chee Kiong Tong, 9–25. Singapore: Times Academic Press.

Barnes, Trevor J., and James S. Duncan, eds. 1992. *Writing Worlds: Discourse, Text, and Metaphor in the Representation of Landscape.* London and New York: Routledge.

Bassett, Keith. 1993. "Urban Cultural Strategies and Urban Cultural Regeneration: A Case Study and Critique." *Environment and Planning A* 25: 1773–88.

Bedlington, Stanley S. 1978. *Malaysia and Singapore: The Building of New States.* London: Cornell Univ. Press.

Benjamin, Geoffrey. 1988. *The Unseen Presence: A Theory of the Nation-State and its Mystifications.* Working Paper No. 19. Singapore: National Univ. of Singapore, Department of Sociology.

———. [1976] 1997. "The Cultural Logic of Singapore's 'Multiracialism.' " In *Understanding Singapore Society,* edited by Jin Hui Ong, Chee Kiong Tong, and Ern Ser Tan, 67–85. Singapore: Times Academic Press.

Berg, Lawrence D., and Robin A. Kearns. 1996. "Naming as Norming: 'Race,' Gender, and the Identity Politics of Naming Places in Aotearoa, New Zealand." *Environment and Planning D: Society and Space* 14, no. 1: 99–122.

Betts, Russell Henry. 1975. "Multiculturalism, Meritocracy, and the Malays of Singapore." Ph.D. diss., Massachusetts Institute of Technology.

Bianchini, Franco. 1993. "Culture, Conflict, and Cities: Issues and Prospects for the 1990s." In *Cultural Policy and Urban Regeneration: The West European Experience,* edited by Franco Bianchini and Michael Parkinson, 199–213. Manchester and New York: Manchester Univ. Press.

Binney, Marcus, and Max Hanna. 1978. *Preservation Pays: Tourism and the Economic Benefits of Conserving Historic Buildings.* London: SAVE Britain's Heritage.

Blaut, James. 1980. "A Radical Critique of Cultural Geography." *Antipode* 12: 25–29.

Boddy, T. 1983. "The Political Uses of Urban Design: The Jakarta Example." In *The Southeast Asian Environment,* edited by D. R. Webster, 31–47. Ottawa: Univ. of Ottawa Press.

Boorstin, Daniel. 1992. *The Image: A Guide to Pseudo-Events in America.* New York: Vintage.

Brady, Diane. 1995. "Romancing the Arts: Singapore Sets Stage for Cultural Tourism." *The Wall Street Journal* 1 Dec.

Bromley, Rosemary D. F., and Gareth A. Jones. 1995. "Conservation in Quito: Policies and Progress in the Historic Centre." *Third World Planning Review* 17, no. 1: 41–59.

Brown, David. 1994. *The State and Ethnic Politics in Southeast Asia.* London: Routledge.

Buckley, Charles. B. [1902] 1984. *An Anecdotal History of Old Times in Singapore.* Singapore: Oxford Univ. Press.

Burgess, Jacquelin. A. 1979. "Place-Making: The Contribution of Environmental Perception Studies in Planning." *Geography* 64, no. 4: 317–26.

Burgess, Jacquelin, and John Gold, eds. 1982. "On the Significance of Valued Environments." In *Valued Environments*, 1–9. Boston: Allen and Unwin.

Burton, S. 1993. "History with a Bottom Line." *Time* 12 July: 36–37.

Cartier, Carolyn. 1993. "Creating Historic Open Space in Melaka." *The Geographical Review* 83, no. 4: 359–73.

———. 1997. "The Dead, Place/Space, and Social Activism: Constructing the Nationscape in Historic Melaka." *Environment and Planning D: Society and Space* 15: 1–32.

———. 1998. "Preserving Bukit China: The Cultural Politics of Landscape Interpretation in Melaka's Chinese Cemetery." In *The Last Half Century of Chinese Overseas*, edited by S. Elizabeth, 65–79. Hong Kong: Hong Kong Univ. Press.

Castells, Manuel. 1992. "Four Asian Tigers with a Dragon Head: A Comparative Analysis of the State, Economy, and Society in the Asian Pacific Rim." In *States and Development in the Asian Pacific Rim*, edited by Richard Appelbaum and Jeffrey Henderson, 33–70. Newbury Park, Calif.: Sage.

Center for Contemporary Cultural Studies (CCCS). 1982. *The Empire Strikes Back: Race and Racism in '70s Britain.* London: Hutchinson Education.

Chan, Chee Seng. 1975. "Speech Delivered at the Vesak Celebrations of the Singapore Buddhists Vesak Celebration Committee." In *Ministry of Social Affairs: Speeches, Statements, Press Conferences, and Interviews, 1974–1976.* 25 May. Singapore: Information Division, Ministry of Culture.

Chan, Heng Chee. 1971. *Singapore: The Politics of Survival.* Singapore: Oxford Univ. Press.

———. 1985. "Legislature and Legislators." In *Government and Politics in Singapore*, edited by Jon S. T. Quah, Heng Chee Chan, and Chee Meow Seah, 71–91. Singapore: Oxford Univ. Press.

Chan, Heng Chee, and Hans Dieter Evers. 1973. "Nation-Building and National Identity in Southeast Asia." In *Building States and Nations: Analyses by Region*, Vol. 2, edited by S. N. Eisenstadt and S. Rokkan, 301–19. Beverly Hills, Calif.: Sage.

Chang, T. C. 1997. "Heritage as a Tourism Commodity: Traversing the Tourist-Local Divide." *Singapore Journal of Tropical Geography* 18: 46–68.

Chang, T. C., Simon Milne, Dale Fallon, and Corinne Pohlmann. 1996. "Urban

Heritage Tourism: The Global-Local Nexus." *Annals of Tourism Research* 23: 284–305.

Cheah, Boon Kheng. 1999. "The Rise and Fall of the Great Melakan Empire: Moral Judgment in Tun Bambang's Sejarah Melayu." *Journal of the Malaysian Branch of the Royal Asiatic Society* 71, pt. 2: 103–21.

Chen, Peter S. J. 1983. "Singapore's Development Strategies: A Model for Rapid Growth." In *Singapore: Development Policies and Trends,* edited by Peter S. J. Chen, 3–25. Singapore: Oxford Univ. Press for the Institute of Asian Affairs in Hamburg.

Cheng, Lim Keak. 1985. "Reflections on the Changing Roles of Chinese Clan Associations." In *Geography and the Third World,* edited by Ismail Ahmad and Jamaludin Md. Jahi, 62. Bangi, Selangor: Penerbit Universiti Kebangsaan Malaysia.

Chia, Karen. 1997–98. "Experiencing Sacred Places: The Negotiation of Authenticity by Tourists and Worshippers." Academic exercise, National Univ. of Singapore.

Chidester, David, and Edward T. Linenthal. 1995. Introduction to *American Sacred Space,* edited by David Chidester and Edward T. Linenthal, 1–42. Bloomington: Indiana Univ. Press.

Chiew, Seen Kong. 1990. "Nation-Building in Singapore: An Historical Perspective." In *In Search of Singapore's National Values,* edited by Jon S. T. Quah, 6–23. Singapore: The Institute of Policy Studies and Times Academic Press.

Chua, Beng Huat. 1983. "Re-opening Ideological Discussion in Singapore: A New Theoretical Direction." *Southeast Asian Journal of Social Science* 11: 31–45.

———. 1991a. "Race-Relations and Public-Housing Policy in Singapore." *Journal of Architectural and Planning Research* 8, no. 4: 343–54.

———. 1991b. "Not Depoliticized but Ideologically Successful: The Public-Housing Program in Singapore." *International Journal of Urban and Regional Research* 15, no. 1: 24–41.

———. 1992. "Australian and Asian Perception of Human Rights." In *Australia's Human Rights Diplomacy,* edited by Ian Russell, Peter Van Ness, and Beng Huat Chua, 87–97. Canberra: Australian Foreign Policy Publication Program, Australian National Univ.

———. 1995a. *Communitarian Ideology and Democracy in Singapore.* London: Routledge.

———. 1995b. "That Imagined Space: Nostalgia for Kampungs." In *Portraits of*

Places: History, Community, and Identity, edited by Brenda S. A. Yeoh and Lily Kong, 222–41. Singapore: Times Editions.

———. 1997a. "Between Economy and Race: The Asianization of Singapore." In *Space, Culture, and Power: New Identities in Globalizing Cities*, edited by Ayse Oncu and Petra Weyland, 23–41. London and New Jersey: Zed Books.

———. 1997b. *Political Legitimacy and Housing: Stakeholding in Singapore*. London: Routledge.

———. 1998. "Culture, Multiracialism, and National Identity in Singapore." In *Trajectories*, edited by Chen Kuan-Hsing, 186–205. London: Routledge.

Clarke, Michael. 1982. *The Politics of Pop Festivals*. London: Junction Books.

Clifford, James. 1988. *The Predicament of Culture: Twentieth-Century Ethnography, Literature, and Art*. Cambridge: Harvard Univ. Press.

Clutterbuck, Richard. 1984. *Conflict and Violence in Singapore and Malaysia, 1945–1983*. Singapore: Graham Brash.

Cockburn, Cynthia. 1977. *The Local State: Management of Cities and People*. London: Pluto.

Cohen, Anthony P. 1982. "Belonging: The Experience of Culture." In *Belonging: Identity and Social Organization in British Rural Cultures*, edited by A. P. Cohen, 1–17. Manchester: Manchester Univ. Press.

Cohen, Sarah. 1991. "Popular Music and Urban Regeneration: The Music Industries of Merseyside." *Cultural Studies* 5: 332–46.

———. 1993. "Ethnography and Popular Music Studies." *Popular Music* 12: 123–38.

Cohen, S., and N. Kliot. 1992. "Place-Names in Israel's Ideological Struggle over the Administered Territories." *Annals of the Association of American Geographers* 82: 653–80.

Commentary. 1993. Singapore: Univ. of Singapore Society.

The Committee on Heritage Report. 1988. Singapore: Committee on Heritage.

Conservation Within the Central Area with the Plan for Chinatown. 1985. Singapore: Urban Redevelopment Authority.

Constitution of the Republic of Singapore. 1985. Singapore: Government Printing Office.

Crang, Mike. 1994. "On the Heritage Trail: Maps and Journeys to Olde Englande." *Environment and Planning D: Society and Space* 12: 341–55.

Daly, Gerald. 1996. "Migrants and Gatekeepers: The Links Between Immigration and Homelessness in Western Europe." *Cities* 13, no. 1: 11–23.

Daniels, Stephen. 1989. "Marxism, Culture, and the Duplicity of Landscape." In *New Models in Geography: The Political Economy Perspective,* Vol. 2, edited by Richard Peet and Nigel Thrift, 196–220. Boston: Unwin Hyman.

————. 1993. *Fields of Vision: Landscape Imagery and National Identity in England and the United States.* Princeton, N.J.: Princeton Univ. Press.

Das, S., and R. Harindranath. 1995.*Nation-State, National Identity, and the Media.* Module Four. Unit 22. M.A. in Mass Communication. England: Leicester Univ.

de Certeau, Michel. 1984. *The Practice of Everyday Life.* Translated by S. Rendall. Berkeley: Univ. of California Press.

Department of Statistics. 1983. *Economic and Social Statistics: Singapore, 1960–1982.* Singapore: Department of Statistics.

Devan, Janadas. 1999. "My Country and My People: Forgetting to Remember." In *Our Place in Time: Exploring Heritage and Memory in Singapore,* edited by Kian Woon Kwok, Chong Guan Kwa, Lily Kong, and Brenda Yeoh, 21–33. Singapore: Singapore Heritage Society.

Dix, Gerald. 1990. "Conservation and Change in the City." *Third World Planning Review* 12, no. 4: 385–406.

Drakakis-Smith, David W., and Yue-man Yeung. 1977. "Public Housing in the City States of Hong Kong and Singapore." OP-8. Canberra: Development Studies Center, Australian National Univ.

Duby, Georges. 1985. "Ideologies in History." In *Constructing the Past: Essays in Historical Methodology,* edited by J. Le Goff and P. Nova, 151–65. Cambridge: Cambridge Univ. Press.

Duncan, James S. 1985. "Individual Action and Political Power: A Structuration Perspective." In *The Future of Geography,* edited by Ron J. Johnston, 174–89. London: Methuen.

————. 1990. *The City as Text: The Politics of Landscape in the Kandyan Kingdom.* Cambridge: Cambridge Univ. Press.

Duncan, James, and Nancy Duncan. 1988. "Rereading the Landscape." *Environment and Planning D: Society and Space* 6: 117–26.

Dwyer, Claire, and Astrid Meyer. 1995. "The Institutionalisation of Islam in the Netherlands and in the UK: The Case of Islamic Schools." *New Community* 21, no. 1: 37–54.

————. 1996. "The Establishment of Islamic Schools: A Controversial Phenomenon in Three European Countries." In *Muslims in the Margin: Political Responses to the Presence of Islam in Western Europe,* edited by W. A. R. Shadid and P. S. van Koningsveld, 218–42. Kampen, The Netherlands: Kok Pharos Publishing House.

Edensor, Tim. 1997. "National Identity and the Politics of Memory: Remembering Bruce and Wallace in Symbolic Space." *Environment and Planning D: Society and Space* 29: 175–94.

Ee, Tiang Hong. 1997. *Responsibility and Commitment: The Poetry of Edwin Thumboo*. Singapore: Center for Advanced Studies and Singapore Univ. Press.

Eitel, Ernest J. 1985. *Feng-Shui*. Singapore: Graham Brash.

Emmerson, Donald K. 1984. "Southeast Asia: What's in a Name?" *Journal of Southeast Asian Studies* 15: 1–21.

Faist, Thomas, and Hartmut Haussermann. 1996. "Immigration, Social Citizenship, and Housing in Germany." *International Journal of Urban and Regional Research* 20, no. 1: 83–98.

Featherstone, Michael. 1993. "Global and Local Cultures." In *Mapping the Futures: Local Cultures, Global Change*, edited by J. Bird, B. Curtis, T. Putnam, G. Robertston, and L. Tickner, 169–87. London and New York: Routledge.

Fitch, James Marston. 1982. *Historical Preservation: Curatorial Management of the Built World*. New York: McGraw-Hill.

Fonseca, Rory. 1976. *Growth, Transition, and the Urban Environment: A Reference Frame for Singapore*. Working Paper No. 50, Department of Sociology, National Univ. of Singapore.

Foucault, Michel. 1979. *Discipline and Punish: The Birth of the Prison*. Translated by Alan Sheridan. London: Penguin Books.

———. 1980a. "The Eye of Power." In *Michel Foucault: Power/Knowledge, Selected Interviews and Other Writings, 1972–1977*, edited by Colin Gordon, 146–65. New York: Harvester.

———. 1980b. "Power and Strategies." In *Michel Foucault: Power/Knowledge, Selected Interviews and Other Writings, 1972–1977*, edited by Colin Gordon, 134–45. New York: Harvester.

———. 1980c. "Two Lectures." In *Michel Foucault: Power/Knowledge, Selected Interviews and Other Writings, 1972–1977*, edited by Colin Gordon, 78–108. New York: Harvester.

———. 1984. "Truth and Power." In *The Foucault Reader*, edited by Paul Rabinow, 51–75. Harmondsworth: Penguin.

Freedman, Maurice. 1967. "Ancestor Worship: Two Facets of the Chinese Case." In *Social Organisation: Essays Presented to Raymond Firth*, edited by Maurice Freedman, 80–91. London: F. Cass.

Frith, Simon. 1991. "Knowing One's Place: The Culture of Cultural Industries." *Cultural Studies from Birmingham* 1: 135–55.

Gee, G. K. 1995. "Geography, Nationality, and Religion in Ukraine: A Research Note." *Journal for the Scientific Study of Religion* 34, no. 3: 383–90.

Gee, K. K., and M. L. Chee. 1981. "Deliberate Urbanization: The Singapore Experience." In *Urbanization and National Development in Asia,* edited by Victor F. S. Sit and Koichi Mera, 95–108. Hong Kong: Comparative Urbanization Project, University of Hong Kong.

Gereffi, Gary. 1996. "The Elusive Last Lap in the Quest for Developed-Country Status." In *Globalization: Critical Reflections,* edited by James Mittelman, 53–82. London: Lynne Rienner.

Giddens, Anthony. 1987. *The Nation-State and Violence.* Vol. 2, *A Contemporary Critique of Historical Materialism.* Cambridge: Polity Press.

Gifford, Paul. 1998. "Chiluba's Christian Nation: Christianity as a Factor in Zambian Politics, 1991–1996." *Journal of Contemporary Religion* 13, no. 3: 363–81.

Glick Schiller, Nina, Linda Basch, and Christine Szanton-Blanc. 1995. "From Immigrant to Transmigrant: Theorising Transnational Migration." *Anthropological Quarterly* 68, no. 1: 48–63.

Goh, Chok Tong. 1988. "Our National Ethic." *Speeches: A Bimonthly Selection of Ministerial Speeches* 12, no. 5: 12–15.

———. 1993. "Guarding the Sacred Institutions of Marriage and Family." *Speeches: A Bimonthly Selection of Ministerial Speeches* 17, no. 3: 28–33.

———. 1999. *Prime Minister's National Day Rally Speech 1999.* Singapore: Ministry of Information and the Arts.

Goh, Keng Swee. 1956. *Urban Incomes and Housing: A Report of the Social Survey of Singapore, 1953–54.* Singapore: Department of Social Welfare.

Gooneratne, Yasmine. 1986. "Edwin Thumboo: Ulysses by the Merlion." In *Critical Engagements: Singapore Poems in Focus,* edited by K. Singh, 7–16. Singapore: Heinemann Asia.

Gopal Baratham. 1999. Untitled article. *Silver Kris.* Official magazine of Singapore Airlines.

Gordon, Colin. 1980. Afterword in *Michel Foucault: Power/Knowledge, Selected Interviews and Other Writings, 1972–1977,* edited by C. Gordon, 229–59. New York: Harvester.

Goss, Jon. 1988. "The Built Environment and Social Theory: Towards an Architectural Geography." *Professional Geographer* 40: 392–403.

Gramsci, Antonio. 1973. *Letters from Prison.* New York: Harper and Row.

Gruffudd, Pyrs. 1994. "Back to the Land: Historiography, Rurality, and the Nation in Interwar Wales." *Transactions: Institute of British Geographers,* n.s., 19: 61–77.

Guehenno, Jean-Marie. 1995. *The End of the Nation-State.* Translated by Victoria El-
    liott. Minneapolis: Univ. of Minnesota Press.

Halfacree, Keith H., and Rob M. Kitchin. 1996. "Madchester Rave On: Placing the
    Fragments of Popular Music." *Area* 28: 47–55.

Hall, Stuart, and Thomas Jefferson, eds. 1976. *Resistance Through Rituals: Youth Sub-
    cultures in Post-War Britain.* London: Hutchinson Education/Center for Contem-
    porary Cultural Studies.

Hall, Stuart, et al. 1978. *Policing the Crisis: Mugging, the State, and Law and Order.* Lon-
    don: Macmillan.

Handler, Richard. 1987. "Heritage and Hegemony: Recent Works on Historic
    Preservation and Interpretation." *Anthropological Quarterly* 6: 137–41.

Hardy, Dennis. 1988. "Historical Geography and Heritage Studies." *Area* 20:
    333–38.

Harvey, David. 1979. "Monument and Myth." *Annals of the Association of American Ge-
    ographers* 69: 362–81.

Harvey, David. W. 1989. *The Urban Experience.* Oxford: Blackwell.

HDB Annual Report. 1961. 1964. 1968. 1972. 1978–79. 1979–80. Singapore: Hous-
    ing and Development Board.

Heng, Hock Mui. 1993. "Public Symbols in Singapore: A Study of the Civic and
    Cultural District." Academic exercise, National Univ. of Singapore.

Hill, Michael, and Kwen Fee Lian. 1995. *The Politics of Nation-Building and Citizenship.*
    London: Routledge.

Ho, A. P. 1990. "The Maintenance of Religious Harmony Bill." *Mirror* 15 Apr.: 1–4.

Hobsbawm, Edward, and Terence Ranger, eds. 1983. *The Invention of Tradition.* Cam-
    bridge: Cambridge Univ. Press.

A Home for the Arts: The Substation. 1996. Singapore: The Substation.

Homes for the People. n.d. Singapore: Housing and Development Board.

Hooson, David. 1994. "Afterword: Identity Resurgent—Geography Revived." In
    Geography and National Identity, edited by David Hooson, 367–70. Oxford:
    Blackwell.

Housing and Development Board (HDB). 2002. *Housing a Nation.* Available online
    at: www.hdb.gov.sg.

Housing and Development Board Files. Deposited at the National Archives, Singapore.

Huntington, Richard, and Peter Metcalf. 1979. *Celebrations of Death: The Anthropology
    of Mortuary Ritual.* Cambridge: Cambridge Univ. Press.

Jackson, Kenneth T., and Camilos Jose Vergara. 1989. *Silent Cities.* New York:
    Princeton Architectural Press.

Jackson, Peter, and Jan Penrose. 1993. "Introduction: Placing 'Race' and Nation." In *Constructions of Race, Place, and Nation*, edited by Peter Jackson and Jan Penrose, 1–23. London: UCL Press.

Jacobs, Jane M. 1993. " 'Shake 'im this country': The Mapping of the Aboriginal Sacred in Australia: The Case of Coronation Hill." In *Constructions of Race, Place, and Nation*, edited by Peter Jackson and Jan Penrose, 100–18. London: UCL Press.

Jacobs, Jane M. 1996. *Edge of Empire: Postcolonialism and the City*. London: Routledge.

Johnson, Nuala. 1995. "Cast in Stone: Monuments, Geography, and Nationalism." *Environment and Planning D: Society and Space* 31: 51–65.

Jumabhoy, R. 1994. "Taking on Wings." In *Singapore 1994*, 1–7. Singapore: Ministry of Information and the Arts.

Jupp, Peter. 1993. "Cremation or Burial? Contemporary Choice in City and Village." In *The Sociology of Death: Theory, Culture, and Practice*, edited by David Clark, 169–97. Oxford: Blackwell Publishers/The Sociological Review.

Kampong Glam Historic District. 1995. Singapore: Urban Redevelopment Authority.

Kandiah, Shamala. 1987. "Women in a Patriarchy." Academic exercise, National Univ. of Singapore.

Kaye, Barrington. 1960. *Upper Nankin Street Singapore: A Sociological Study of Chinese Households Living in a Densely Populated Area*. Singapore: Univ. of Malaya Press.

Kho, Ee Moi. 1979–80. "Religion and State in Singapore, 1959–1978." Academic exercise, National Univ. of Singapore.

Khoo, Su Nin. 1993. *Streets of Georgetown Penang: An Illustrated Guide to Penang's City Streets and Historic Attractions*. Penang, Malaysia: Janus Print and Resources.

Khublall, Nat, and Belinda Yuen. 1991. *Development Control and Planning Law in Singapore*. Singapore: Longman.

King, Anthony D. 1990. *Urbanism, Colonialism, and the World Economy: Cultural and Spatial Foundations of the World Urban System*. London: Routledge.

Knight, David B. 1985. "Commentary: Perceptions of Landscapes in Heaven." *Journal of Cultural Geography* 6, no. 1: 127–40.

Kobayashi, Audrey. 1989. "A Critique of Dialectical Landscape." In *Remaking Human Geography*, edited by Audrey Kobayashi and Susan Mackenzie, 164–83. London: Unwin Hyman.

Koh, Tai Ann. 1989. "Culture and the Arts." In *Management of Success: The Moulding of Modern Singapore*, edited by Kernial S. Sandhu and Paul Wheatley, 710–48. Singapore: Institute of Southeast Asian Studies.

Kong, Lily. 1993a. "Ideological Hegemony and the Political Symbolism of Religious Buildings in Singapore." *Environment and Planning D: Society and Space* 11: 23–45.

————. 1993b. "Negotiating Conceptions of Sacred Space: A Case Study of Religious Buildings in Singapore." *Transactions, Institute of British Geographers*, n.s., 18, no. 3: 342–58.

————. 1996. "Popular Music in Singapore: Local Cultures, Global Resources, and Regional Identities." *Environment and Planning D: Society and Space* 14: 273–92.

————. 1997. "Popular Music in a Transnational World: The Construction of Local Identities in Singapore." *Asia Pacific Viewpoint* 38, no. 1: 19–36.

————. 1999. "Cemeteries and Columbaria, Memorials and Mausoleums: Narrative and Interpretation in the Study of Deathscapes in Geography." *Australian Geographical Studies* 37, no. 1: 1–10.

————. 2000a. "Culture, Economy, Policy: Trends and Developments." *Geoforum* 31: 385–90.

————. 2000b. "Cultural Policy in Singapore: Negotiating Economic and Socio-Cultural Agendas." *Geoforum* 31: 409–24.

————. 2001. "Mapping 'New' Geographies of Religion: Politics and Poetics in Modernity." *Progress in Human Geography* 25, no. 2: 211–33.

Kong, Lily, and Jasmine S. Chan. 1997. "Women and the State in Singapore: Continuity and Change." Paper presented at the ASEAN Inter-University Seminar on Social Development, Pekan Baru, Indonesia, 16–19 June.

Kong, Lily, and Brenda S. A. Yeoh. 1994. "Urban Conservation in Singapore: A Survey of State Policies and Popular Attitudes." *Urban Studies* 31: 247–65.

————. 1997. "The Construction of National Identity Through the Production of Ritual and Spectacle: An Analysis of National Day Parades in Singapore." *Political Geography* 16, no. 3: 213–39.

Kuo, Eddie C. Y. 1987. *Confucianism and the Chinese Family in Singapore: Continuities and Changes.* Working Paper No. 113, Singapore: National Univ. of Singapore, Department of Sociology.

Kuo, Eddie C. Y., Jon Quah, and Chee Kiong Tong. 1988. *Religion and Religious Revivalism in Singapore.* Singapore: Ministry of Community Development.

Kuo, Eddie C. Y., and Aline K. Wong. 1979. *The Family in Contemporary Singapore.* Singapore: Singapore Univ. Press.

Kwok, Kian-woon 1993. "The Problem of 'Tradition' in Contemporary Singapore." In *Heritage and Contemporary Values*, edited by Arun Mahizhnan, 1–24. Singapore: Times Academic Press.

Kwok, Kian-woon, Lily Kong, Pao Kun Kuo, Chong Guan Kwa, William Lim,

Beng Luan Tan, and Brenda Yeoh. 1999. "Our Place in Time: A Preliminary Reflection." Introduction to *Our Place in Time*, edited by Kian-woon Kwok, Chong Guan Kwa, Lily Kong, and Brenda Yeoh, 1–14. Singapore: Singapore Heritage Society.

Lai, Ah Eng. 1995. *Meanings of Multiethnicity: A Case Study of Ethnicity and Ethnic Relations in Singapore*. Kuala Lumpur: Oxford Univ. Press.

Laquian, Aprodicio A. 1996. "The Multi-Ethnic and Multicultural City: An Asian Perspective." *International Social Science Journal* 48, no. 1: 43–54.

Lasswell, Harold D. 1979. *Signatures of Power*. New Brunswick, N.J.: Transaction Books.

Lau, Kak En. 1994. *Singapore Census of Population 1990: Statistical Release 6, Religion, Childcare, and Leisure Activities*. Singapore: SNP Publishers.

Lee, Hsien Loong. 1989a. "The National Identity: A Direction and Identity for Singapore." In *Speeches: A Bimonthly Selection of Ministerial Speeches*, Vol. 131. Singapore: Information Division, Ministry of Communications and Information.

Lee, Hsien Loong. 1989b. "Speech Delivered on 30 April at the Inauguration of the Parliament of Religions Organised by the Ramakrishna Mission in Singapore." In *Speeches: A Bimonthly Selection of Ministerial Speeches*, Vol. 132. Singapore: Information Division, Ministry of Communications and Information.

Lee, Khoon Choy. 1967. "The Role of the Singapore Arts Council." Speech delivered at the Rotary Club, 12 Oct., Singapore.

Lee, Kuan Yew. 1991. *Lee Kuan Yew on the Chinese Community in Singapore*. Singapore: Singapore Chinese Chamber of Commerce and Industry; Singapore Federation of Chinese Clan Associations.

Lee, Raymond L. M., and Susan E. Ackerman. 1997. *Sacred Tensions: Modernity and Religious Transformation in Malaysia*. Columbia: Univ. of South Carolina Press.

Lefebvre, Henri. 1991. *The Production of Space*. Translated by Donald Nicholson-Smith. Oxford: Blackwell.

Leiris, M. 1938. "The Sacred in Everyday Life." Translated in *The College of Sociology 1937–39*, edited by D. Hollier, 24–31. Minneapolis: Univ. of Minnesota Press.

Leitner, Helga, and Peter Kang. 1999. "Contested Urban Landscapes of Nationalism: The Case of Taipei." *Ecumene* 62: 214–33.

Lewandowski, Susan J. 1984. "The Built Environment and Cultural Symbolism in Post-Colonial Madras." In *The City in Cultural Context*, edited by John A. Agnew, James Mercer, and David E. Sopher, 237–54. Boston: Allen and Unwin.

Ley, David. 1989. "Modernism, Post-Modernism, and the Struggle for Place." In

The Power of Place: Bringing Together Geographical and Sociological Imaginations, edited by J. A. Agnew and J. S. Duncan, 44–65. Boston: Unwin Hyman.

Ley, David, and Kris Olds. 1988. "Landscape as Spectacle: World's Fairs and the Culture of Heroic Consumption." *Environment and Planning D: Society and Space* 6: 191–212.

Lip, Evelyn. 1979. *Chinese Geomancy.* Singapore: Times Books International.

Living the Next Lap. 1991. Singapore: Urban Redevelopment Authority.

Lodge, George C. 1987. "Introduction: Ideology and Country Analysis." In *Ideology and National Competitiveness: An Analysis of Nine Countries*, edited by George C. Lodge and Ezra Vogel, 9–10. Boston: Harvard Business School Press.

Low, Vivienne. 1993–94. "Upgrading of Public Housing." Academic exercise, National Univ. of Singapore.

Lowenthal, David. 1985. *The Past is a Foreign Country.* Cambridge: Cambridge Univ. Press.

————. 1994. "European and English Landscapes as National Symbols." In *Geography and National Identity*, edited by David Hooson, 15–38. Oxford: Blackwell.

Lowenthal, David, and Martyn J. Bowden, eds. 1975. *Geographies of the Mind.* Oxford: Oxford Univ. Press.

Ludden, David, ed. 1996. *Contesting the Nation: Religion, Community, and the Politics of Democracy in India.* Philadelphia: Univ. of Pennsylvania Press.

"Maintenance of Religious Harmony Bill." 1991. In *The Statutes of the Republic of Singapore.* Rev. ed., chapter 167a. Singapore: Government Printing Office.

A Manual for Kampong Glam Conservation Area. 1988. Singapore: Urban Redevelopment Authority.

Massey, Doreen. 1993. "A Global Sense of Place." In *Studying Culture*, edited by Ann Gray and Jim McGuigan, 232–40. London: Edward Arnold.

Mattar, Ahmad. 1977. "Speech Delivered at a Tea Party to Welcome New Members of the Majlis Ugama Islam Singapura." In *Ministry of Social Affairs: Speeches, Statements, Press Conferences, and Interviews, 1977–1979.* 17 Oct. Singapore: Information Division, Ministry of Culture.

————. 1988. "Speech Delivered at the Dawoodi Bohra's Prophet Muhammad's Birth Celebrations." In *Singapore Government Press Release: November-December 1988.* 13 Nov. Singapore: Information Division, Ministry of Communications and Information.

McConnell, Shean. 1981. *Theories for Planning.* London: Heinemann.

Meyrowitz, Joshua. 1985. *No Sense of Place.* Oxford: Oxford Univ. Press.

Ministry of National Development. 1987. *Annual Report*. Singapore: Ministry of National Development.

Minutes of Meeting of the Advisory Committee on the Naming of Roads and Streets (MMAC-NRS). n.d. Files 2/67, 70/59, and 515/59, Dewan Bahasa Files. Ministry of Culture National Archives, Singapore.

Mitchell, K. 1997. "Conflicting Geographies of Democracy and the Public Sphere in Vancouver, B.C." *Transactions, Institute of British Geographers* 22: 162–79.

National Arts Council Annual Report. 1996. Singapore: National Arts Council.

National Theatre Trust Annual Report 1961–62. 1962. Singapore: National Theatre Trust.

Naylor, Simon K., and James R. Ryan. 1998. "Ethnicity and Cultural Landscapes: Mosques, Gurdwaras, and Mandirs in England and Wales." Paper presented at the "Religion and Locality Conference," Univ. of Leeds, 8–10 Sept.

Offe, Claus. 1984. *Contradictions of the Welfare State*. Cambridge, Mass.: MIT Press.

Ohmae, Kenichi. 1995. *The End of the Nation State: The Rise of Regional Economies*. London: Harper Collins.

Olwig, Kenneth R. 1993. "Sexual Cosmology: Nation and Landscape at the Conceptual Interstices of Nature and Culture; or, What Does Landscape Really Mean?" In *Landscape Politics and Perspectives*, edited by Barbara Bender, 307–43. Oxford: Berg.

Ong, Teng Cheong. 1990. "Opening Speech Delivered at the People's Action Party Women's Wing Seminar on 'Family and Core Values,' " 1 July, PUB Auditorium, Singapore.

Ooi, Giok Ling. 1993. "The Housing and Development Board's Ethnic Integration Policy." In *The Management of Ethnic Relations in Public Housing Estates*, edited by Giok Ling Ooi, Sharon Siddique, and Kay Cheng Soh, 4–24. Singapore: Times Academic Press and The Institute of Policy Studies.

Pain, Rachel. 1991. "Space, Sexual Violence, and Social Control: Integrating Geographical and Feminist Analyses of Women's Fear of Crime." *Progress in Human Geography* 15: 415–31.

Pannell, Kerr, and Forster. 1986. *Tourism Development in Singapore*. Singapore: Singapore Tourist Promotion Board.

Parliamentary Debates: Official Report. 1971. 22 Mar. 1972. 2 July, 3 Nov. 1975. 20 Mar. 1977. 16 Mar. 1978. 16 Mar., 7 Apr. Singapore: Government Printing Office.

Parteneau, René, François Charbonneau, Khanh Toan Pham, Ba Dang Nguyen, Hung Tran, Manh Nguyen Hoang, and Thuy Hang Vu. 1995. "Impact of Restoration in Hanoi's French Colonial Quarter." *Cities* 12: 163–73.

Pearson, Harold Frank. 1955. *People of Early Singapore.* London: Univ. of London Press.

Pek San Theng Special Publication. 1988. Singapore.

Pemberton, John. 1994. "Recollections from Beautiful Indonesia Somewhere Beyond the Postmodern." *Public Culture* 6: 241–62.

Penrose, Jan. 1993. "Reification in the Name of Change: The Impact of Nationalism on Social Constructions of Nation, People, and Place in Scotland and the United Kingdom." In *Constructions of Race, Place, and Nation,* edited by Peter Jackson and Jan Penrose, 27–49. London: UCL Press.

Perry, Martin, Lily Kong, and Brenda Yeoh. 1997. *Singapore: A Developmental City State.* Chichester: John Wiley.

Philo, Chris. 1992. "Foucault's Geography." *Environment and Planning D: Society and Space* 10: 132–61.

Philp, Janette, and David Mercer. 1999. "Commodification of Buddhism in Contemporary Burma." *Annals of Tourism Research* 261: 21–54.

Phua, Siew Chye, and Lily Kong. 1996. "Ideology, Social Commentary, and Resistance in Popular Music: A Case Study of Singapore." *Journal of Popular Culture* 301: 215–31.

Pieterse, Jan N. 1994. "Globalisation as Hybridisation." *International Sociology* 92: 161–84.

Pirie, Gordon H. 1984. "Letters, Words, Worlds: The Naming of Soweto." *African Studies* 43: 43–51.

"Planning Act." 1990. *The Statutes of the Republic of Singapore.* Rev. ed. Singapore: Government Printing Office.

Porteous, J. Douglas. 1988. "Topocide: The Annihilation of Place." In *Qualitative Methods in Human Geography,* edited by John Eyles and David M. Smith, 75–93. Cambridge: Polity Press.

Pugh, Cedric. 1989. "The Political Economy of Public Housing." In *Management of Success: The Moulding of Modern Singapore,* edited by Kernial Singh Sandhu and Paul Wheatley, 833–59. Singapore: Institute of Southeast Asian Studies.

PuruShotam, Nirmala 1993. "The Normal Family: A Study of Ideological Reformulations Concerning the Family in Singapore." Paper presented at the Third Malaysia-Singapore Forum, National Univ. of Singapore, Singapore, 1–4 Nov.

Quah, Jon S. T. 1990a. "National Values and Nation-Building: Defining the Problem." In *In Search of Singapore's National Values,* edited by Jon S. T. Quah, 1–5. Singapore: The Institute of Policy Studies and Times Academic Press.

———. 1990b. "Searching for Singapore's National Values." In *In Search of Singa-*

pore's National Values, edited by Jon S. T. Quah, 91–105. Singapore: The Institute of Policy Studies and Times Academic Press.

Quah, Stella. 1983. "Social Discipline in Singapore." *Southeast Asian Journal of Social Science* 14: 266–89.

Rabinow, Paul. 1989. "Governing Morocco: Modernity and Difference." *International Journal of Urban and Regional Research* 13: 32–46.

Radcliffe, Sarah. 1996. "Gendered Nations: Nostalgia, Development, and Territory in Ecuador." *Gender, Place, and Culture* 31: 5–21.

Radcliffe, Sarah, and Sallie Westwood. 1996. *Remaking the Nation: Place, Identity, and Politics in Latin America*. London: Routledge.

Raja-Singam, S. D. 1939. *Malayan Street Names: What They Mean and Whom They Commemorate*. Ipoh: Mercantile Press.

Relph, Edward. 1976. *Place and Placelessness*. London: Pion.

Report of the Committee on Performing Arts. 1988. Singapore.

Report of the Committee on the Standardization of Street Names in Chinese (RCSSNC). 1970. Singapore: Government Printing Office.

Report of the Committee Regarding Burial and Burial Grounds. 1952. Colony of Singapore: Government Printing Office.

Report of the Sub-Committee on the Service Sector. 1985. Singapore: Economic Committee.

"Republic of Singapore 1989." 1991. *Government Gazette*. Singapore.

Richman, Joel. 1983. *Traffic Wardens: An Ethnography Of Street Administration*. Manchester: Manchester Univ. Press.

Robins, Kevin. 1991. "Tradition and Translation: National Culture in its Global Context." In *Enterprise and Heritage: Crosscurrents of National Culture*, edited by John Corner and Sylvia Harvey, 21–44. London: Routledge.

Robinson, David. 1989. "The Language and Significance of Place in Latin America." In *The Power of Place: Bringing Together Geographical and Sociological Imagination*, edited by John A. Agnew and James S. Duncan, 157–84. Boston: Unwin Hyman.

Rogers, Ali. 1995. "Cinco de Mayo and the 15th January: Contrasting Situations in a Mixed Ethnic Neighbourhood." In *The Urban Context: Ethnicity, Social Networks, and Situational Analysis*, edited by Ali Rogers and Steve Vertovec, 117–40. London: Berg.

Rose, Gillian. 1994. "The Cultural Politics of Place: Local Representation and Oppositional Discourse in Two Films." *Transactions, Institute of British Geographers* 19: 46–60.

Salaff, Janet W. 1988. *State and Family in Singapore: Restructuring an Industrial Society.* Ithaca, N.Y.: Cornell Univ. Press.

Sasitharan, T. n.d. *Artistic Statement.* Available online at: www.substation.org.sg.

Scheefers, P., J. Lammers, and J. Peters. 1994. "Religious and Class Voting in the Netherlands, 1990–1991: A Review of Recent Contributions Tested." *Netherlands Journal of Social Sciences* 301: 5–24.

Scott, James C. 1998. *Seeing Like a State: How Certain Schemes to Improve the Human Condition Have Failed.* New Haven, N.J., and London: Yale Univ. Press.

Shapiro, Michael J. 1994. "Moral Geographies and the Ethics of Post-Sovereignty." *Public Culture* 6: 479–502.

Shared Values. 1991. Singapore: Singapore National Printers.

Shaw, Gareth, and Allan M. Williams. 1994. *Critical Issues in Tourism: A Geographical Perspective.* Oxford: Blackwell.

Shils, Edward. 1968. "The Concept and Function of Ideology." In *International Encyclopedia of the Social Sciences,* Vol. 7, edited by D. L. Sills, 66–76. New York: Macmillan.

Siddique, Sharon. 1989. "Singaporean Identity." In *Management of Success: The Moulding of Modern Singapore,* edited by K. S. Sandhu and P. Wheatley, 563–77. Singapore: Institute of Southeast Asian Studies.

Simmie, J. 1974. *Citizens in Conflict: The Sociology of Town Planning.* London: Hutchinson Education.

Singapore 21 Committee. 1999. *Singapore 21 Vision.* Available online at: www.gov.sg/Singapore21/keyideas4.html.

Singapore Facts and Pictures. 1978. Singapore: Publicity Division, Ministry of Culture.

Singapore's Family Values. 1994. Singapore: Ministry of Community Development.

Singapore: Global City for the Arts. 1995. Singapore: Singapore Tourist Promotion Board and Ministry of Information and the Arts.

Singapore Government Press Release. 1973. 26 Apr., 25 Nov. 1974. 30 Nov. 1987. 3 Oct. 1988. 13 Dec. Singapore: Information Division, Ministry of Culture.

Singapore Heritage Society and Associated Consultants. 1997. *Enhancement of Chinatown Experience Pre-qualification Stage Tender.* Singapore: Singapore Heritage Society.

Singapore Planning Department. 1967. Technical Paper No. 48. Singapore: Government Printing Office.

Singapore Tourism Board. 1996a. *Tourism 21. Vision of a Tourism Capital.* Singapore: Singapore Tourism Board.

————. 1996b. *Destination Singapore: The Arts Experience.* Singapore: Singapore Tourism Board.

Singapore Tourist Promotion Board. 1971–72. *Annual Report 1971–72.* Singapore: Singapore Tourist Promotion Board.

————. 1972–73. *Annual Report 1972–73.* Singapore: Singapore Tourist Promotion Board.

————. 1993–94. *Annual Report 1993–94.* Singapore: Singapore Tourist Promotion Board.

————. 1989, 1990, 1991, 1999. *Singapore: Official Guide.* Singapore: Singapore Tourist Promotion Board.

Slater, Terry R. 1984. "Preservation, Conservation, and Planning in Historic Towns." *The Geographical Journal* 1503: 322–34.

Sloane, David Charles. 1991. *The Last Great Necessity: Cemeteries in American History.* Baltimore, Md.: The John Hopkins Univ. Press.

Smith, Anthony D. 1993. "The Nation: Invented, Imagined, Reconstructed?" In *Reimagining the Nation,* edited by Marjorie Ringrose and Adam J. Lerner, 9–28. Buckingham, Pa.: Open Univ. Press.

Smith, Christopher J. 1995. "Asian New York: The Geography and Politics of Diversity." *International Migration Review* 291: 59–84.

Sng, Poh Yoke. 1986. "The End of the Birth of an Art." *Sunday Times,* 17 Aug.

Sorkin, Michael. 1992. "Introduction: Variations on a Theme Park." In *Variations on a Theme Park,* edited by Michael Sorkin, xi-xv. New York: Noonday Press.

The Straits Times. 1964. 16 May. 1967. 1 Mar., 10 June. 1970. 13 June. 1972. 20 Aug. 1976. 7 Mar. 1977. 11 Nov. 1978. 17 Jan. 1978. 9 Feb., 18 May, 7 Oct. 1979. 15 June, 7 Sept., 16 Oct. 1982. 4 Dec. 1983. 23 Dec. 1984. 8 Jan., 9 Jan., 13 Jan., 26 Feb. 1985. 19 Feb., 6 Apr., 22 Dec. 1986. 9 Apr., 23 Nov. 1987. 4 Jan., 19 Mar., 20 Mar., 17 Aug. 1988. 3 Mar., 29 Apr., 25 June. 1989. 10 Jan., 25 Feb., 19 June, 12 July. 1990. 6 Jan., 21 Jan., 24 Feb., 7 Aug. 1991. 23 Sept., 16 Oct., 23 Oct., 27 Dec., 1992. 3 Apr., 11 Apr., 14 Apr., 21 Apr., 29 Aug. 1994. 22 July, 23 July, 27 July, 30 July, 1 Aug., 9 Aug., 12 Aug., 22 Aug. 1995. 14 July, 27 Aug., 30 Aug., 31 Aug., 17 Oct., 4 Nov. 1996. 29 Jan., 5 Feb., 16 Mar., 22 Apr., 26 Apr., 1 May, 5 June, 10 July, 15 July. 1997. 14 Aug., 30 Aug., 10 Oct. 1998. 29 Sept., 22 Nov., 12 Dec. 1999. 16 Mar., 22 Mar., 9 Apr., 27 May. 2000. 18 Feb.

Stump, R. W. 1988. "Toponymic Commemoration of National Figures: The Case of Kennedy and King." *Names* 36: 203–16.

Sullivan, Gerald, and S. Gunasekaran. 1994. *A Study of Motivations of Emigrants from Singapore to Australia.* Singapore: Institute of Southeast Asian Studies.

The Sunday Times. 1994. 28 Aug. 1995. 19 Feb. 1996. 21 Jan. 1998. 20 Dec.

Tailford, E. J. 1995. *A Guide to Mount Vernon Complex.* Singapore: Environmental Health Department, Ministry of Environment.

Tamney, Joseph B. 1988. "Religion and the State in Singapore." *Journal of Church and State* 30: 109–28.

Tay, Kheng Soon. 1991. "Heritage Conservation—Political and Social Implications: The Case of Singapore." *Singapore Institute of Architects Journal* Mar./Apr.: 37–41.

Teather, Elizabeth K. 1998. "Themes from Complex Landscapes: Chinese Cemeteries and Columbaria in Urban Hong Kong." *Australian Geographical Studies* 361: 21–36.

Teh, Cheang Wan. 1969. "Public Housing." In *Modern Singapore,* edited by J. B. Ooi and H. D. Chiang, 171–80. Singapore: Univ. of Singapore Press.

———. 1975. "Public Housing in Singapore: An Overview." In *Public Housing in Singapore,* edited by S. H. K. Yeh, 1–21. Singapore: Singapore Univ. Press.

Teo, Peggy. 1994. "Assessing Socio-cultural Impacts: The Case of Singapore." *Tourism Management* 15: 126–36.

Teo, Peggy, and Shirlena Huang. 1996. "A Sense of Place in Public Housing: A Case Study of Pasir Ris, Singapore. *Habitat International* 202: 307–25.

Teo, Siew Eng. 1986. "New Towns Planning and Development in Singapore." *Third World Planning Review* 8: 252–71.

Teo, Siew Eng, and Lily Kong. 1997. "Public Housing in Singapore: Interpreting 'Quality' in the 1990s." *Urban Studies* 343: 441–52.

Tham, Seong Chee. 1984. *Religion and Modernization: A Study of Changing Rituals among Singapore's Chinese, Malays, and Indians.* Tokyo: The Center for East Asian Cultural Studies.

Thomas, Michael J. 1982. "The Procedural Planning Theory of A. Faludi." In *Critical Readings in Planning Theory,* edited by Chris Paris, 13–26. Oxford: Pergamon.

Thompson, John B. 1981. *Critical Hermeneutics.* Cambridge: Cambridge Univ. Press.

Tong, Chee Kiong. 1988. *Trends in Traditional Chinese Religion in Singapore.* Singapore: Ministry of Community Development.

Tong, Chee Kiong, and Anne L. Schiller. 1993. "The Anthropology of Death: A Preliminary Overview." *Southeast Asian Journal of Social Science* 212: 1–9.

Tuan, Yi Fu. 1974. "Space and Place: Humanistic Perspective." In *Progress in Geogra-*

phy, edited by Chris Board, Richard J. Chorley, Peter Haggett, and David R. Stoddart, 211–52. London: Edward Arnold.

Tunbridge, John E. 1984. "Whose Heritage to Conserve? Cross-cultural Reflections upon Political Dominance and Urban Heritage Conservation." *Canadian Geographer* 28: 171–80.

Turnbull, C. Mary. 1989. *A History of Singapore, Malaysia, and Brunei.* Sydney: Allen and Unwin.

Urban Redevelopment Authority (URA). 1990. *Procedures for Recovering Possession of Rent-Controlled Premises.* Singapore: Urban Redevelopment Authority.

URA Annual Report. 1974–75—1988–89. Singapore: Urban Redevelopment Authority.

Van der Veer, Peter, and Hartmut Lehmann, eds. 1999. *Nation and Religion: Perspectives on Europe and Asia.* Princeton, N.J.: Princeton Univ. Press.

Van Grunsven, Leo. 1992. "Integration versus Segregation: Ethnic Minorities and Urban Politics in Singapore." *Tijdschrift voor Economische en Sociale Geografie* 833: 196–215.

Vasil, Raj. 1988. *Governing Singapore: Interviews with the New Leaders.* Singapore: Times Books International.

Wagner, Philip L., and Marvin W. Mikesell. 1962. "General Introduction: The Themes of Cultural Geography." In *Readings in Cultural Geography*, edited by Philip L. Wagner and Marvin W. Mikesell, 1–24. Chicago: The Univ. of Chicago Press.

Wallis, Roger, and Krister Malm. 1984. *Big Sounds from Small Peoples.* London: Constable.

Wang, Gungwu. 1988. "The Study of Chinese Identities in Southeast Asia." In *Changing Identities of the Southeast Asian Chinese since World War II*, edited by Jennifer W. Cushman and Gungwu Wang, 1–21. Hong Kong: Hong Kong Univ. Press.

Warren, James. 1994. "A Strong Stomach and Flawed Material: The Making of a Trilogy, Singapore, 1870–1940." Abstract of paper presented at the Institute of Southeast Asian Studies, Singapore, 12 Sept.

Warren, Stacey. 1993. " 'This Heaven Gives Me Migraines': The Problems and Promises of Landscapes of Leisure." In *Place/Culture/Representation*, edited by James Duncan and David Ley, 173–86. London: Routledge.

Waterman, Stanley. 1998. "Place, Culture, and Identity: Summer Music in Upper Galilee." *Transactions, Institute of British Geographers* 23: 253–67.

Watson, James L. 1988. "The Structure of Chinese Funerary Rites: Elementary Forms, Ritual Sequence, and the Primacy of Performance." In *Death Ritual in*

Late Imperial and Modern China, edited by J. L. Watson and E. S. Rawski, 11–19. Berkeley: Univ. of California Press.

Watts, Michael J. 1992. "Space for Everything: A Commentary." *Cultural Anthropology* 7: 115–29.

Weekly, Kathleen. 1999. "Nation and Identity at the Centennial of Philippines Independence." *Asian Studies Review* 233: 337–50.

Western, John. 1985. "Undoing the Western City?" *Geographical Review* 75: 335–57.

Wok, Othman. 1971. "Speech Delivered at a Hari Raya Gathering Organised by the Toa Payoh Mosque Building Committee." In *Ministry of Social Affairs: Speeches, Statements, Press Conferences, and Interviews, 1971–1973.* 11 Dec. Singapore: Information Division, Ministry of Culture.

————. 1974a. "Speech Delivered at the Pasir Panjang Koran Reading Competition." In *Ministry of Social Affairs: Speeches, Statements, Press Conferences, and Interviews, 1971–1973.* 17 July. Singapore: Information Division, Ministry of Culture.

————. 1974b. "Speech Delivered at a Meeting with New Members of the Majlis Ugama Islam Singapura." In *Ministry of Social Affairs: Speeches, Statements, Press Conferences, and Interviews, 1974–1976.* 25 Oct. Singapore: Information Division, Ministry of Culture.

Wolch, Jennifer, and Michael Dear. 1988. *The Power of Geography.* London: Unwin Hyman.

Wong, Kwei Chong, et al. 1984. *Report of the Tourism Task Force.* Singapore: Ministry of Trade and Industry.

Wong, Poh Kam, and Chee Yuen Ng. 1993. "Singapore Coping with a Maturing Economy." *Southeast Asian Affairs* 313–24.

Wood, Richard L. 1994. "Faith in Action: Religious Resources for Political Success in Three Congregations." *Sociology of Religion* 554: 397–417.

Wynne, Derek, ed. 1992. *The Culture Industry.* Aldershot: Avebury.

Yeh, Stephen H. K. 1972. *Homes for the People: A Study of Tenants' Views on Public Housing in Singapore.* Singapore: Housing and Development Board.

Yen, Ching-Hwang. 1986. *A Social History of the Chinese in Singapore and Malaya, 1800–1911.* Singapore: Oxford Univ. Press.

Yeo, George. 1989. "Importance of Heritage and Identity." In *Speeches: A Bimonthly Selection of Ministerial Speeches,* Vol. 131. Singapore: Ministry of Communications and Information.

Yeo, George Y. B. 1991. "Building in a Market Test for the Arts." In *Speeches: A Bimonthly Selection of Ministerial Speeches,* Vol. 15. Singapore: Publicity Division, Ministry of Information and the Arts.

————. 1992. "Promoting the Arts." In *Speeches: A Bimonthly Selection of Ministerial Speeches*, Vol. 16. Singapore: Publicity Division, Ministry of Information and the Arts.

————. 1993. "An International Market for the Arts." In *Speeches: A Bimonthly Selection of Ministerial Speeches*, Vol. 17. Singapore: Publicity Division, Ministry of Information and the Arts.

————. 1994. "Singapore Arts Centre: Taking Shape." In *Speeches: A Bimonthly Selection of Ministerial Speeches*, Vol. 184. Singapore: Publicity Division, Ministry of Information and the Arts.

Yeoh, Brenda S. A. 1991. "The Control of 'Sacred' Space: Conflicts over the Chinese Burial Grounds in Colonial Singapore, 1880–1930." *Journal of Southeast Asian Studies* 222: 282–311.

————. 1992. "Street Names in Colonial Singapore." *The Geographical Review* 82: 313–22.

————. 1996. *Contesting Space: Power Relations and the Urban Built Environment in Colonial Singapore.* Oxford: Oxford Univ. Press.

Yeoh, Brenda S. A., and Lily Kong. 1994. "Reading Landscape Meanings: State Constructions and Lived Experiences in Singapore's Chinatown." *Habitat International* 184: 17–35.

————. 1995. "Place-Making: Collective Representations of Social Life and the Built Environment in Tiong Bahru." In *Portraits of Places: History, Community, and Identity in Singapore*, edited by Brenda S. A. Yeoh and Lily Kong, 88–115. Singapore: Times Editions.

Yeoh, Brenda S. A., and W. P. Lau. 1995. "Historic District, Contemporary Meanings: Urban Conservation and the Creation and Consumption of Landscape Spectacle in Tanjong Pagar." In *Portraits of Places: History, Community, and Identity in Singapore*, edited by Brenda S. A. Yeoh and Lily Kong, 46–67. Singapore: Times Editions.

Yeoh, Brenda S. A., and Boon Hui Tan. 1995. "The Politics of Space: Changing Discourses on Chinese Burial Grounds in Post-war Singapore." *Journal of Historical Geography* 212: 184–201.

Ying Fo Fui Kun. 1989. *165th Anniversary Commemorative and Souvenir Publication, 1822–1987.* Singapore: Ying Fo Fui Kun.

Zelinsky, Wilbur. 1975. "Unearthly Delights: Cemetery Names and the Map of the Changing American Afterworld." In *Geographies of the Mind*, edited by David Lowenthal and Martyn J. Bowden, 171–95. Oxford: Oxford Univ. Press.

————. 1983. "Nationalism in the American Place-Name Cover." *Names* 31: 1–28.

————. 1994. "Gathering Places for America's Dead: How Many, Where, and Why?" *Professional Geographer* 461: 29–38.

Zukin, Sharon. 1991. *Landscapes of Power: From Detroit to Disney World.* Berkeley: Univ. of California.

Index

Italic page number denotes illustration.

Barnes, Trevor J., 203

Basch, Linda, 1

Bassett, Keith, 200

Beach Road, 135, 147, 150

Bedlington, Stanley S., 31

Benjamin, Geoffrey, 34, 35, 58n,
    205

Berg, Lawrence D., 23

Betts, Russell Henry, 36

Bianchini, Franco, 28, 200

Binney, Marcus, 88

Black Box, 166, 185–86

Blair Plain, 135

Blaut, James, 16

Boat Quay, 135

Boddy, T., 24

Boon Lay Community Centre, 168

Boorstin, Daniel, 158, 159

Bourdieu, Pierre, 24

Bowden, Martyn J., 17

Brady, Diane, 180, 184

British East India Company, 29, 108

Bromley, Rosemary D. F., 24

Brown, David, 33

Browning, Robert, 128

Buckley, Charles B., 149

Buddhism, 75, 86

Bugis Street, 136

building and construction industry, 99

building heights, varying, 97

Bukit China (Melaka, Malaysia), 17–18

Bukit Pasoh, 135, 139n

Bukit Pasoh Extension, 135

Bulim, 63

Burgess, Jacquelin A., 47, 91

burial grounds. *See* Chinese Burial
    Grounds

Burials Committee, 55–56

Burton, S., 136

Bussorah Street, 148–49

Cairnhill, 135

Canning, Fort, 136, 196

Cartier, Carolyn, 17–18

Castells, Manuel, 46

cemeteries, Chinese. *See* Chinese burial
    grounds

Central Provident Fund (CPF), 96, 96n,
    99, 112, 113

Chai, Chong Yii, 91

Chan, Chee Seng, 90

Chan, Heng Chee, 30, 32, 34, 47

Chan, Jasmine S., 44

Chan, Soo Sen, 111

Chang, T. C., 136, 140

Chee, M. L., 102

Chen, Peter S. J., 47

Cheng, Lim Keak, 58

Chia, Karen, 87

Chidester, David, 18

Chiew, Seen Kong, 32

Chinatown: bilingual street signs in, 127;
    conservation in, 134, 136, 139–46;
    living conditions in 1950s, 94; as
    manifestation of Singapore's Asian
    roots, 206; racial segregation under
    the British, 108, 118; shophouses, 139,
    140, *141*, 145; tourism served by
    redevelopment of, 144–45, 146, 208;
    in tourist guide training, 86–87;
    traditional Chinese trades, 140, 141,
    141n, 143–44

Chinese: Chinese street names in Jurong
    Industrial Estate, 124; as "clear" racial
    category, 35; conflict with Malays in
    public housing, 109–10;
    Confucianism, 38, 43, 54; as
    congregating in particular estates,
    109; cremation by, 56, 58–59, 62–64,
    67–72, 73–74; high school riots of
    1950s, 32; and Malay toponyms, 121;

Kwang Teck Suah cemetery, 62
Kwok, Kian-woon, 131, 132

Lai, Ah Eng, 109
Land Acquisition Act, 60
landscape: as constantly reinterpreted,
    15; in construction of nations, 1–3,
    7–28, 202; in exercise of power, 15; as
    ideological, 2–3, 14–15, 202, 204;
    material and imagined elements of, 14;
    as multicoded space, 15; norms and
    forms in shaping of, 15; politics of,
    14–17; in Singapore state's nation-
    building, 204; as sites of conflict and
    negotiation, 16; social construction of,
    14
landscapes of aesthetics, 162–200;
    defined, 4; as ideological, 204; local
    versus global forces in, 26–28; as
    luxury rather than necessity, 6. *See also*
    arts
landscapes of death. *See* deathscapes
landscapes of heritage, 131–61; defined,
    4; heritage tourism, 24, 136–38; as
    ideological, 204; as luxury rather than
    necessity, 6; as mapping history onto
    territory, 23–26, 160, 206; the
    Merlion, 152–59; resistance to state-
    propelled, 160, 208–9; thematic
    development, 137–38, 139, 142, 145.
    See also conservation; national symbols
landscapes of religion, 75–93; as
    landscapes of sentiment, 5; political
    dimensions of, 18–20. *See also* religious
    buildings
landscapes of sentiment: core meanings of
    life related to, 5; defined, 4; as
    ideological, 204. *See also* deathscapes;
    landscapes of religion

language: Chinese dialects, 126, 210;
    Mandarin dialect, 37, 123, 194. *See also*
    multilingualism
Laquian, Aprodicio A., 21
LaSalle SIA, 169
Lasswell, Harold D., 24
Latin America, 10, 22
Lau, Kak En, 76, 127
Lee, Hsien Loong, 39, 89, 133
Lee, Khoon Choy, 36, 188
Lee, Kuan Yew, 40, 77, 84, 92, 154,
    175
Lee, Raymond L. M., 18
Lee, Tzu Pheng, 157, 158
Lefebvre, Henri, 13
Lehmann, Hartmut, 18
Leitner, Helga, 201
Lewandowski, Susan J., 22
Ley, David, 27, 46, 47, 79, 208
Lian, Kwen Fee, 30–31, 34, 38, 39, 42, 44,
    43
Li Cheng, 69–72
Lim, Nang Seng, 154
Lim, Nee Soon, 126, 126n, 127
Lim, Pee Boon, 154
Lim, Pee Nee, 154
Linenthal, Edward T., 18
Lip, Evelyn, 53
Little India, 86, 118, 127, 134, 135,
    136
Liu, Kang, 162, 163
Liu, Thai Ker, 180
Living the Next Leap (Urban Redevelopment
    Authority), 48, 197
Lodge, George C., 38, 41
Lorong Lew Lian housing estate,
    105–6
Low, Vivienne, 106
Lowenthal, David, 10, 17, 88, 132
Ludden, David, 18

Madrasah Aljunied Al-Islamiah (Aljunied
 Arab School), 147, 149–52
Madrasah Alsagoff (Alsagoff Arab
 School), 147, 150–52
Mahizhnan, Arun, 184
Maintenance of Religious Harmony Bill,
 77
Majlis Ugama Islam Singapura (Muslim
 Religious Council; MUIS), 89
Malabar Muslim Jama-Ath, 148, 150
Malays: as "clear" racial category, 35;
 conflict with Chinese in public
 housing, 109–10; as congregating in
 particular estates, 109; constitutional
 protection of, 77–78, 89–90;
 Malayanizing street names, 119–22,
 206; in Raffles's race-based planning,
 108; sense of their own significance, 3;
 Shared Values and, 39. *See also*
 Kampong Glam
Malaysia: Bukit China cemetery, 17–18;
 colonial street names changed, 22;
 Singapore Chinese burying their dead
 in, 63; Singapore in Federation of
 Malaysia, 3, 29, 30; state religion in,
 76
Malm, Krister, 26
Mandai columbarium-*cum*-crematorium
 complex, 62, 70
Mandarin dialect, 37, 123, 194
Marine Parade Community Club, 168
Marine Parade housing estate, 109
marriage, housing policy favoring,
 111–15
Masjid Hajjah Fatimah, 86
Massey, Doreen, 8
Mass Rapid Transit (MRT) stations, 81,
 88, 121n
Master Plan (1965), 57, 65, 66
"Master Plan attitude," 47

materialism, 37, 49
Mattar, Ahmad, 91
Mercer, David, 18
meritocracy, 36, 37, 193, 204
Merlion, 152–59; commercialization of,
 155; as national symbol, 156–59, 191,
 206, 209; the Sentosa Merlion,
 155–56, 157, 159; statue at river's
 mouth, 154; as tourist attraction, 154,
 155, 156, 158, 209
Merlion Park, 154
Merlion Walk, 156
Merlion Week, 155
Metcalf, Peter, 51
Meyer, Astrid, 19
Meyrowitz, Joshua, 26, 27
MGS Auditorium, 169
Mikesell, Marvin W., 144
millennium celebrations, 160–61
Ministry of Culture Cultural Affairs
 Division, 175
Mitchell, K., 21
MND Auditorium, 167
monumental forms, 24–25
Moses, Robert, 46–47
mosques, 79, 80, 81, 86, 88, 89
Mountbatten Community Centre, 168
Mount Sinai estate, 122
Mount Vernon columbarium-*cum*-
 crematorium complex, 61, 61–62, 72
multiculturalism: the arts and, 192–94,
 207; Committee on Heritage on, 133,
 134; race and, 34; religious buildings
 and, 88–90; in Singapore state
 ideology, 32, 76, 77, 204; and street
 naming, 122, 124, 125
multilingualism: the arts and, 192; race
 and, 34–35; in Singapore state
 ideology, 32, 204; and street naming,
 122, 124, 206